THE BROADVIEW GUIDE TO WRITING

THE BROADVIEW GUIDE TO WRITING

Doug Babington and Don LePan

broadview press

Ca_____ _uing in Publication Data

_ _gton, Doug.
_ Broadview guide to writing

SBN 0-921149-76-X

1. English language — Rhetoric. 2. Report
    Writing. I. LePan, Don, 1954-   . II. Title.

LB2369.B32 1991   808'.042 C91-093625-0

broadview press   in the US: broadview press
P.O. Box 1243   269 Portage Rd.
Peterborough, Ontario   Lewiston, NY
K9J 7H5   Canada   14092   USA
(705)743-8990   (705)743-8990

CONTENTS

to Anatole Broyard
(1920-1990)

and to Ann

PREFACE

The late Thomas Weiskel, in his full and very persuasive book on the Romantic sublime, includes a sentence that could easily serve as the testimony of many university essay-writers: "We are reading along and suddenly occurs a text which exceeds comprehension, which seems to contain a residue of signifier which finds no reflected signified in our minds." Perceptual imbalance, intellectual intimidation — these are the very real difficulties of learning and scholarship that often stop students dead in their tracks. Many write little of value, for themselves or their audiences, because they avoid difficulties by turning to the easy solutions described by James Moffett as "glorified book-reporting or the filling in of instances to fit someone else's generalization." Good writing, it seems to me, is very much a matter of attitude, not just for students but for all scholars and all writers. Of course, surviving a term paper in political theory, or discussing narrative perspective in D.H. Lawrence, may seem like anything but a sublime experience. It is, nevertheless, in "constituting a fresh relation" between writer and topic that success in writing begins. Several other components of that success are also addressed in this book, including logic, style, paragraphing, grammar, and research. My principal source of knowledge and material has been the experience of teaching writing for over ten years. I owe a great deal to students and colleagues at Queen's University. And, for their stimulating research on inquiry and the epistemology of writing, I am particularly indebted to Janice Lauer, Linda Flower, and John R. Hayes.

Doug Babington

To the above I need only add my thanks to the many academics who have offered advice on this project, and in particular to Michael Hornyansky of Brock University and Sheila Trant of

Centennial College, both of whom offered detailed criticisms that were enormously helpful.

Don LePan

INTRODUCTION

Open any book to no page in particular. Turn it upside down. What appears is a strange pattern of black marks and white spaces — the essential stuff of any writer's efforts. Reading that pattern, different on every page of text, means (for most of us North Americans) moving from left to right and from top to bottom. With the page right side up, those black marks become symbols of a sound ("s") or an image ("door") or a concept ("oppression") or even an emotion ("!") — while the white ones run the necessary interference, establishing the spaces and divisions that help writers make their meanings.

Selecting symbols and arranging them (left to right, top to bottom) so that they communicate sensibly is every writer's occupation. Nothing more, in the end. But at the beginning, and every step along the way, the experiences of writers can be very frustrating and uncertain, whether they work in journalism, business, the performing arts, advertising, sports, politics, or — where so many really get their start — at a university, writing essays.

Because it deals with writing, *The Broadview Guide* deals with ways of handling frustration and uncertainty. But a grim primer on pain-survival it certainly is not. Satisfaction, discovery — and even playfulness — are all part of the demanding and worthwhile experience shared by capable writers in every field of professional endeavour; we hope we have succeeded in reflecting at least something of all of these.

Part One of *The Broadview Guide* discusses the four essentials that every essay-writer must develop: voice, ideas, fluency, and collaboration. As with every completed text, its black and white symbols are arranged sequentially, moving from left to right and top to bottom. There are, however, plenty of cross-references built into its organization; the authors have tried to stress the **non**-sequential aspect of the reading process — and writing process — by frequently inserting parenthetical numbers that refer readers to complementary pages in the book. For example, "**thesis** (27, 88)" is our way of promoting *The Broadview Guide* as an actual handbook — one that rewards a hands-on approach to its own usage.

Often the parenthetical page numbers refer to Part Two, where we provide a detailed survey of points of English grammar and usage. Grammatical jargon is there, because a common vocabulary concerning the structure of our language is well worth learning. There are usually clear reasons, after all, why the pieces of an effective sentence fit together the way they do; highlighting those reasons is one important purpose of *The Broadview Guide*.

However, since every native speaker and writer of English uses participles, for example, before learning to label them as "participles," Part Two stresses in particular a common sense approach. The various points can be understood while making little or no reference to the grammatical terms themselves; the emphasis throughout is on showing through example. The repeated use of a 'worth checking' and 'revised' structure in the presentation of these examples is designed to encourage the student to focus on the process of revising and improving his writing. And, by choosing examples from highly respected writers as well as from student writing, we attempt throughout to underscore the point that *everyone's* writing can benefit from careful checking and revision; no student should be demoralized by the presence of imperfections in a final draft — let alone a first one. The process of working towards better writing is a continual one; it may never be easy, but it can be truly rewarding.

Reprinted in the middle of the book — between Part One and Part Two — is the complete text of a university essay: "Research and Racism: A Question of Academic Freedom" by Mary C. Dillon. It addresses the controversy surrounding the work of Philippe Rushton, psychology professor at the University of Western Ontario, who began delivering lectures by videotape in the fall of 1990 because of fears that his presence in the classroom might spark violence. The topic is fascinating and — more important for our purposes — the writing is clear and thoughtful. We refer to Ms. Dillon's essay frequently, as an important part of *The Broadview Guide*'s system of cross-references.

STYLE AND STRUCTURE

VOICE WORK: ATTITUDE, AUDIENCE, PURPOSE

What does it mean, 'the writer's *voice*'? It is a voice that a mute voice cannot speak; nothing is vocalized in the final draft, on the paper that the reader sees. At one time all reading was done aloud — in the 5th century Augustine remarks upon the

peculiarity of reading silently. But even reading aloud gives sound to the *reader's* voice, not the writer's. Ultimately, the voice of a writer is a silent force between two minds.

Of course, silence has its disadvantage; it lacks intonation, and thus can easily be misinterpreted. For example, the sentence "I was really thrilled to see them again" could, given the appropriate intonation by a speaker, become drippingly ironic — not the least bit sincere. The spoken tone of voice is an audible transmission, controlled and clearly manipulated. But the mute writer must find other ways to transmit tone and meaning, carefully arranging symbols on the page so as to minimize misinterpretation by his or her eventual readers.

---

attitude

attitude Not an easy task, and one that must begin with a mental *attitude* of self-confidence and self-assertion. A competent writer's voice is born from a position of power over the assignment at hand, the resources at hand, and the deadline that looms ahead. If no real power is felt to exist, then it must be manufactured:

> "Three-thousand words in five days? Not a problem."

> "There are definitely ways in which Milton's verse disappoints me."

> "This professor of mine is about to really learn something."

Of course, establishing full control at the outset of the writing process is impossible. "How do I know what I think," wrote E. M. Forster, "until I see what I have to say?" The point is that writers see what they have to say — they start writing — only by believing in themselves. Some manufactured power at the outset will lead to real power along the way.

Weak writing, then, can often be traced to an attitude problem. The passive writer-in-waiting views his or her blank pages like some ominous battlefield whose land-mines will commence exploding with the first timid step forward. Passiveness and timidity combine to abort the writer's fledgling voice. But **active** confrontation with an assignment, however tough that assignment may first appear, allows the voice to grow. As one sociology professor advises (in notes distributed to all her students),

> In writing the work, do not be afraid to give your own views. It is of considerable interest to the tutor to know what students think about the material, and especially what they think they have learned from the exercise. If you find material obscure or unconvincing say so, but always give the reasons.

audience

Attention to attitude, which gives birth to a writer's voice, is often followed by attention to *audience*, which modifies that voice. Competent writers realize the folly of locking themselves in to any set formulas of style or organization — because these things often change, depending upon the demands or expectations of a given audience. "Avoid the passive voice," cautions one professor of English literature. "Reports **must** be written in the third person, passive voice, and past tense," announces the professor of chemistry. What's a writer to do? Listen carefully, for one thing, and ask questions. Look over past essays written for similar audiences. Conformity to reasonable audience expectations — like writing in English instead of Hindustani — does not mean slavish imitation. Ideas can be strong and original, evidence can be compelling, even as a writer writes to please, say, the grammatical or bibliographical preferences of his or her readers-to-be.

An example from the world of academic publishing illustrates the sort of concessions good writers make to their audiences—and points up something important about the

audience

introductions

VOICE WORK: ATTITUDE, AUDIENCE, PURPOSE

matter of writing introductions to essays. Here are the introductory paragraphs from two articles that recently appeared in the Canadian journal *Queen's Quarterly*. First, from Susan P. C. Cole's "The Legacy of Terry Fox":

> More than nine years have elapsed since Terry Fox began his run across Canada to raise money for cancer research and eight years have passed since his death from the disease he sought to conquer. The events of the early 1980s surrounding Terry's Marathon of Hope can now be viewed with some perspective, and one might begin to answer a number of questions. Could the medical profession do more for Terry if he were alive today than they were able to do when he was first stricken with cancer? How has the money raised been spent? What has been the impact of his run on the efforts of the cancer research community in Canada? Has Terry's dream been kept alive? This article will address these questions and discuss the influence of Terry Fox and his Marathon of Hope on cancer research in Canada.

Second, from Neil Jumonville's "The New York Intellectuals' Defence of the Intellect" :

> Recently a number of studies of the New York intellectuals have laboured to explain their apparent journey from the political left to the centre over the past 50 years. These accounts found that the New York group sold its earlier Trotskyism for a share of bourgeois life (Wald, 1989), or that conservatism accompanied a greater sense of Jewish identification (Bloom, 1988), or that a modernist cosmopolitanism weakened their leftist commitments (Cooney, 1990). Curiously, these works have ignored the more obvious explanation that the process of wrestling with their own conceptions of themselves as intellectuals comprised the greatest influence on their outlook. Members of the New York group saw themselves primarily as intellectuals, and their political movement to the centre was prompted by their need to define the proper function of the intellectual in the new era following World War II.

VOICE WORK: ATTITUDE, AUDIENCE, PURPOSE

Cole is a pharmacologist, used to writing for other scientists, while Jumonville is a historian, used to writing for other humanists. Their approaches to an article's introductory paragraph differ as a result. After clearly announcing her topic, the scientist poses a series of relevant questions and then confirms for her readers what the article will accomplish. (She would be in trouble with the English professor who instructs his students to "avoid telling the reader about your writing; stick to your **topic** instead. Cut phrases such as "We will examine," and "This paper will show that.") The humanist also begins with a clear announcement of his topic, but that is where the similarity ends. He immediately carves out the argumentative territory of his essay, moving from opposing views — of Wald, Bloom, and Cooney — to his own **thesis statement** (18) in the final two sentences of the paragraph. (Jumonville would find more favour with the English professor: "I consider it conventional, and therefore essential, that your thesis be stated in the **last** sentence of paragraph one.")

Like most scientific writers, Susan Cole saves her argumentative assertions — the answers to questions posed in the introductory paragraph — for the "Conclusion" of her article. This bottom-heavy approach, which contrasts with the top-heavy approach of Neil Jumonville, is dictated — in part — by knowledge of the intended audience. Such knowledge no competent writer can afford to lack.

Notice that neither Cole nor Jumonville ignored the profile of the *Queen's Quarterly's* audience. Both were able to maintain their discipline-specific methods of introduction because of that journal's editorial policy: "Articles are interdisciplinary in nature and are intended to have a broad appeal." Certainly, the more diverse the audience, the more freedom a writer may enjoy in decisions of organization and style. Many university essay-writers tend to err, however, in the other direction: by envisioning an audience of one — namely, the professor responsible for the assignment. Even if she may, in fact, be the only one who will read the paper, it is better to write not only for the professor but also for one's peers, for the other people in the lecture hall or classroom, so as to avoid unnaturally stilted language and overly grandiose assertions. In writers' worlds, the most successful voices are the least strained.

purpose

purpose   But even with diligent attention to attitude and audience, some very important voice work remains to be done. No writer can get on with the business of filling up pages and sorting out paragraphs unless some compelling *purpose* for it all exists. "What's it all about?" "Why am I sitting here losing sleep and working myself into a state of anxious indigestion?" Such questions must be raised and must be answered — at least partially: "I don't believe the writer should know too much where he's going," says James Thurber. "If he does, he runs into old man blueprint — old man propaganda." Certainly no good journalist follows an editor's blueprint and no good university essayist follows a professor's blueprint. But each requires a purpose, one that is more than the mere desire to earn this month's salary or this term's B+ in history.

The stated assignment is an obvious place to begin. "Discuss the rise to power of Francisco Franco." Or "Thoroughly explain the advances in kidney dialysis technology since the 1960s." Or "Analyze the connections between Margaret Atwood's poetry and her novels." Very few writers are absolutely free to devise their own purposes. Most receive orders or commands ("Discuss" "Explain" "Analyze"), either from some external figure of authority or from inside their own writerly consciences. Such commands are usually quite vague and open-ended, though. It's enough to make an honest writer quiver and squirm:

> How am I supposed to discuss the rise to power of Francisco Franco? That could take years! And what is "Discuss" supposed to mean? Do I tell the story of the Spanish Civil War? Do I try to ascertain Franco's psychological makeup, or to analyze socio-economic influences at work at the time? How does my professor feel; what exactly is she expecting with this paper, anyway?

If she's a professor who really cares about writing, she's expecting some tension to be located and resolved. Purpose in writing comes from tension, from the writer's personal sense of things out of kilter, in conflict:

> This clash engenders puzzlement, curiosity, a sense of enigma, sometimes of wonder, a pressure to restore equilibrium. While some people suppress such tension, the inquirer, the learner, strives to resolve it by searching for new understanding, by going beyond the known.

What Janice Lauer is actually recommending here is a sublime experience, through which "the inquirer, the learner" confronts an essay topic in much the same way that King Lear confronts the stormy heath or Alice confronts her Wonderland. Worthy purposes are often a little off-beat, a little idiosyncratic, even a little bit fantastic. They turn otherwise formulaic, impersonal, encyclopedia-entry essays into essays of personally distinct intellect. Competent writers can write personally without being subjective and intellectually without being pretentious or false.

What if (returning to Francisco Franco) a prospective writer is bothered by the whole notion of "power" in the world of Spanish politics and warfare? Ignoring that abstract and difficult word might very well short-circuit her ability to handle the assignment — whereas grappling with its **definition** (39) might *be* sufficient purpose to set her writing in gear. Rather than half-heartedly narrating a string of events from the 1930s or explaining the political parties of that era, she would be motivated to write by the personal tension and ambiguity surrounding a single word in the assignment. What does the Spanish Civil War suggest about the nature of power? Suddenly, the paper has a focus. From here it is only a step or two to a **thesis statement** — a statement of the writer's intentions, which expresses concisely what the essay as a whole will attempt to show.

> Like most fascists, Franco saw power as an end in itself, not merely as a means to achieving other ends.

Unlike the topic, the thesis statement expresses a purpose and a point of view. It should be strong, clear, concise and meaningful. It should be limited in its scope to what can realistically be shown in the available space. It need not be original, but it should not be self-evident, either. It need not be simple, but it should be concise — a sentence, two at the most. It need not declare anything earth-shattering, but it should not be trivial.

Effective thesis statements are molded to fit both the length of their essays and the expertise of their writers. There is no logical sense in asserting, at the outset of a 3000-word history paper, that "every military leader since Attila the Hun has repeated his mistakes" or that "all politicians who supported American intervention in Vietnam qualifiers were morally corrupt." The vocabulary of absolutes ("every" "all" "best" "only" etc.) always commits a writer to universal coverage — and authoritative knowledge — of his topic. Chances are he has neither time and space for the former nor

THESIS STATEMENTS: SOME EXAMPLES

worth checking   Art is important to society in many ways, and I will talk about them in this essay. One of the artists I will focus on is Robert Mapplethorpe, the subject of much recent controversy.

   thesis

   statements

Yawn. The statement is too general and too vague to have significance.

revised   The art of Robert Mapplethorpe deserves to be exhibited — and at public expense — even if most people find it abhorrent.

This statement is more precise, more limited, more interesting.

worth checking   In this paper I will examine various reasons for launching the war against Iraq in 1991.

This is statement of topic rather than thesis. It's also wordy.

revised   The US and its allies had a relatively strong moral case for launching the war against Iraq in 1991, but it is difficult to accept that their motives for doing so were entirely pure.

Suddenly there is an argument being made.

worth checking   The purpose of this essay is to explore the interplay between poetry and the novel. I will prove that good poets don't usually write good novels and vice versa.

Full points for ambition, but it's the subject for a book, not a term paper. (At most, a short paper might justifiably speculate about such a large question in its conclusion; the main focus should be much narrower.) Also, the statement is far too bold in its generalization ("What about Thomas Hardy?" the professor will ask. "What about Boris Pasternak?").

revised   Ondaatje's characters seem thin and unreal to the reader — alternately brittle and transparent. Paradoxically, however, it may be precisely these qualities that allow the poetic power of his prose — at once brutal and fragile — to strike the reader with full force.

A much narrower but still controversial thesis exploring the connections between poetry and prose.

sufficient education for the latter. Strength in argumentative writing often comes from a willingness to qualify assertions and to acknowledge that contrary points of view are, if not

VOICE WORK: ATTITUDE, AUDIENCE, PURPOSE

convincing, at least intelligent and comprehensible. Words such as "often", "usually", "largely", and phrases such as "for the most part," "to a great extent" are not necessarily signs that the writer is cowardly or lacks the courage of his convictions; more frequently they are indications that he is careful.

* * *

All of the above rests on one important presupposition — that the student understands the topic he is given. What if one is uncertain not only as to 'what the professor wants', but also as to what she *means*? This should not be thought of as an indication that the student is stupid; it is far worse to plunge blindly ahead in the hope that one has grasped the topic — and the conviction that it would be shameful to expose one's ignorance to one's professor — than it is to be honest about one's uncertainty. After all, the language of assignments, like academic language generally, *is* often difficult. Here, for example, is the gloss to an assignment provided by a sociology professor to his students:

> The assignment involves learning to think sociologically and to present a sociological argument. The process involved is analogous to "inductive" reasoning (or what some sociologists refer to as "grounded theory") in that the object is to start from where you are at and refine your thinking such that you develop general statements that represent the character of human social activity and that are capable of being treated with reference to empirical reality.

No student should be ashamed of asking for a clarification here. This, the language of intellectual discourse, involves concepts, all of which are made up of abstract nouns — words representing things that cannot be seen or heard or appreciated by any physical sense. Consequently, concepts are difficult to grasp, especially when the abstract noun is preceded by an equally abstract adjective: "empirical reality," for example, or "sociological argument," or (turning to

this very paragraph) "intellectual discourse," or (turning to Mary Dillon's essay) "academic freedom." By the time they graduate, students are expected to have learnt to deal comfortably with abstract and difficult concepts. But they're not expected to be comfortable from the outset; in the face of uncertainty and confusion, *ask*!

* * *

Once the topic is clearly understood, though, generating purpose is — at university or college — the responsibility of the students, not the professors. Every assignment ever dreamed up by the latter group could be reduced to a single imperative: "Respond!" Once lethargy and timidity are shunned (**attitude**), and once the eventual readers are clearly in mind (**audience**), then any writer who is not brain-dead will be able to locate tension in the course material or in the statement of topic. To resolve that tension becomes the essay's **purpose**, one that may well change or expand or contract during the writing process but without which no writer's voice can ever be called complete.

VOICE WORK: ATTITUDE, AUDIENCE, PURPOSE

THE BIG IDEAS: READING, MAPPING, DIALOGUE

Something is bothering Mary C. Dillon. She doesn't like Philippe Rushton's theoretical ideas—not in the least. But it's more than that. Something bothers her about the way those ideas are being circulated, publicized, analyzed. Mary would like to sort out what amounts to a gut reaction. She'd like to deal with some wordless tension by working with words. The time to write an essay has arrived because Mary C. Dillon has a purpose.

The final draft of her essay on Rushton (109-115) is exactly that: the *final* residue of an intense thinking process, during which the purpose in her gut found articulate expression in a few big ideas and in the material supporting them. This mental refinement — from purpose to ideas — is usually the most mysterious and satisfying phase of the writing process: "The initial delight is in the discovery of something I didn't know I knew," the American poet Robert Frost once said, knowing from long experience that writing and thinking grow together like Siamese twins — mutually supportive and absolutely bound.

reading

First among activities that assist writers in discovering their own thoughts is *reading*. According to another celebrated   reading

American poet, Walt Whitman, it requires no less self-confidence and self-assertion than writing itself:

> Books are to be call'd for, and supplied, on the assumption that the process of reading is not a half-sleep, but, in the highest sense, an exercise, a gymnast's struggle; that the reader is to do something for himself, must be on the alert, must himself or herself construct indeed the poem, argument, history, metaphysical essay — the text furnishing the hints, the clue, the start or framework. Not the book needs so much to be the complete thing, but the reader of the book does.

There is no such thing as a frozen, immutable text whose lofty message can only be unlocked by a single, privileged, correct reading. Rather, each reader constructs the text anew. Even when faced with assigned chapters by world-famous intellectuals, he or she must be ready to respond. Whitman is right: reading is valuable because it provides "the hints, the clue, the start or framework" of the reader's own text.

In practice, this means taking notes. As work begins for many a writer, paper and pencil are nearby. Or paper and pen, or word-processor (if it happens to be compact and portable). Thoughts and insights can strike at any time, but they also have a way of evaporating quickly — so it's wise to be prepared. From the word "*Go!*", writing things down is central to the writing process. Some reading writers favour the pencil-in-the-margin approach, which yields brief and pointed reactions (such as "Bad logic" or "?" or "!" or "Yes!" or "Ho hum"). Others keep sheets of paper handy, to work up some preliminary sentences — or even paragraphs. Either way, the objective is to use reading as a catalyst in the discovery of ideas on the mind. (This is not the only purpose of note-taking, of course; they are also crucial as a research tool — see below, page 95.)

For many people who are reading to survive at universities, though, note-taking seems like a utopian luxury enjoyed in some distant time warp. There are simply too many pages of too many books and articles to plough through. Among such burdened readers, the most fortunate and effective are those who hang on to their pens by forfeiting some text: they *do* take notes, but they read selectively. Before ploughing through anything in an assigned reading, they skim over the introduction, the lead sentences of paragraphs, and the conclusion. In other words, they conduct a reconnaissance mission, based on strategic knowledge of most essays' terrains. The likely result is an accurate sense of the essay's thesis, key terminology, range of evidence, and logical organization. Such readers will then select passages for sustained and thorough surveillance, according to the purposes developed in their own voice work.

mapping

In the beginning, when the task at hand is choosing a topic or considering what aspects to focus on to build a thesis, a writer's thinking may be quite unstructured. Indeed, it's a positive benefit — in the early stages particularly — to play with ideas, to think loosely, to allow a wide range of notions to jostle together in the brain — and on paper as you make rough notes.

mapping

As the topic comes into focus, though, a bit more structure is necessary; the writer needs to begin building an outline of the path the argument will take. But at this stage no one wants to feel that the structure of the argument is cast in

THE TRADITIONAL OUTLINE

...Having collected so much information, you now begin to sort, grouping like items together....(Some items don't become members of a group easily; they resist and struggle until you force them to join.) Like all writers, you are feeling a bit anxious at this stage of the composing process.

So, when you remember what you were taught in school about a proper *outline*, you feel as if you might be getting somewhere. You write down

> Introduction

and you feel a bit better. In need of good feelings at this unsettling stage of composing, you go ahead with what Mr. Jones taught you in Grade 7, or Miss Ashworth showed you in Grade 10:

> I. Introduction
> II.
>   A.
>   B.
>   1.
>   2.
>   C.
> III.
>   A.
>   1.
>   2.
> IV. Conclusion

What a relief!...

This kind of outline can be useful as a memory device: it reminds you to mention certain parts of your research. But it also has serious flaws . . . For one thing, it makes no

stone; it shouldn't be. Now is the time for the second crucial activity that leads to a writer's thought-discoveries: *mapping*. Unlike a first draft — or a traditional outline — mapping ignores the inevitable sequence (left to right, top to bottom) of the essay-to-be. It provides, instead, a **spatial** rendition of emerging ideas, concerns, and questions to be answered;

estimate of the essay's *proportions*: it can fail entirely to account for the volume of each element...[Moreover], even the most intricately ordered and labelled outline can fail to generate the strong *topic* you need to keep your reader on track and to ward off ambiguity....The schoolroom outline can mislead you into thinking you have a topic, when all you really have is a general name for what you are talking about....

Sometimes the successful writer might conceive of his topic when he reviews his outline and spots disconnection; aware of the gap, he comes up with the meaningful connection, the proposition that justifies these two things being said next to each other.

Or sometimes the topic might emerge when the writer is composing his first draft: trying to get from section III to section IV, he finds himself stuck for a "transition." ...Other times, the topic arrives as the essay *plan* is developing, as the writer works on organizing his material and designing an argument. Then the outline or plan itself constructs the connections that have to be made, and itself generates the strong complex topic that makes the essay coherent and meaningful.

Janet Giltrow, Academic Writing

Giltrow makes clear that, although it can unquestionably help some writers to use an outline as well as a map at the outset of the writing process, no outline should be regarded as cast in stone before the writing begins. For more on outlines see page 50.

the writer can thereby realize more clearly which ones are aligned or inter-dependent, which ones are dominant, and which less important. Furthermore, he can literally centre his material around the biggest idea of them all — the **thesis**, the argumentative assertion that his entire essay will be constructed to support.

THE BIG IDEAS: READING, MAPPING, DIALOGUE

Return to the example of Mary C. Dillon. As her "Works Cited" list shows (116), she read several articles, academic and otherwise, and even listened to the CBC in order to sort out her gut reaction to Philippe Rushton's work. With notes from this research, she was able to map out an essay yet to be written (see facing page).

Several times while reading, Mary had come upon the phrase "academic freedom" and jotted down in her notes: "This term isn't clear" or "Unclear concept." As the starred command in her mapping reveals, the essay will certainly strive to "explain this term." **Definition** (39) will be one of her key writing strategies.

The identification of such strategies, whose common aim is to support the thesis, is yet another dividend of mapping. Every writer uses them because they are all natural modes of

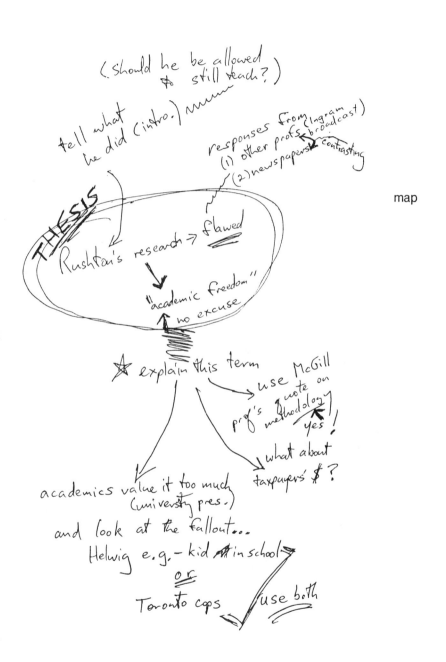

map

THE BIG IDEAS: READING, MAPPING, DIALOGUE

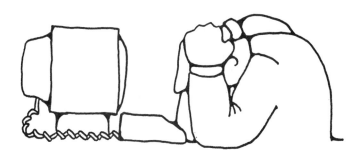

human thought. **Definition** appears in Mary's map but so does **narration** ("tell what he did"), **example** ("Helwig e.g. - kid in school"), **cause and effect** ("academics value it too much . . . and look at the fallout"), and **contrast** ("other profs / newspapers"). We will return to these modes of thought and writing shortly (37-53).

Because Mary's mapping happens to be a very accurate preview of her essay (this will not always be the case), it is possible to pinpoint sentences in the final draft that represent each writing strategy. In the middle of paragraph two, for example, she writes: "Curiously, while the press furiously covered the story, Rushton's colleagues were generally quiet." Thus she articulates the **contrast** that emerged through mapping. Two sentences later, with the mention of geneticist Joseph Cummings, another strategy arises: "Joseph Cummings" is an **example** of the category "colleagues." Here contrast flows into example, just as fluidly as narration flows into argument in paragraph one — where Mary briefly tells the story of what Rushton did before presenting her thesis statement. Fluidity, overlap, merger, and convergence are all characteristic of writing strategies, because those strategies represent a miraculously complex and kinetic field of energy: the human mind.

As Mary's work demonstrates, many big ideas can get together on paper for the first time through mapping. A few appear in the form of questions ("Should he be allowed to teach?" "What about taxpayers' $s?"); another is crystallized through images ("fallout", "kid in school", "Toronto cops"). All of them, however, radiate from and connect to the biggest of the big ideas — Mary's thesis concerning Rushton's research. Its two-pronged appearance on the map carries over to the final draft (at the end of paragraph one): "Evaluation of Rushton's work and its impact reveals that his research is faulty, and to support his rights using academic freedom ignores the rights of students and the interests of the public." Because it is a thesis statement, this sentence's strategy is **argument**. But the argumentative strength of any thesis depends entirely on its strategic accompaniment, which — even in a short essay like Mary's — is diverse. Mapping is an invaluable aid in managing the diversity of any writer's text.

What is one to do, though, in the presence of a feeling that it is somehow *impossible* to get down to the actual *writing*? One doesn't have to be a professional writer to experience what is known as 'writer's block'. Almost all of us know the experience of sitting down to write, notes and map or outline close to hand. 'Perhaps my plan needs a bit more fiddling', we think. 'Now what was it again that Smith and Sapsucker said about all this? Maybe I should check that passage again...And maybe I should get a new pen to write

writer's block

THE BIG IDEAS: READING, MAPPING, DIALOGUE

with. Or delete some of the stuff on this disc so I'll be sure to have enough space for the essay...A coffee might help...' It may be a comfort to know that instructors do this as well. Many's the time that a professor will say, "I'm working on a paper dealing with such and such. It's pretty much done; all I have to do is write it up." The professor knows as well as the student that this is a convenient fiction — that the writing is the main business, not just an afterthought. But to the academic, as to the student, it sometimes seems just too daunting.

How can this problem be avoided? The simplest and quickest way is to write anything at all. To force the pen to move over the paper (the cursor keys to start clicking) quite literally writing   anything that comes to mind, whether coherent or not, whether on or off the topic. Within fifteen or twenty minutes at the most suddenly one is writing quickly and profusely on the chosen topic. The writing won't, of course, display perfect grammar, spelling or punctuation. Nor will it be perfectly organized. But at this stage none of that matters.

Once a writer has begun writing fluidly on the topic, it does *not* pay to pause when she hits a point in the argument that requires an example or a reference that's not handy. Instead, she should jot down a note in the margin ('find example—Taylor's book?' or 'support this with quotation—gravediggers' scene?') and keep on going! There will be plenty of time later to check for the required item, and chances are that doing so now will mean losing the flow of the argument.

Eventually the moment comes to set down the pen for a few minutes and take stock of the words on the page or the

THE BIG IDEAS: READING, MAPPING, DIALOGUE

screen: to decide how much fits in, and where, what needs fleshing out, what should be scrapped. It may be the time to start revising the map in the light of what's been discovered while writing. For, as every experienced writer knows, writing is *not* simply a process of putting down on paper what is already known in the writer's mind. The very act of writing inevitably (but often quite unexpectedly) forces the writer to see things differently, to combine ideas in unanticipated ways.

---

dialogue

A third activity, *dialogue*, is a complement to reading and mapping in the formulation of an essay's big ideas.

<u>dialogue</u>

Its importance is continuously proven these days by the success and rapid growth of writing centres at universities throughout North America. There people talk about writing, often in groups of two, often focusing on material brought along by one of them — some preliminary notes, mapping, paragraphs. Questions get asked, and answered, concerning the essay's thesis and the suitability of writing strategies intended for its support. Such dialogue is immediately encouraging for a writer-in-process, who steps from the solitary turbulence of his work and finds an attentive ear and sympathetic heart (most writing centre tutors are writers of some kind themselves). Dialogue can help ensure that the writer fully understands the topic (20). Dialogue can help ensure that a writer in pursuit of big ideas does not get his priorities backwards. Dialogue can be invaluable as an aid to curing many of the specific germs that can infect writing style and corrupt purpose, as it can to correcting the mechanical mistakes (detailed in Part Two) that can so easily distract the reader from the ideas being discussed.

Often, though, it may not be possible to see someone at a Writing Centre about each essay. One should also be ready and willing to show your writing to friends, classmates — and of course instructors — at any stage. Too often we look at our work as sacrosanct; we are embarrassed by its weaknesses, shy of showing it to others before it's what we like to think of as perfect. And if at that late stage others see imperfections, we are too easily hurt. Ironically, the more experienced and confident a writer is, the more she is usually willing and eager to seek out dialogue — and criticism — from others. She has developed even within herself a critical stance towards her work; she knows it is not and will never be perfect; but she knows as well that dialogue with others is always a way to improvement, and is in itself a stimulating and enjoyable activity.

DOUBLE FLUENCY: LOGICAL AND STYLISTIC

Smooth easy flow. Effortless movement. In a word, *fluency* — something that any finished piece of writing is much better off with than without. As all experienced writers know, however, the appearance of effortlessness and ease is superficial; the final draft of an essay is a marvelously opaque surface, showing readers none of the turbulence that is so much a part of the writing process. This section of *The Broadview Guide* will try to create some transparency in that surface — and peer down at the two principal sources of movement and flow.

logical fluency

Because most university essays are argumentative, their strength depends greatly on *logical fluency*. Assertions need to be clearly supported by reasons, and those reasons need to be convincing and . . . well . . . logical. "Try to be more clear, convincing, and *logical* in future papers," advises many a well-meaning professor. Easier said than done. Fortunately, experience has taught competent writers some useful approaches — and some speciific cautions.

A first step towards logical fluency is to be aware of **premises** in the back of the mind. Most writing starts with certain *conscious* premises; Mary Dillon, for example, has clearly begun with the premise "Rushton is wrong"; she

premises

non-sequiturs

> ## THAT'S WHY SO MUCH RICE IS CONSUMED IN CHINA
>
> The effect on the reader if the writer does not show the links in his argument is a sense that what one is reading does not follow (in Latin *non sequitur*) from what one has just read. It's worth remembering the expression *non sequitur* — as *Globe & Mail* sportswriter Marty York didn't:
>
> > Reporting the possibility of mean old George Bell's being traded to the Philadelphia Phillies, Marty York asks, "is it a *non sequitur* for George Bell to exist in the city of Brotherly Love? "
> >
> > The answer, if he really wants one, is no.
> >
> > It may be an irony, a contradiction, an inconsistency, or even *nihil ad rem*. But it is not a *non sequitur*. That's why so much rice is consumed in China.
> >
> > (Robertson Cochrane, letter to the *Globe & Mail*, Oct. 1990)

moves later to more specific conscious premises in her argument, such as "academic freedom protects only methodologically rigorous work" (52). Consciously held premises such as these are useful and indeed necessary steps in building an argument. But we also all hold *unconscious* premises — general beliefs, automatic assumptions, with the power to covertly direct our critical thinking. "I cannot possibly have anything worthwhile to say on this topic" is an example; if allowed to lurk in the back of the mind, this premise — this crisis of attitude (12) — will paralyze an essay's development. "Children over five years of age are just miniature adults" is a premise that could lead an editorialist to call for a return to corporal punishment in our schools. "Capitalism is in all circumstances the best system" is a premise that would certainly cloud a writer's judgement and reduce her capacity for understanding if she were writing an essay on the economic system of medieval Europe, or that of traditional Inuit society. Premises, be they strong or weak, do not always appear in the text of an essay. All the more reason, then, for every writer to examine hers attentively, so that the essay's logic will be intentional, not inadvertent.

elaboration

Even a clear and manageable thesis will be ineffective unless the writer carefully elaborates every one of its parts. It is all too easy when writing to assume that the reader will make all the same logical connections that he has, and because of that to omit what seem to him to be obvious steps in the argument. Here again it is useful to keep trying to imagine the reader, to keep asking, "Am I making everything clear for someone who has *not* done the research I have and does *not* know anything of my argument beyond what I have told him. In conversation it's easy enough for the other person to interrupt by saying, "I can't follow your reasoning there." The reader can never do the same. elaboration

modes of thought / modes of writing

It is traditional to classify essays as falling into categories such as descriptive, narrative, and persuasive or argumentative. In practice, such distinctions are largely artificial; few essays are written purely in one form. The most common pattern for college and university essays is broadly speaking argumentative — the writer is trying to prove a point — but most arguments also incorporate elements of description, narration and so forth. thought / writing

It is true, though, that we use different mental processes

for different sorts of writing, and it may be helpful to examine the different modes of writing in connection with some of these processes: classification, abstraction, generalization, narration, and causal thought.

---

classification

---

classification Classification is the process of sorting into groups. Mental act of classifying can be enormously complex; how well we learn to do it will have a lot to do with how well we learn to write with logical fluency.

comparison Classification is particularly important to essays that make comparisons or draw contrasts. If the writer is comparing the Canadian economy with that of the United States, for example, she will sort the data or other evidence she has assembled into various classes: sizes of the two economies; strengths of particular economic sectors (manufacturing, services, government etc.); trade; banking and interest rates; geographical and climatic inputs; and so on. In doing so she will need to make a number of choices. What will go in and what will be left out? In large part this will be dictated by the thrust of her argument. (Essays of comparison and contrast, like other essays, must have a purpose; they should never be merely lists.) She must be careful, certainly, not to make the selection on a random or arbitrary basis.

Then there are questions of where given topics should appear in the paper. Should the essay deal with all aspects of one country's economy first, and then turn to the economy of the other country? Usually this approach results in a weaker paper structurally; it is probably better to compare manufacturing with manufacturing, banking with

under the classification of government or that of banking? Should the impact of defense spending on the two economies be dealt with under government spending or under manufacturing? She may well find half way through the writing process that a given topic fits better under another classification, and end up revising entire paragraphs and moving them from one place to another in the essay in order to increase its level of logical fluency. (Here of course, is where computers come into their own.)

Classification is of equal importance if the essayist is writing description in a descriptive mode: telling what something looks like or how it works. (This mode of writing is particularly common in the sciences.) If the writer is describing the behaviour patterns of the beaver, for example, he may decide to group them into headings such as feeding, dam- and lodge-building, and breeding habits. He will probably also want to discuss how the anatomy of the animal and its behaviours (193) are adapted to each other — perhaps pausing after each category of behaviour has been described to relate it to particular anatomical features. Here we may see clearly how naturally paragraphing follows classification.

Classification is also vital to another mode of writing — definition definition. Sometimes an entire essay may have a question of definition as its focus:

- 19th and 20th Century Definitions of 'Liberalism'
- The Concept of Metonymy in Sixteenth Century Rhetoric and in Deconstructionist Criticism
- 'Making Love' from the 1950s to the 1990s

In such cases the writer describes or analyses the ways in which a term or concept has been understood differently in different eras. How did the term 'liberal', which in the nineteenth century implied firm opposition to government intervention in the economy, come to imply the very opposite a hundred years later? How did 'making love', once understood to refer to acts of courtship that stopped short of the sexual act, come in the 1960s to refer to *nothing but* the sexual act? And how do such changes in definition reflect or even cause broader changes in social attitudes?

Definition can also be an important part of other sorts of essays, as another look at Mary Dillon's paper illustrates. She offers two definitions of academic freedom — one in paragraph 3 and one in paragraph 4. Under Roy's definition, with its proviso about "methodologically rigorous work," Dillon feels Rushton's research can be excluded from the class of research that deserves protection under the principle of academic freedom. The definition is thus central to her argument.

Notice that Dillon does not refer to any dictionary definition. She is aware that dictionary definitions are usually inadequate to the needs of academic writing. Indeed, if a term has a meaning particular to an academic discipline, dictionary definitions can be downright misleading.

---

generalization and abstraction

generalization and abstraction Generalization is the process of moving from an observation or conclusion about a single thing or a small number to a conclusion about all or most of that group. Abstraction, on the other hand (20), is at its most basic level the isolation of some particular quality of a thing from the rest of its properties — the consideration of the colour of a particular object, for example.

Many people are a bit hazy on the difference between abstraction and generalization — not surprisingly, since the two are related activities that we often perform simultaneously. Perhaps the best way of keeping them straight is to remember (as Christopher Hallpike puts it) that "while the opposite of 'general' is 'particular', the opposite of 'abstract' is 'concrete'":

> *Emotions* is a broad general category; *love* and *hate* are particular emotions. (Neither is a concrete thing.)
>
> The redness of the Canadian flag is an abstraction; the flag itself is a concrete thing.
>
> (We may also, of course, speak of one particular Canadian flag or of the Canadian flag in general, or of all flags in general; there can be numerous levels of both abstraction and generalization.)

Most essays involve shifts not only from the general to the particular and back again but also from one level of generalization to another:

- An art history essay on Chippendale chairs would probably refer to particular examples from the 18th century studio of Thomas Chippendale himself, generalize about all chairs of that type, generalize further about the furniture of the period, and perhaps generalize at one higher level about how and why such designs suited the overall sensibilities of 18th century England.

- An English literature essay might make a general claim about Jane Austen's use of irony. It might then descend one level of generality to discuss the differences in the degree to which the generalization applies in the various novels. It might then move to a lower level of generality, distinguishing between the scenes in Northanger Abbey that are suffused with the characteristic Austen sense of irony and those (apparently

> remaining from the first draft of the novel) that are almost pure melodrama with no irony to them whatsoever. Finally, the essay would doubtless give particular examples — quote sentences or paragraphs that exemplify an ironic tone and a melodramatic one.

Both abstraction and generalization are important mental processes for any writer; they help us, as Janet Giltrow puts it, to "name and manage otherwise unruly details." But writers have to learn to use them with care. As a rule, generalizations must be supported by evidence. (Generalizations that are commonplaces may be made without support; one does not need to provide evidence in support of the generalization that dogs have four legs or that war is terrible thing, or cite sources to back up a claim that Jane Austen has been widely admired for her use of irony.) If an essay makes any claim that is not generally accepted (and if it is an interesting essay it usually will make several such claims), the claim must be supported either inductively or deductively (51). If the reasoning is inductive, the writer must be particularly careful to show that he is aware when his generalizations do not apply in all cases. He should make clear if he is writing about the way the beaver build lodges that not all beaver do so; river beaver have quite different quarters and behave differently in other ways as well.

And he should be precise. "Most Canadians voted against the Free Trade Agreement in the 1988 election" is an imprecise generalization. "In the 1988 election most Canadians voted for parties that opposed the Free Trade Agreement" is more accurate. Such concern for precision may seem like pedantry; is there any difference between the two statements? Yes, there is. In that election many Canadians who opposed Free Trade nevertheless voted for the Progressive Conservatives, just as many Canadians who supported Free Trade voted for the Liberals or New Democrats. Free Trade was the most contentious issue in the campaign, but not the only one; it *was* an election, not a referendum. Being careful about such distinctions is an important part of what is involved in a college or university education.

---

narration

The mode of thought involved in narratives is a very simple narration one: one thing happens, and then another thing happens, and then another thing happens.... Narration is particularly useful in an academic context when the writer is describing the steps in a procedure, such as a scientific experiment. (The body of a lab report is normally largely taken up by narration, though the most important sections — outlining the hypothesis, drawing conclusions, etc. — will not be written in a narrative mode.)

Narrative is the most straightforward mode of thinking and of writing, but in academic work it should normally be used sparingly. There is a special temptation to employ the narrative mode in writing history or literature (45) essays. In a few cases this may be appropriate. If the writer is discussing the Watergate scandal during the administration of Richard Nixon, for example, the narrative mode may well be the best one to adopt; the sequence is a complex one, and getting it straight is crucial to establishing the degrees of guilt (who knew what when) of those

---

WRITING ABOUT LITERATURE

For as long as literature has been taught as an academic subject students who care about the feelings books engender in them have sometimes felt that the analysis of literary works is an act of dissection: a process that somehow removes the feelings that are what they value about the work. They are taught not to write *I think* and *I feel* (82), to think in the abstract terms of theme, image, symbol and character. They are taught that — unlike works of history or psychology or philosophy — works of fiction or poetry are often texts that do not directly say what the author means; the students are not supposed to commit the *intentional fallacy* of confusing what the characters in a literary work say with what the author herself feels or believes. They are taught to look at the text not in the context of the real world in which they live but in the context of other texts, and of the ideologies current at the time the text was created.

What they are sometimes not taught, but what they should never forget, is that an essay need not lose sight of the feelings that literary works give rise to. Indeed, literary analysis that starts with those feelings, that never loses sight of those feelings is often literary analysis of the greatest depth and the highest order. To discuss the symbols or imagery of a text, or the ways in which character is conveyed, or the structure of the plot is not to deny the feelings the work gives rise to, but to attempt to understand them — to explain how it is that the work can have such an effect on the reader. That we are often unsure of the author's own beliefs and feelings does nothing to detract from the strength of the beliefs and feelings of the characters, or those of the reader.

---

involved. But the narrative should be introduced in support of the writer's argument. It must not overwhelm the ideas.

---

cause and effect

cause and effect A great deal of university and college writing involves discerning and analyzing causes and effects. Whereas the

To relate a text to other texts is not to deny its value — or to suggest that a work cannot speak powerfully to us even across many centuries. Rather it is to attempt to understand how that value is relative, and has particular roots in a given culture and ideology. In all these areas, the understanding that comes through analysis and discussion can help to deepen our feeling for literary works; it should never be allowed to destroy that feeling.

Some particular cautions follow:

- sources: Consult critical works, but don't rely on them to make the argument. The main points of an essay about literature should always be supported by direct reference to the text(s).
- verb tense: Use the present tense when writing about literature (141).
- quotation: Exercise care in integrating quotations into the essay (162, 280).
- story line: Avoid summaries of the story line of a text: summarize and paraphrase where necessary, but write with the understanding that the reader has read the work(s) being discussed. Like essays in most other Arts and Social Sciences disciplines, English essays should discuss the topic and present an argument — not tell a story.
- Keep the historical context in which the text was written in mind. Comment on or explore the manner in which the female characters in Austen's novels occupy subservient positions in society, but don't condemn the author as you might someone living in the 1990s for holding reactionary or sexist views. If writing about the rhythm and metre of the fourteenth-century poem 'Sir Gawain and the Green Knight' be aware of the poetic conventions prevalent at the time.

natural connectives in narrative writing are "and" and "then", the natural connectives in writing about causes and effects are words such as "because" and "therefore". These **connectives** (and how they relate to causes and effects) are treated fully below (55, 213). Here we offer three additional points.

Events often have more than one cause, and claims must   multiple causes often be justified by more than one reason. This sounds straightforward enough, but it is easy to forget, as the following examples show.

Many of the arguments against the war against Iraq in 1991 took this form:

> The Americans are fighting because they believe the oil reserves of the Gulf region are of strategic and economic importance to them. This is not a good moral justification for going to war. Therefore we should not be fighting.

To begin with, this sort of argument confuses explanation with justification. To ask what American motives were is to ask *why* they went to war — a very different thing from asking if they *should* have gone to war. Quite possibly they may have done "the right deed for the wrong reason."

Beyond this, however, the argument assumes that if one explanation can safely be advanced for an action, it is also safe to conclude that it is the *only* explanation. Surely it is entirely possible that the US and its allies went to war *both* out of a self-interested desire to protect oil reserves *and* out of a genuine desire to resist aggression? There may well have been other reasons, too.

A similar blindness to multiple causes and reasons afflicts the reasoning of many on the other side of the fence. The gist of the argument of George Bush and Brian Mulroney was this:

> In an act of brutal aggression, Iraq invaded and annexed Kuwait, killing many of its citizens in the process. Aggression must be resisted. Therefore we should go to war.

Like the anti-war argument above, this is incomplete reasoning; it fails to allow for any multiplicity of causes, reasons, and effects. What if Iraq had a legitimate historical claim on the territory of Kuwait (which, like Iraq, was carved out what had been a part of the Ottoman Empire by the British)? It might also be that, even if Saddam Hussein's actions were totally unjustifiable, *and* even if he could be driven out of Kuwait with the minimum of casualties on both sides, that the negative side effects of war would be sufficiently great as to outweigh the benefits of resisting aggression. If, for example, war could be seen as likely to lead to generations of increased instability and hardship throughout the region, then the virtues of resisting aggression become far less clear cut.

A useful distinction in sorting out the relative importance of multiple causes, effects and reasons is that between necessary and sufficient conditions. The presence of oxygen is a necessary condition for there to be fire; there can be no fire without oxygen. But it is not a *sufficient* condition; everything in the presence of oxygen does not automatically catch fire.

necessary and sufficient conditions

Similarly (in the argument discussed above), George Bush and Brian Mulroney are in effect arguing that the fact that Iraq had invaded and annexed another sovereign country was in itself a sufficient condition to justify going to war. Someone arguing against going to war in the same circumstances might claim that the invasion of one country by another was a necessary condition for going to war, but not a sufficient one — that other, additional justification was required. And a third person might say that the invasion constituted neither a necessary nor a sufficient condition; that we should stay out of such affairs in any circumstances.

Anther useful distinction — particularly in the sciences and social sciences — is between cause and correlation. Again, this may be made clear by example. A recent study has

cause and correlation

shown that the rate of breast cancer in women has increased markedly over the past twenty years. Over the same period, the average childbearing age has also increased dramatically. Now it is *possible* that the connection between those two occurrences may be causal in nature — that, for example, waiting until later in life to have children increases one's risk of breast cancer. But researchers caution that we should not assume this to be the case; more research needs to be done. As it stands, the connection is merely a correlation: an interelationship of variable qualities. In this case, over the same period and under the same conditions, both variables increased.

When a correlation between two things exists,

- there may be a common cause or common causes for both
- one may cause the other (or help to cause the other; again, more than one cause may be involved)
- the two may happen coincidentally as a result of quite separate causes

* * *

Let us now look once more now at the structure of Mary Dillon's essay, this time from the point of view of the way in which she has employed the mental processes of generalization and abstraction, classification, and sorting out causes and effects. Let's look first at the way in which she moves back and forth between the general and the particular:

- paragraph (1)   An introduction both to the general issues at stake (including the abstract concept of academic freedom) and to the particular case (she outlines the thrust of Rushton's controversial paper). The paragraph concludes with Dillon's **thesis statement**: "Evaluation of Rushton's work and its impact reveals that his research is faulty, and to support his rights using academic freedom ignores the

rights of students and the interests of the public."
- paragraph (2) Descends to the particular, discussing reactions to Rushton's views both in the popular media and in the scientific literature.
- paragraphs (3) and (4) Ascend to high levels of abstraction and generalization to discuss the nature of the concept of academic freedom. The last sentence of each paragraph, however, descends again to the particulars of the Rushton case.
- paragraphs (5) and (6) The opening two sentences of paragraph (5) make the transition to a discussion of particulars: the effects of Rushton's work.
- paragraph (7) Ascends once more to a high level of generalization and abstraction to draw a conclusion.

Now let's look at how Dillon has employed classification. According to her, the grounds on which Rushton's theories may be criticised are in three classes:

- a) purely emotional: they are morally repugnant (Dillon refers to this in paragraph (2).)
- b) the scientific argument that the research is "methodologically unsound", "bad science". Dillon details this argument in paragraph (2) and refers to it again in paragraphs (4) and (5).
- c) the argument that the publication of Rushton's claims creates undesirable social effects. Dillon discusses these effects in paragraphs (5) and (6).

Of the three she dismisses (a) as "nothing more than emotionally charged denial of morally repugnant ideas" (paragraph 2). She also implicitly rejects (c) as a sufficient reason for silencing Rushton: "ideas should not be silenced because of their likely unpopularity " she allows at the beginning of paragraph 4. Dillon does not argue that explosive or socially damaging effects of research are in themselves sufficient to justify the denial of academic freedom. It is only because she also has concluded that Rushton's work is "methodologically unsound" that she advocates that

outline

Intro. — what happened?
— outline Rushton's conclusions
— outline reaction: focus on
1) Rushton's science (accuracy)
2) academic freedom

Response in more detail
— journalists + emotional response
— scientists: largely quiet but
rebuttal — Ingram
Zuckerman + Brody

Academic freedom — the case against
— principle should not be used to
support bad science
— Roy definition: sound methodology needed

Academic freedom — the case for
— Ingram definition
— case for protecting Rushton's rights
(Horn, Pederson quotes)

Effects of Rushton
— explosive topic
— race — grade 5 e.g., Toronto
— reinforce bad stereotypes
— In university: the effect in class
— Western should not allow him to teach

Conclusion
— freedom of students as well as scientists
— freedom of taxpayers — know money
well spent
— acad. freedom not more important
than acad. competence / responsibility

This outline of Mary Dillon's paper shows how a writer may
use an outline during the writing process as an aid to the
organization — and reorganization — of the argument. For
more on outlines see 26-27.

students should not be "subjected" to his views.

One can readily imagine a different structure to the essay:
one that would have begun in the same way, but then
discussed the bad effects of Rushton's research before
dealing with the question of its scientific soundness. That
structure could work, but it would be unlikely to work as

well as the one Dillon has adopted. She does not argue that all academics who produce a piece of methodologically unsound work should be prevented from teaching, but only that research which is *both* bad science *and* harmful in its effects goes beyond the bounds of what should be allowed as academic freedom. And she clearly wishes to emphasise the latter more than the former. Here as elsewhere, Dillon is following good writing practice — saving her most important point to the last.

---

inductive and deductive reasoning

Logical reasoning operates in conjunction with several of the processes we have been discussing. To better understand its operation in the formulation of an argument, let's turn again to Mary Dillon's **thesis statement** at the end of her essay's first paragraph(110). She is logically bound by that sentence to demonstrate (1) that Rushton's research is faulty, and (2) that supporting his rights using "academic freedom" ignores the rights of both students and the public. These are not unrealistic demands, but how can Mary be sure —as she writes — that the elaboration of her thesis is sufficient? Working from notes and mapping, she first decides to cover the faultiness of Rushton's research in paragraph two, whose topic sentence in the final draft reads, "Controversial work is unlikely to go unnoticed or unchallenged, and Rushton's research was no exception." The logical core of that paragraph is its **inductive** method of supporting the thesis: Mary cites Rushton's "peers" (Joseph Cummings, "those who took the time to evaluate") as detailed evidence for her general conclusion that "no academic who evaluated Rushton's work found it to be

reasoning

induction

scientifically acceptable."

The second part of Mary's thesis is elaborated in paragraphs three, four, five, and six (as her mapping prefigured, the question of "academic freedom" and its consequences dominates this writer's thinking). Her logical fluency is particularly apparent towards the end of paragraph four, where she rejects one definition of academic freedom ("a licence to say anything and everything one wants") in favour of David Roy's (112). Seizing on one aspect of his definition, she concludes that "in the requirement for sound methodology . . . Rushton's work clearly falls beyond what can be protected by academic deduction freedom . . . ." This statement expresses a **deductive** method of reasoning, which can be visualized in outline form:

(a) THE PRINCIPLE OF ACADEMIC FREEDOM SHOULD PROTECT ONLY METHODOLOGICALLY RIGOROUS WORK.

and

(b) RUSHTON'S WORK IS NOT METHODOLOGICALLY RIGOROUS.

Therefore:

(c) ACADEMIC FREEDOM DOES NOT PROTECT RUSHTON'S WORK.

Mary has supported part of the essay's thesis (c) by introducing a restriction on the meaning of "academic freedom" (a). Her logical method here — moving from that general restriction ("methodologically rigorous work") to a specific case ("Rushton's work") — is deductive, in contrast to the inductive method of paragraph two.

Like writing strategies, logical methods are natural modes of human thought; no writer sits down at her desk and plans to think deductively or inductively. Nevertheless, every competent writer is able to stand back from his work-in-progress and notice such methods taking shape. In doing so, he is evaluating the **evidence** for the conclusions that constitute his **thesis** statement. Such evaluation is crucial to logical fluency.

---

subordination: an essay's paragraphs

For many pages now, *The Broadview Guide* has been **paragraphs** discussing something that is impossible to *fully* describe in words — the transfer of human thought from mind to paper. Various natural functions of the mind have been bravely named: for example, **contrast, narration, argument, induction, deduction, logical transition.** Certainly, the more a writer can be conscious of these functions while working on the draft of an essay, the better off she will be. But that won't always happen. From time to time, writers' brains go on functioning — and writers keep on writing — in a less-than-fully-conscious-of-where-this-paper-is-going sort of condition. What saves the day at those moments is the **paragraph**. A competent writer will start new paragraphs on no surer a hunch than, "Something's gotta change here." Perhaps on reflection, or by looking back at the preliminary mapping of the essay, he will realize that example must give way to comparison or that deduction must be followed by summation. Until such useful analysis kicks in, though, paragraphing is a compass; it gives visual form to the emerging sections of any essay. Of course, the movement from a first draft to a final draft may well require reordering of those sections. Paragraphs may have their original

DOUBLE FLUENCY: LOGICAL AND STYLISTIC

start a new
paragraph

"WHEN NAPOLEON LEFT ELBA HE..."

There is a degree of flexibility when it comes to the matter of where and how often to start new paragraphs. Sometimes a subtle point in an argument will require a paragraph of almost an entire page to elaborate; occasionally a single sentence can form an effective paragraph. Here are some general guidelines.

a) in narration
- whenever the story changes direction ("This was the moment Mulroney had been waiting for...", "When Napoleon left Elba he...")
- when there is a gap in time in the story ("Two weeks later the issue was raised again in cabinet...")

b) in description:
- whenever you switch from describing one place, person or thing to describing another ("Even such a brief description as this has been is enough to give some sense of the city and its pretensions. Much more interesting in many ways are some of Ontario's smaller cities and towns... ")

c) in persuasion or argument:
- when a new topic is introduced ("There can be little doubt that Austen's asides on the literary conventions of her time provide an amusing counterpoint to her story. But does this running commentary detract from the primary imaginative experience of *Northanger Abbey*?")
- when there is a change in direction of the argument ("To this point we have been looking only at the advantages of a guaranteed annual income. We should also ask, however, whether or not it would be practical to implement.")

d) when changing from one mode to another
- Description, narration and argument are commonly blended together in writing. If, for example, the essay moves from describing an experiment to analyzing its significance, it's a good time to start a new paragraph. If it moves from telling where Napoleon went and what he did to discussing why events unravelled in this way, the same holds true.

---

sequence shattered and reconstituted, a fact of writers' lives that leads to the fifth caution on logical fluency: never underestimate the power of subordination.

In a nutshell, subordination is a grammatical gesture — the addition of a "subordinating conjunction" (127) — that turns a complete sentence (e.g., "It is true that ideas should not be silenced because of their likely unpopularity") into a sentence fragment (e.g., "While it is true that ideas should not be silenced because of their likely unpopularity"). This example comes from the beginning of Mary Dillon's fourth paragraph (112). Because the first half of her sentence (before the comma) is subordinated, the second half (after the comma) need not be. Grammatically, the second half is stronger; it could stand alone as a complete sentence. Its logical function is to introduce the topic of the new paragraph. Meanwhile, the first half — the grammatically weaker "subordinate clause" — nods back in the direction of the just-completed paragraph, restating the position of the University of Western Ontario administration.

Thus, the grammar of subordination mirrors the logic of an essay's transition from one sub-topic to the next. It allows any paragraph to acknowledge — in its lead sentence — the preceding paragraph's material, while still introducing (and grammatically asserting) its own. This can greatly enhance logical fluency, especially for the writer who tends to change the sequence of her paragraphs during the process of drafting and redrafting an essay.

---

connectives

If the paragraphs and the sentences in an essay are to connectives convey a sense of logical fluency to the reader, **connectives** are of vital importance. Mary Dillon uses one in the final phrase of her third paragraph: "and *therefore*, it [academic freedom] should not be supported or defended by the University of Western Ontario." Like others of its kind (*however, consequently, nevertheless, furthermore, admittedly, still, accordingly*), the word *therefore* is a writer's road sign, indicating to readers where the logic of the essay is headed. (See Part Two for a full treatment of the ways in which such words can be used.) Mary's use of "therefore" conveys a clear message: "Because of what was just asserted, the following can be reasonably asserted." Thus she very concisely establishes a **logical transition** between two sections of the essay. Sometimes a phrase may be needed instead of a single word (*by contrast, in addition, for example, to summarize, all in all*), but in either case writers should be very careful: an essay's fluency often depends on matching connectives with their correct logical contexts.

---

repetition

repetition Fluent or not, no essay can go on forever. Its conclusion is the logical inevitability that every writer can count on. Writing that conclusion is, however, a challenge worthy of eliciting a further caution: "Learn the difference between repetitiveness of ideas and repetition of ideas." The former is sleep-inducing for readers, a sign of an unimaginative and perhaps even desperate writer. Clearly, then, we can conclude that repetitiveness is sleep-inducing for readers, a sign of an unimaginative and perhaps even desperate writer. Ho hum.

Repetition, on the other hand, underlines the logical core of an essay — its thesis — without merely plagiarizing sentences from the introduction. For instance, Mary Dillon's sixth paragraph not only repeats the argumentative essence of her thesis ("academic freedom" and "faulty work") but also presents a new angle on it: "it is the freedom of all taxpayers to know that public money is not used to support [such] researchers."

She has withheld, until the conclusion, an idea that first reached paper during her mapping (page 29, bottom right corner of the map). She has also introduced a vivid figure of speech — "cancerous myths that spread" — as another means of engaging her readers, not just reminding them.

Of course, methods of repetition can be as varied as writers' purposes. Appearing in the issue of *Queen's Quarterly* quoted earlier (13) is an article by Sylvia Ostry entitled "New Developments in Trade Policy." Its thesis, a vision of the world's economic future, foresees "a gradual, largely invisible transformation of the world trading system, a transformation that is unplanned and therefore essentially unpredictable." (Some of the most compelling and clear thesis statements, by the way, can be those that express uncertainty or limited knowledge.) Because her logical focus is the future, Ms. Ostry begins the essay's conclusion with a question: "So what are the policy options?" After briefly identifying two such options, she returns to the interrogative mode: "Can or will the US exercise leadership without hegemony? And if not the US, then who?" End of article. The posing of thoughtful questions, while consistent with the essay's thesis ("a transformation that is . . . essentially unpredictable"), is not mere repetitiveness; a specific factor is introduced (US leadership) that keeps readers thinking.

conclusions

* * *

DOUBLE FLUENCY: LOGICAL AND STYLISTIC

Logical fluency is, essentially, a writer's ability to keep thinking so that his readers will too. To let the meaning choose the word and not the other way round. To resist work-saving formulas and, instead, to be independently responsible for a composition of language whose logical coherence is unique. After all, the pieces of no two essays come together in precisely the same way, so every writer must make good sense — every time out — as if for the very first time.

stylistic fluency

Unfortunately, the achievement of logical fluency does not guarantee the achievement of its necessary other, *stylistic fluency.* Consider, for example, these meticulously thought-out instructions for patrons of the Bank of Nova Scotia:

> The annual rental fee for the lease of the box is subject to change from time to time by the Bank either giving notice in writing to the lessee by mailing the notice to the lessee at the address given hereunder (or such address as the lessee may from time to time in writing instruct the Bank to substitute thereof) and any such notice shall be deemed to have been duly given when mailed, or by posting a notice in a readily accessible place in the branch of the Bank.

Or this paragraph from a university student's critique of an assigned reading:

> Rembar simply uses refutation to make a greater distinction between impeachment and the judiciary system. Refutation, in this instance, clarifies the distinction. The natural confusion which exists initially is suppressed as Rembar offers explanation. The effect has tremendous influence and we progressively take stance with Rembar's viewpoint.

Neither writer is thoughtless or incompetent, but each has developed a case of what James Thurber once called "inflammation of the sentence structure." Fortunately, this stylistic disease is curable, provided the patient is willing to rehabilitate his **diction** (choice of words) and **syntax** (arrangement of words).

---

diction

As George Orwell warned repeatedly, the great danger of English is its insidious power over the human thought process. Words come in familiar, formulaic packages that often leap from a writer's pen or keyboard before she's had

diction

a chance to really think. Worse yet, the familiar and formulaic tends to be hypnotic; writers are often unaware that Language is leading Thought on its leash:

> Ready-made phrases come crowding in. They will construct your sentences for you — even think your thoughts for you, to a certain extent — and at need they will perform the important service of partially concealing your meaning even from yourself . . . This invasion of one's mind by ready-made phrases . . . can only be prevented if one is constantly on guard against them, and every such phrase anaesthetizes a portion of one's brain.

Four eyes are better than two when it comes to sighting an invasion force. In dialogue with another person, any university essay-writer will resist more strongly the temptations of ready-made academic prose (what Northrop Frye calls "verbal cotton wool"). Such temptations are very real. For example, how easy it would have been for Mary Dillon, an experienced consumer of university writing, to summon a lifeless introductory sentence from her general memory-bank:

tyranny of words

Certain	definite	elements	can be	identified
Several	key	components		illuminated
Three	crucial	factors		underlined
		aspects		isolated
		facets		
		areas		

. . . when discussing the topic of Philippe Rushton's research.

Even the most attentive writers can inadvertently slip into this passive game of fill-in-the-blanks, dulling their topics (and their minds!) with phrases like "Certain crucial facets" or "Three key elements" or "Several definite components" or (even worse) "Certain crucial facets and several definite components." Usually there is nothing at all "definite" or "certain" about such writing. Rather, its anaesthetized perpetrator conjures up vague categories — factors, areas, components, etc. — without having any specific material to fill them in. "What is above all needed," insists Orwell, "is to let the meaning choose the word, and not the other way about." He's absolutely right.

Many people believe that their writing will be made more impressive by using long, unusual words and long, complicated sentences. About one percent of us are capable of impressing in this way; the rest of us only end up making more mistakes than we would have done otherwise, and looking rather foolish. Even the best writers try to avoid difficult or unusual words if they can find a simple way to say the same thing. On the other hand, no one likes to read an essay entirely composed of four-letter words. As in so much else to do with writing, variety is the goal to strive for.

Because they are involved in intellectual discourse (20), <u>abstract words</u> academic and professional writers must rigorously monitor their use of abstract and conceptual nouns. Too dense a concentration will sap an essay's clarity; the ideas will be — as the overused idiom has it — too difficult to grasp. But the idiom is apt: readers can't put their hands on something that is too airy. They require, and deserve, a balance between abstraction and solidity. Mary Dillon leans towards the abstract when she uses the word "effects" four times in her fifth paragraph . Fortunately, enough ballast is inserted, through the use of examples, to preserve clarity: "a man ... asked by his son" ; "policemen ... being accused" ; "shootings of black youths" ; "(a) black student feeling uncomfortable." Competent writers choose from several techniques —

A TANZANIAN FOG

Almost any combination of abstract words can create fuzziness of meaning unless the writer exercises extreme care. Look at the following passage, for example:

abstract
words

> There are two features of Nyerere's view in 1968 of the transition to socialism which distinguish it from his earlier view. First, the trends in Tanzanian society which he felt would soon greatly increase the strength of the opposition to socialism led him to a greater sense of urgency about the need seriously to set in train the transition to socialism. Second, in 1967 he had a much clearer perception of the initiatives the government should take to achieve an effective transition to socialism.
>
> This new perception of the transition to socialism owed much, of course, to the character of the socialist society which Nyerere finally hoped to achieve. It was however very much shaped as well by his understanding of the political realities of Tanzania in 1967. It has been Nyerere's ideas on the transition to socialism rather than his vision of a transformed Tanzania which have had a direct and major impact upon policy and politics in the years since 1967.
> (Cranford Pratt, *The Critical Phase in Tanzania*)

This is the sort of thing English professors have in mind when they tell their students to use concrete words rather than abstractions. By itself there is nothing wrong with any of the words *features, transition, socialism, distinguish, trends, opposition, perception, initiatives, perception, transition, socialism, character, socialist society, understanding, political realities, ideas, transition, socialism, vision, transformed,*

including example, definition, reference to data, metaphor (67), and quotation — in order to keep their abstract diction out of the rhetorical clouds.

impact or *policy*. But put them together in a string like this—unbroken by any words like *dog*, or *box*, or *tree*, or *paper*—and you have writing that puts even the most determined reader to sleep. Moreover, the writer who consistently uses such words is likely to find himself circling round and round in a fog. (It should not be inferred that Cranford Pratt is such a writer; the point of including a passage from a book by this distinguished professor is rather that even the best writers must be wary of such problems.) Let's try the first paragraph again:

> By 1968 Nyerere had realised how deeply and strongly the currents of opposition to socialism flowed; he would have to move fast. But he had also realised much more clearly by this time what the government could do to speed up the process.

Some academics might complain that this version is too journalistic, but at least it has the virtue of clarity. What about the second paragraph? Pratt seems to be saying something like this:

> How much did Nyerere's vision of socialism itself have to do with the change in his view of how it should be achieved? Some, of course, but not much. It is his concept of how the vision should be achieved rather than the vision itself that has shaped Tanzanian politics since 1967.

Does this in fact say anything of importance? I think not, and would recommend cutting the entire paragraph. But until one trims some of the verbal foliage away, it is difficult to see how little is being said.

Word-choosing can also be perilous whenever a writer's topic involves jargon, that is, technical or specialized vocabulary. "In order to ensure that a truly regional renal care delivery structure will be optimally functional, there

jargon

must be patient accessibility to a number of interdigitated modalities of care," writes the medical essayist, forgetting simplicity in his pursuit of kidney doctors' respect. Chances are he has misconstrued his audience, anyway; even professionals at ease with the jargon of their own specialty would prefer "work well" to "be optimally functional" or "several interconnected clinics" to "a number of interdigitated modalities of care." Who really wants to hear, "the plan is more philosophical than operational in terms of framework," rather than "the plan is still an idea; it hasn't

---

PRESTIGIOUS BODY CLEANING SYSTEMS

doublespeak George Orwell coined the word *doublespeak* in *1984* to describe the use of language to disguise one's true meaning. This is a variant of jargon that one should try particularly hard to avoid. Here are a few humorous but saddening examples:

Original	The government must deal with the issue of revenue enhancement.
Translation	The government will have to raise taxes.
Original	Our guest rooms feature the most prestigious body cleaning systems.
Translation	We have good bathtubs.
Original	We provide outplacement consulting to companies involved in downsizing their operations.
Translation	We advise companies on how best to fire people.

These examples are taken from the *Quarterly Review of Doublespeak*, which is published by the National Council of Teachers of English, 1111 Kenyon Rd., Urbana, Ill. 61801.

---

been tried and it may not work."

The abuse of jargon is as much a problem of psychology as it is of English grammar and usage. It comes from people being more concerned with making themselves sound knowledgeable and intellectual than with acquiring knowledge or developing their intelligence; more concerned with making their ideas sound important than with thinking them through and expressing them clearly. Unfortunately, most students are sufficiently impressionable to be taken in by the pretence that jargon puts forward. Even more sadly, many working adults who should know better are just as easily taken in. The best way to safeguard against jargon is simplicity of expression. Writers who are always willing to revise their choices, who realize that no word in any draft of an essay is inevitable, will best resist being hypnotized by jargon.

Here is a list of commonly used jargon words and expressions that are usually best avoided:

access	counterproductive
enhance	familiarize
finalize	impact
implement	interface
liaise	opt for, option
parameter	point in time
previous to	prior to
prioritize, priorize	specificity
structure	totality
utilize	viable
-wise (money-wise, sales-wise, weather-wise etc.)	

---

figures of speech

Yet another ingredient in such stylistic fluency is **figurative language**, the persuasive use of images from beyond the realm of the essay's primary topic — most commonly in the

figures of speech

> ### WHAT *IS* A PARAMETER?
>
> A small case study in the abuse of jargon:
>
> > The very fact that these articles [criticising the government] have been published in *Pravda* tells the reader something of consequence. It indicates that these are the parameters within which debate has been sanctioned by the Central Committee of the party.
> >
> > (*The Guardian*, June 1987)
>
> jargon   The jargon word here is of course *parameters*. This word has a very specific technical meaning in mathematics (a quantity that is constant in the case being considered, but is a variable in other cases), and should not be used in other contexts. It gained currency out of a confusion with *perimeter* (the boundary of a closed area), and out of people's desire to use words that sound impressive but are clearly understood by neither writer nor reader. *Sanction* is another troublesome word in the passage — it would be a perfectly good word if it had not come to take on two diametrically opposed meanings. Here one presumes it means to *approve of*, but it is possible that it means to *restrict* instead. Because of such ambiguity the word is probably best avoided in this context. Let's try again:
>
> > The very fact that these articles [criticising the government] have been published in Pravda tells the reader that the Central Committee of the party has allowed debate in these areas.
>
> Notice the other changes made: cutting the wordy "tells the reader something of consequence", and changing from a passive verb (*has been sanctioned*) to an active one (*has allowed*). This change puts the subject (*the Central Committee*) at the beginning of the second clause, and allows us to cut "It indicates." The final result is a sentence that is a good deal simpler and shorter. One cannot be fooled into thinking it says anything particularly profound, but nor does one have to waste any time in puzzling out what the writer means.

form of metaphors or similes. Images appeal to readers' senses and can therefore give life and clarity to abstract diction.

"Metaphors may either enliven prose or deaden it; it is all in how you use them." In that sentence there are two metaphors; the verbs *enliven* and *deaden* both implicitly compare writing to a living thing. As this suggests, a metaphor is a comparison of one thing to another made through the use of a word or words that do not apply literally. "My love is a red, red rose" is a metaphor. "My love is *like* a red, red rose" is a simile ; the difference is simply that in a simile the fact that one is making a comparison is made explicit through the use of words such as *like* or *as if*, whereas the comparison is left to be understood in a metaphor.

An example: in his famous essay on politics and language, Orwell complains about those people who believe that "any

metaphor

A SHOT IN THE ARM TO BOTH LEGS

A dead metaphor all too often becomes a mixed metaphor as well. Mixed metaphors occur when we are not really thinking of the meaning of the words we use. "If we bite the bullet we have to be careful not to throw the baby out with the bathwater"; "we will leave no stone unturned as we search for an avenue through which the issue may be resolved". As soon as one really thinks about such sentences one realizes that the bullet is really better off out of the baby's bathwater, and that the best way to search for an avenue is not to turn stones over. A mixed metaphor is of course capable of providing more unintentional humour than almost any other form of verbal slip. One recent CBC newscast suggested that "now Chretien is out on a limb because his colleagues pulled the rug out from under him." Another, concerning inflation, asserted that "the man in the street has trouble keeping his head above water." And we should not forget the poor Nevada senator who wrote, "The advent of these sleek coaches should provide a tremendous shot in the arm to both legs of the Nevada passenger train system." Revenge of the clichés.

mixed metaphor

---

struggle against the abuse of language is a sentimental archaism, like preferring candles to electric light, or hansom cabs to aeroplanes." His introduction of a difficult concept ("sentimental archaism") is followed by two similes, ones whose vivid and simple images are immediately accessible.

Of course, as Orwell himself warns, dull or overly familiar figures of speech can undermine not only stylistic but also logical fluency. Most people's writing is more laced with metaphorical language than they realise. Phrases such as the following are all too familiar to us: *that will be the acid test*; *the United States is a melting pot*; *he's barking up the wrong tree*; *I threw caution to the winds; this reorganization lays the foundation for future change; we were told that we would have to bite the bullet; the government's move has paved the way for a resumption of talks; we are opening up new horizons; the university is a hotbed of unrest.*

For the most part these are what are known as **dead metaphors** — metaphors that have been used so frequently that they no longer conjure up any physical image in the minds of those who hear or read them. When we hear the phrase "miss the boat" we do not think of a boat, any more than we think of pavement when we hear the expression "paved the way for." It is a moot point whether a dead metaphor is better than no metaphor at all, but certainly a fresh metaphor is far better than either. Instead of *paved the way*, for example, what about *blazed a path?* Instead of a *hotbed* try a *cauldron.* Instead of "nipping something in the bud", try "digging up the seedlings". It may take a little longer, but the improvement in style will be worth it.

Of course, so many people have been using metaphors for so long that it is extremely difficult to find a fresh one for every situation. One useful compromise is to try to bring dead metaphors to life by using them in new ways. For example, no one thinks of a wave in this sentence:

> The Prime Minister has been riding a wave of popular support since his election.

Mention the wave again in a slightly different way, however, and it becomes water again to the reader:

> The Prime Minister has been riding a wave of popular support since the election. The question now is when that wave will crest.

> The company wanted to nip the spreading unrest among its employees in the bud before it became a tangled, snake-infested jungle.

dead metaphor

syntax

syntax *The Broadview Guide* begins by talking about "black marks on a page" moving "from left to right and from top to bottom" (5). It begins, in other words, by talking about syntax, which can so disrupt stylistic fluency that even experienced journalists will produce some embarrassingly wacky sentences:

> (1) Two injured men, trapped in a 101-foot abandoned mine shaft for almost five years, were rescued over the weekend after they lit a fire to attract the attention of passers-by.
>
> (2) The macadamia was named for Dr. John MacAdam, an enthusiastic scientist who promoted the nut in its native Australia, and was dubbed "the perfect nut" by Luther Burbank.

At times, words and phrases seem to have wills of their own, teaming up unexpectedly to completely undermine writers' intended meanings. Like some subversive magnet, the word "trapped" (in the first sentence) lures the prepositional phrase "for almost five years" to its side. And, in sentence 2, the verbal phrase "was dubbed" ignores the macadamia and aligns itself instead with poor Doctor MacAdam.

Writers must, however, shoulder the blame for such syntactical insurrections. They may not know the grammatical jargon — may not know that "a past participle preceding the object of a preposition will surrender control of a subsequent prepositional phrase to a second past participle that precedes either of the two prepositional phrases in question." But they must know that the phrase "for almost five years" in the first example is controlled by the word "trapped" — *not* the word "abandoned." They may not know that "the second of two past-tense verbs in the passive voice, instead of aligning itself to the subject word of the sentence, will align itself to the relative pronoun that introduces an adjective subordinate clause, when that clause modifies a noun in apposition to the object of a prepositional phrase syntactically adjacent to the first past-tense verb in the passive voice." But they must know that in the second example the verb "was dubbed" refers to "the scientist" — *not* the nut.

Very rare is the writer who thinks in grammatical terms as she writes. Nevertheless, successful writers develop an eye for the syntax of English grammar by allowing time between successive drafts of an essay: a good night's sleep enhances objectivity, so that the person who wrote the sentences can respond more as their eventual readers will respond.

---

rhythm

A writer's pursuit of stylistic fluency is not complete without attention to the music created by words and sentences — to the **rhythm** of language. The most predictable syntax in the grammar of English is SUBJECT-VERB-PREDICATE, as in the sentence, "The effects are disturbing." Disturb that predictability, and a writer like Mary Dillon is on her way (in paragraph five) to rhythmical distinctiveness: "Less obvious, but equally disturbing, are the effects this work could have in places like Toronto . . . . "

An important element in rhythmical distinctiveness is balance. Sometimes a pleasing balance is achieved simply by restating the same idea through the same grammatical structure:

Academic freedom is not a license to say everything and

confusion
of meaning

DEVELOPING POSSIBLE ENGINE TROUBLE

When a writer is not taking in the meaning of all the words
he has been writing, confusion is bound to result:

worth checking　　It was thought that by their very existence the
tanks would prevent the need for their ever
being used in combat.

(Can a need be prevented?)

revised　　The tanks were intended as a deterrent; it
was thought that they would never be
needed in combat.

worth checking　　With inflation running at about 1.8 percent in
the United States, approximately 0.5 per cent
in Japan and actually falling 0.9 per cent in
West Germany, only Italy has a higher
inflation rate than Canada among the seven
industrialized nations.*(The Globe and Mail)*

(Inflation cannot fall, though the *rate* of inflation can.)

revised　　Inflation is running at about 1.8 percent in the
United States and approximately 0.5 per cent
in Japan. Prices in West Germany have
actually fallen 0.9 per cent in the past year.
Among the seven industrialized nations, only
Italy has a higher inflation rate than Canada.

worth checking　　An Oakville tree nursery turned into an
emergency airstrip for the Duke and Duchess
of York yesterday afternoon when the
helicopter carrying them to Niagara Falls
developed possible engine trouble. *(Toronto
Star, Aug. 25, 1987)*

(An engine cannot develop possible trouble.)

revised　　An Oakville tree nursery turned into an
emergency airstrip for the Duke and Duchess
of York yesterday afternoon when the
helicopter carrying them to Niagara Falls
apparently developed engine trouble.

---

anything one wants; a carte blanche is not equated with a
Ph.D.

Sometimes balance may be achieved by placing words or phrases in apposition:

> Haldeman was Nixon's closest confidant, his most influential advisor.

> The generality of the images here has the effect of *balance* opening up the scene to the reader, of allowing her to graft her own archetypes of 'river' and 'hill' and 'woods' onto the story.

Often paired connectives ("if...then", "either...or", "not only...but also") can help in achieving balance. But here, as always, the writer must be careful that the words are in the right places; otherwise the fragile element of balance is lost:

Worth checking Hardy was not only a prolific novelist but wrote poetry too, and also several plays.

Revised Hardy was not only a prolific novelist but also a distinguished poet and a dramatist.

(The noun "novelist"is balanced by the later nouns "poet" and "dramatist".)

Worth checking The experiment can either be performed with hydrogen or with oxygen.

Revised The experiment can be performed with either hydrogen or oxygen.

(The choice is between the two gasses, not between performing and doing some other thing.)

Worth checking To subdue Iraq through sanctions, the United Nations felt, was better than using military force.

Revised To subdue Iraq through sanctions, the United Nations felt, was better than to use military force.

(The infinitive "to subdue" is balanced by the infinitive "to use"

Worth checking	In 1972 there was a stop-McGovern movement and a stop-Carter movement in 1976. (The Globe and Mail, July, 1988)
Revised	In 1972 there was a stop-McGovern movement and in 1976 a stop-Carter movement.
or	In 1972 there was a stop-McGovern movement and in 1976 there was a stop-Carter movement.

Repetition of some grammatical phrase, then, allows readers to sense a pattern in the writing. To feel that pattern. To conclude that pattern.

* * *

If parallel structure has been used to balance the parts of a sentence, even long sentences can be made easily digestible to the reader. Let's look again to Mary Dillon's essay for an example:

> It is a freedom that academics hold almost as dearly as the basic freedom of expression; for this reason, those who support Rushton's right to research, although recognising his work as profoundly distasteful and offensive, say that "the offensiveness of an idea says nothing about its truth or falsehood," and that to silence him "would serve neither the cause of academic freedom nor the advancement of knowledge."

Notice here how careful Dillon has been to balance *"that* 'the offensiveness...'" with *"that* to silence him...".

But even careful balancing cannot make a steady diet of long sentences palatable; a rich source of rhythm in any well-written essay is the short sentence, a highly visible minority in the academic world of long, drawn-out sentences. No writer naturally thinks, as she is drafting an essay, "Now I must remember to vary the length of my sentences." But when she comes to revise her work — particularly if she has allowed

a day or two to elapse after completing the rough draft —
she is better able to notice if and when the writing becomes
too dominated either by very long sentences or by very short
ones. She is able too to notice such things as a
preponderance of "there is..." and "it is..." sentences:

worth checking	It is important to consider the cultural as well as the economic effects of Free Trade. In 1988 there were many people who argued that these would be even more significant, and would inevitably cause the disappearance of Canada as a distinct cultural entity.
revised	Free Trade has cultural as well as economic effects. In 1988 many argued that these would be even more significant; that they would eventually cause the disappearance of Canada as a distinct cultural entity.

By making such changes as these, even when there are no
actual errors in her rough draft, the careful writer is able —
with very little effort expended — to make her prose clearer,
crisper, and more concise. And by doing so she makes things
considerably easier for her reader.

DOUBLE FLUENCY: LOGICAL AND STYLISTIC

---

voice

As many authorities have pointed out, in most cases writers can make their sentences less wordy and more effective by using the active voice rather than the passive.

worth checking	The election was lost by the premier. (Passive—7 words)
revised	The premier lost the election. (Active — 5 words)
worth checking	Union power was seen by them to have constrained the possibilities for full investment, and for achieving full employment. (from the first draft of a manuscript by a professor)
revised	The shareholders thought that union power had constrained the possibilities for full investment, and for achieving full employment.

It is too extreme, however, to suggest with George Orwell that you should "never use the passive when you can use the active." Writers often want for perfectly good reasons to keep the focus of their writing on the recipient of an action rather than its agent. In such cases they are quite right to use the passive voice:

Fifty milliliters of the solution were added to the serum.

I added fifty milliliters of the solution to the serum.

John Paul Getty 3rd was released in Italy after a 2.8 million dollar ransom had been paid.

His kidnappers released John Paul Getty 3rd in Italy after they had been paid a 2.8 million dollar ransom.

To the reader of a chemistry paper it is of no concern who added the fifty milliliters; that they were added is what matters, and there the focus of the sentence should be. Similarly in the second example, it is more appropriate to keep John Paul Getty 3rd as the subject of the sentence than to shift the focus to his kidnappers.

The vice, then, is not the passive voice *per se*, but the wordiness it sometimes gives rise to.

---

sexist language

In recent years, syntax and diction have participated equally in attempts to resolve an important issue of stylistic fluency —the elimination of sexist language. The healthy revolution in attitudes towards gender roles has created some awkwardness in English usage — though not nearly so much as some have claimed. *Chairperson*, or even simply *chair* is an unobjectionable non-sexist replacement for *chairman*, and *humanity* may serve for *mankind*. Nor is one forced into *garbageperson* or *policeperson*; *police officer* and *garbage collector* are entirely unobjectionable even to the linguistic purist.

The nouns will no doubt sort out themselves; the pronouns are more difficult. Most writers now agree that the use of *he* to represent both sexes is unacceptable. Yet *he/she, s/he* or *he or she* are undeniably awkward. Another solution is to avoid the singular pronoun as much as possible either by repeating nouns ("An architect should be aware of the architect's clients' budgets as well as the architect's grand schemes") or by switching to the plural ("Architects should be aware of their clients' budgets as well as of their own grand schemes"). Of these two the second is obviously preferable. But a third strategy — the one we have adopted in this book — eliminates awkwardness entirely. Like more and more texts, this book alternates between the masculine pronoun "he" and the feminine pronoun "she" when referring to a single, generic member of a group. A

sexism

"she"
"he"

THE 3-YEAR-OLD TV ADDICT

"That really is extraordinary!" I remarked to my tenant, whom I shall call Mark Doe, as I looked up from the newspaper. "It says here that the average person has seen over 375,000 television advertisements by the time she's twenty-one." In fact the newspaper had *not* said "she"; that was merely how I had paraphrased it.

A puzzled expression came over Mark's face. He looked from me to my five-year-old son, Dominic. Clearly he was still baffled. Finally his gaze fixed on my three-year-old daughter, Naomi. He was no longer puzzled; he was astounded.

"*She's* seen all those ads?" he asked incredulously.

As I had done at his age, he had simply assumed that "the average person" would always be a "he". I carefully explained to him that "she" could also be used to refer to people in general, male and female. Happily, he seemed to understand; in such small ways are our attitudes often changed.

---

cautionary note accompanies this strategy, however; be careful not to asssign *he* to all the professors, executives, or doctors; and *she* to all the students, secretaries, or nurses.

Choosing one noun or pronoun over another or deciding to alternate between *he* and *she* are decisions of diction. Another book might eliminate sexist language syntactically; in place of the sentence "He must attempt resolution of the problem" might appear "Resolution of the problem must be attempted." The first sentence, an example of active voice, has the subject word ("He") performing the action ("must attempt") — whereas the second sentence, an example of passive voice, has the subject word ("Resolution") receiving the action of the verb ("must be attempted").

The passive-voice version allows the masculine pronoun to disappear; the only place it *could* appear in the revised syntax of the sentence would be at the very end: "Resolution of the problem must be attempted by him." By not allowing it to appear, by literally pushing it off the far end of the sentence's syntax, a writer can sidestep the issue of non-sexist language. She — or he — can simply refuse to rely on gender-specific pronouns. Whichever method a writer chooses, it is unquestionably worth the effort; there can no longer be any question that language helps to shape attitudes.

* * *

Pronoun or no pronoun, active or passive — stylistic fluency is indeed an intricate craft. Fortunately, some very sound advice comes from researcher Lilita Rodman: "Whether or not . . . specific agents should be named depends in part on the purpose and audience of the discourse." Purpose and audience — two components of the voice work covered at the outset of this book. Even *grammatical* voice work, in choosing between active and passive, is best guided by two preliminary and essential questions: "What am I out to accomplish? and "Who am I writing for?"

---

tone

While revising her essay, a capable writer can answer both those questions by remembering that one of her purposes is not to rely on emotional appeals to the audience. The voice of logical fluency is not supposed to gush or cajole or insult or amuse or exclaim. The written essay, in particular, is a piece of formal writing, and should be approached as such.

tone

(It is generally regarded as unacceptable, for example, to use slang expressions or contractions [277].) More than that, most readers at universities expect a calm and disinterested **tone**, free of extreme emotion. Thinking rigorously about a topic does not, however, preclude feeling strongly about it. As

---

"A BUNCH OF WORDS": SLANG AND INFORMAL ENGLISH

The following words and expressions are often used in conversation, but not in formal English. The more formal word is listed afterwards.

anyways	anyway
anywheres, anyplace	anywhere
boss	manager, supervisor
bunch (except for grapes, bananas, etc.)	group
buy (as a noun — "a good buy", etc.)	bargain
kid	child, girl, boy
kind of, sort of	rather, in some respects
let's us	let us
lots of	a great deal of
mad (unless the meaning is "insane")	angry
awful	poor, miserable, sick
awfully	very, extremely

Some authorities continue to hold that *awful* should retain its original meaning of "filled with or inspiring awe". In any case, a better replacement can always be found. The same is even more true of the use of the adverb *awfully* as an intensifier to mean *very* ("awfully good," "awfully small", etc.).

could care less	couldn't care less

A few years ago people started to say sarcastically "I could care less" to mean the opposite—that they couldn't care less. Now "I could care less" is taking over, regardless of the tone of voice used, and the meaning of the words themselves is in danger of being lost.

get : should not be used to mean *come, go, be,* or *become*

worth checking	Henry and Jane Seymour got married in 1536, only ten days after the death of Anne Boleyn.
revised	Henry and Jane Seymour were married in 1536, only ten days after the death of Anne Boleyn.

Susan Cole demonstrates in her essay on Terry Fox, sentences that are both logically and stylistically fluent will convey emotion without the need for fanfare:

Terry's Marathon of Hope was a tremendous athletic accomplishment, and the physical punishment to which

---

have got   have

worth checking   He has got two houses and three cars.

revised   He has two houses and three cars.

let's say: This expression should be omitted entirely from essays.   slang

worth checking   Let's say for example a relative dies, a poor family will have to deal with financial worries as well as with their grief.

revised   If a relative dies a poor family will have to deal with financial worries as well as with their grief.

off   (to mean "from")

worth checking   I got it off him for two dollars.

revised   I bought it from him for two dollars.

go   (to mean "say")

worth checking   He goes, "What do you mean?"

revised   He said, "What do you mean?"

put across, get across (one's point)   express, convince

worth checking   He could not get his point across.

revised   He could not persuade us he was right.

well: In conversation well is often added to sentences while you are thinking of what to say. Do not do this in writing.

worth checking   Well, at the end of the war there was some doubt within the Cabinet as to which course to take.

revised   At the end of the war there was some doubt within the Cabinet as to which course to take.

when you get right down to it: usually best omitted; use *otherwise, indeed,* or *in fact.*

> he subjected himself is almost beyond imagining. It is not a
> well-known fact that he was advised before his run that he
> had a heart condition . . . As he approached Thunder Bay in
> late August, he experienced a persistent intense pain in his
> upper chest and he was unable to go any further. Terry's
> run was finished on the first of September, 114 days and
> 3,339 miles after it had begun. (255)

Dr. Cole's style is personal without being subjective. Competent writers are able to preserve objectivity while at the same time conveying their own individual syntax, diction, and — consequently — their own emotional tone.

first person

Notice in particular how Cole — like many another good writer — manages to create a distinctive personal tone without using the first person singular; most academic writers use "I" and "me" infrequently or not at all. The object of a formal essay is normally to present an argument, and they realize that they can best argue their case by presenting evidence rather than by stating that such and such is what they think. Thus many teachers advise their students always to avoid using the first person singular (*I* and *me*) in their writing.

This guideline should not be regarded as a firm and fast rule; George Orwell, often praised as this century's finest essayist, uses *I* and *me* frequently. As the following example illustrates, however, he employs the first person to guide the reader through his argument, not to make the points in that argument:

> If one gets rid of these habits one can think more clearly,
> and to think more clearly is a necessary first step towards
> political regeneration: so that the fight against bad
> English is not frivolous and is not the exclusive concern
> of professional writers. I will come back to this presently,
> and I hope that by that time the meaning of what I have
> said will become clearer. ('Politics and the English Language')

Phrases such as *I think* and *I feel*, on the other hand, will

not help you convince the reader of the strength of your main points.

worth checking   Many authorities assume inflation to be a cause of high interest rates, but I think that high interest rates are a cause of inflation. This essay will prove my argument through numerous examples.

revised   Many authorities assume inflation to be a cause of high interest rates; in fact, high interest rates are often a cause of inflation. Let us take the years 1978 to 1983 in the US as an example.

---

revision

Perhaps the greatest failing among those learning to write <u>revision</u> well is a reluctance to spend sufficient time checking and re-writing. Far too many students — not to mention people in business and bureaucrats — feel that they have essentially finished the job when they have completed a first draft. Far from it: some of the most important parts of the writing process take place after the first draft has been completed.

As Ian Cameron recommends in *For All Practical Purposes*:

A few students feel that they are as likely to make more mistakes in checking and correcting their work as they are to correct the mistakes they have already made, but in fact almost every student is able to improve his or her work at least 15% by checking it slowly and carefully. Remember, you are not checking simply for details such as spelling; you should be trying to replace words, to re-arrange paragraphs, to cut entire sections, to alter almost every sentence.

By its very nature revising is likely to lead to more cuts than additions. Might this not cause damage? "Aren't I more likely to do well," some students may ask themselves, "if I've written more than the prof. asked for?" If the instructor has asked for 1,000 words, they feel they should write 1,500; if 2,500 words are requested, they are sure to top 3,000. Experienced writers have learnt that quantity matters much less than quality; unless an essay is well below the requested number of words the only thing that matters is what it says, and how well it says it.

examinations

exams   When they turn from writing essays to writing essay questions on examinations, many students have a natural — and understandable — tendency to assume that entirely different principles apply. There are differences, of course, but the basic similarities must also be kept in mind. Success in either situation depends upon clearly understanding the task at hand. By zeroing in on the **command words** ("Explain," "Analyze," "Argue," "Compare," "Summarize," etc.), an exam-writer will know precisely what kind of response (explanatory, argumentative, etc.) the professor wants. Reading the exam carefully and with an **attitude** (12) of self-confidence; assessing the relative value of each question, so as to better apportion the time available; remembering (as the essay-writer must) that quantity matters much less than quality: these are the means to the mastery of examinations. Here too are a few additional pointers:

- Examination questions never ask the student to write down all he has in his head on the given topic. If the student is asked to write on Austen's use of irony in *Emma*, he will not do well by recounting the full story of the book, or discussing Emma's character at great length. If asked to comment on the claim that "the Treaty of Versailles caused World War II", he will not do well by simply reciting a list of the main historical developments between the two world wars.

- As in writing essays, the use of a map or plan is an asset. It won't of course be as well thought-out; indeed, it may well be a just a frenzied clutter of words. But it's important to have some sense of structure, and some place to jot down ideas that come to mind unexpectedly. A rough sheet for notes and plans kept always at hand can help.

- Another similarity between essays and essay questions on exams is the importance of checking written work. Make sure nothing important has been left out; make sure the points are expressed concisely and clearly. And avoid writing madly right up to the end of the exam. Again, a well-written short answer is almost invariably better received than a sloppy and long-winded one.

Note: An excellent guide to the peculiarities of exam-writing is *Making Your Mark* by Catherine Taylor et. al, published by the Academic Skills Centre at Trent University.

EXERCISE: Active and Passive

Improve each of the following sentences by changing the verb from the passive voice to the active. You may also be able to make other improvements.

1) Legislation has been passed by the government to ensure that the rights of individuals are protected.

2) After careful deliberation, it has been decided that the application for residential zoning of the building to be changed to commercial will be approved.

3) The economy was subjected to two serious oil price shocks in the 1970s; those with cars were forced to line-up for hours to obtain gasoline, and everyone was affected by inflation.

4) Research in this area was first carried out by Samuel Smith in the 1960s, and was completed after his death by a team directed by Marjorie Mullins.

EXERCISE: Metaphors

Unmix the following metaphors:

1) We don't want to throw the baby out with the bathwater before we check to see if the coast is clear.

2) Unless every clause in the agreement is airtight the deal could come unglued and we'd be left up the creek without a paddle.

3) The government's scorched earth policy in response to the rebels has dampened hopes for an early settlement of the war.

4) We were all swamped by an avalanche of paperwork.

EXERCISE: Slang and Informal English

Rewrite each sentence to eliminate slang words or expressions:

1) She has five kids and fifteen grandchildren.

2) The work he handed in was truly awful.

3) It is kind of difficult to understand why public perceptions of Jimmy Carter changed so quickly.

4) There is a bunch of reasons why the deficit has become so large.

DOUBLE FLUENCY: LOGICAL AND STYLISTIC

EXERCISE: Jargon, Abstraction, and Doublespeak

Translate each of the following into English:

1) The new pen has negative vulnerability to water entry.

2) The building in which the reactor is situated was apparently constructed with a view to structural rather than containment integrity.

3) The former aide to the President tries to help clients strategise whatever their objectives may be vis-à-vis Washington, D.C. or the world.

4) Since data is central to the issue of implementation guidance we believe it is advisable to examine the data that your organization is assembling, in order to maximize the actualization of projects designated for implementation, and to preclude unintended effects.

5) With regard to the staff members' requests for supplements to the level of remuneration, management is of the opinion that it would be injudicious to advocate an increment.

6) With the loss of Challenger we are in a temporary hiatus of shuttle flights. It is certain that we will have a shortfall in the national launch capability in the near term.

7) In considering the multiplicity of factors involved, this essay will also explore possible solutions to the parameters of the problem of the bias that is particularly strongly felt in many American Caucasian communities against ethnic heterogeneity in school transportation arrangements.

COLLABORATION: RESEARCH AND CRITICISM

Stop and think for a moment about the experiences of writers described in this book: putting together a voice; discovering the big ideas for an essay; working out the logical fluency of an argument and the stylistic fluency of phrases, sentences, and paragraphs.   Some of those experiences are collaborative by nature, such as the active, critical reading of texts and the one-to-one dialogue of writing-centre tutorials. There simply is no such thing as a hermetically sealed, independent writer of absolutely personal beliefs and insights. As long as he is acquiring new knowledge, a competent writer succumbs to collaboration, which is an honourable and occasionally miraculous habit to acquire.

using the library

Among the most habit-forming locales for a university essay-writer is the library, where **research** is accomplished. Some will approach research as an endeavour to find and collate old material.   The more imaginative and independent, however, will set out to discover new material, seeking to arrange and examine what already exists in order to present that which has never existed.   In that way, a writer's **thesis** is strengthened through collaborative exposure to the work of others.

Consider the research presented by Mary Dillon at the close of her second paragraph. In an effort to support the

library

first half of her thesis ("Rushton's research is faulty"), she seizes on a specific oversight by Rushton, namely, that "his consideration of diversity within races that may exceed differences between races is poor." Derived from Zuckerman and Brody, whose critique of Rushton appeared in a professional journal, Mary's evidence is a specific example of scientific sloppiness, one that anchors and enhances preceding assertions ("he ... ignorantly uses data"; "his logic is flawed"; "his data selection and analysis are biased"). Her collaboration with Zuckerman and Brody provides the informed perspective of Rushton's professional colleagues, something Mary could not have achieved independently.

But how does one find Zuckerman and Brody?

Research begins in the library with a card catalogue or — more often these days — a computer terminal. Sometimes an instructor will provide the names of at least one or two books or articles in the area to look up; sometimes the

COLLABORATION: RESEARCH AND CRITICISM

researcher will be starting from scratch with only the subject, and will have to make up a list of books from the library data base. Often the researcher is faced with a vast array of material — more than could possibly be taken account of in a single essay, perhaps more than could be read or even skimmed in an entire academic year. How does she choose? In this case it saves time to keep the initial list brief — no more than a handful of books or articles. Then, as the researcher is skimming those, she can notice which other books or articles are referred to most often by the authors; those are the ones she knows she should be aware of in particular, both in order to keep the task of research manageable and to try to ensure that she does not ignore any of the most important authorities on the subject.

The experienced researcher will also notice the publishing company, but not put too much stock in its reputation; the university presses of Oxford, Cambridge, Harvard and Princeton have published a few real clunkers as well as vast amounts of first-rate scholarship. And, because librarians often have standing orders for all books from such prestigious presses as these, a clunker from them is more likely to find its way onto the shelves of a university library than a clunker from Wilfrid Laurier Press or Hackett Publishing.

Finally, the experienced researcher is willing to trust her own judgement: to glance at the Table of Contents and skim quickly through five, ten, even two or three dozen works on a subject and in each case make a snap decision pon its likely usefulness. These decisions are not, of course, irreversible; she may well find that one of the books initially set aside with barely a moment's notice is generally regarded as among the two or three most important works in the field (in which case she will of course return to it with more care). But she must in the first instance have some way of making the mass of material manageable. What of the opposite problem? What if there seems at first to have been little or nothing published on the subject before? Perhaps it's an area on the border with one or more other territories; in that case, surveying those territories may be necessary. Perhaps it's a relatively new subject; in that case — as indeed for any research — it's essential to check the relevant indexes of journal articles. Some of the most important of these for work in the Arts and Social Sciences are as follows:

Humanities Index – covers articles published from 1974 onwards in such disciplines as English, History and Philosophy.

MLA Bibliography – covers articles on English Language and Literature as well as on French, German, Italian, Spanish and so on.

Philosopher's Index — the most comprehensive listing of articles on Philosophy.

Social Sciences Index – covers articles published from 1974 onwards in such areas as Anthropology, Economics, Political Science, Psychology and Sociology.

Social Sciences and Humanities Index – the predecessor of the *Humanities Index* and the *Social Sciences Index* —; covers articles in these fields from before 1974.

The article by Zuckerman and Brody on Rushton's work is listed in the *Social Sciences Index*, and once the student is familiar with the library at his university, finding both the reference work and the article itself is straightforward. But it takes some time to become familiar

with any library. Finding the right research material —
professional journal, book, or otherwise — often means
asking energetic questions. Library staff are trained to know
which standard reference books apply to which academic
disciplines, and where they are located — and to know a

good deal more than that. For instance, the student of
literature who asked her librarian for advice about
researching a paper on the imagery of Keats' poetry might
learn, through polite and persistent interrogation, the value
of a "concordance," a listing of words used by an author,
with citations of the lines or passages in which each word
appears. In that way, she could rapidly determine the
frequency and location of "mortality" in the poems of John
Keats, thereby saving time and enhancing evidence for, say,

a thesis asserting the poet's preoccupation with death. Just one more instance of fruitful collaboration.

The old-fashioned (not to mention sexist) image of the librarian as timid and bespectacled spinster is contradicted mightily by today's experts in "information retrieval and management." More and more research tools are being computerized (*The MLA Bibliography*, for example, is now available on CD-ROM), and expertise with computers is an important professional service offered by modern reference librarians. Writers can and should take advantage of in-library workshops on such topics as "search strategy formulation," "database access," "on-line library catalogues," and "file management."

There are, however, important decisions that must still be made in relative solitude: those having to do with **citation and documentation.** Back from the library, armed with information from secondary sources, a researcher now establishes the collaboration between her own writing and the writing of others. The assertive attitude developed during voice work (11) is crucial at this point, since quotations from experts can easily obscure or overwhelm an essay's thesis. Zuckerman and Brody, as professional psychologists, are more qualified than Mary Dillon when it comes to assessing the logical strengths and weaknesses of Rushton's work. She is the writer, though, and must therefore remain in full control of the essay's argumentative force, while using their psychological expertise as evidence. As paragraph one shows, there is certainly more to Mary's argument than just the faultiness of Rushton's research; her concern over the definition and abuse of academic freedom is paramount. She therefore succeeds in presenting a thesis that is supported **in part** — rather than bullied into submission — by Zuckerman and Brody's very valuable analysis.

plagiarism

Collaborating with a secondary source means acknowledging that source in the final draft of the essay. Otherwise a writer commits **plagiarism**, defined by the *MLA Handbook for Writers of Research Papers* as "the act of using another person's ideas or expressions in your writing without acknowledging the source (21)." In his article for *Queen's Quarterly* (the introduction to which appears on page 14), Neil Jumonville writes, "Dwight Macdonald, a prominent cultural critic in the circle, called the period following World War II 'the gray dawn of peace' (27)." Had he not included Macdonald's name and the quotation marks around Macdonald's phrase and the page reference to Macdonald's book, Jumonville would have been guilty of plagiarism.

plagiarism

Judgement of this writerly crime has no provision, by the way, for malice aforethought; whether or not a writer is willfully deceptive makes no difference. Therefore, the truly competent writers (Neil Jumonville among them) are extremely careful on two counts. First, they keep thorough and well-organized notes while reading and researching, so as not to assume (weeks later) that some vivid turn of phrase (like "the gray dawn of peace") must have come to them (weeks ago) in a burst of inspiration. Second, they continuously assess their eventual audience during the essay-writing process. In his introductory paragraph, Jumonville mentions "political movement to the centre" but provides no citation for this phrase. He assumes, correctly, that the figurative geography of politics (i.e., left - centre - right) will be considered general knowledge by the academically oriented readers of *Queen's Quarterly*. Jumonville didn't invent that geography, nor did he invent the phrase "the gray dawn of peace." Nevertheless, the familiarity of the former allows it to be owned by all — readers and writer alike — whereas the unfamiliarity of the latter requires its acknowledgement.

citation: the MLA system

MLA system   Notice that a parenthetical number is included by Jumonville to cite Dwight Macdonald's original use of the quoted phrase. Like Mary Dillon, he is following a system currently recommended by the *MLA Handbook* (an authoritative guide, published by the Modern Language Association of America). The number refers readers to a page in the work by Macdonald that is listed under "Works Cited" at the end of Jumonville's article:

> **Macdonald, Dwight. Memoirs of a Revolutionist. New York: Farrar, 1964.**

Under the MLA system, which dispenses with the traditional footnote, the parenthetical page reference should include the author's last name **unless** — as in the example from Jumonville — that name is clearly linked to the cited material in the actual text of the essay. Thus, Mary Dillon's citation in her fifth paragraph — (Platiel A3) — provides her readers with the last name of the journalist from whose article the quotation is taken.

Mary's list of "Works Cited" also demonstrates the format

for arrangement of titles (alphabetical, according to authors' last names) and for indentation of successive lines.

citation: the APA system

An alternative to MLA documentation is the "author-date" method recommended by the APA (American Psychological Association) and used widely in both the social and natural sciences. This method is named for its addition of the year of publication to the parenthetical citation: (Sisser 1983, 211). Notice the placement of a comma between the year and the page number. In a list of "Works Cited" entry, the publication date would also follow the author's name: APA system

Sisser, Yolanda. 1983. <u>Sociological oddities</u>. Winnipeg: Clarity Press.

THE MLA SYSTEM

Books

Two or more works by the same author:

Sadler, Doug. Reading Nature's Clues: A Guide to the Wild. Peterborough, Ontario: Broadview, 1987.

- - - . Winter: A Natural History. Peterborough, Ontario: Broadview, 1990.

(In second and subsequent entries the author's name is replaced by three unspaced hyphens.)

A book with two or three authors:

Houston, Susan E., and Alison Prentice. Schooling and Scholars in Nineteenth Century Ontario. Toronto: U of Toronto P, 1989.

(The first author's name appears surname first; the other author's name is in its normal order. Note as well the publisher's abbreviation.)

A book with more than three authors: Only the first author's name is given, followed by "et al." (Latin abbreviation of "et alia" — and others).

An edited or translated book:

Rosengarten, Herbert and Jane Flick (Eds.) The Broadview Reader. Peterborough, Ontario: Broadview, 1987.

Aristotle. Nichomachean Ethics. Trans. Terence Irwin. Indianapolis, IN.: Hackett, 1985.

A work appearing in an anthology or edited collection:

Whitman, Walt. "O Captain! My Captain!" An Introduction to Poetry. Ed. X.J. Kennedy. 6th ed. Boston: Little Brown, 1986. 256.

Adair, John G. "Social Psychological Issues in Research." Social Psychology: Readings for the Canadian Context. Ed. Brian Earn and Shelagh Towson. 2nd ed. Peterborough, Ontario: Broadview, 1990. 167-29.

Scholarly Journals:

Raedts, P. "The Children's Crusade of 1212." Journal of Medieval History 3.4 (1977): 279-325.

Note: "3.4" means Volume 3, number 4. If a periodical is paginated continuously throughout the annual volume you need not give the issue number.

Magazines:

Dolphin, Ric. "Race and Behavior: A Theory Outrages Ethnic and Other Critics." Maclean's 13 Feb. 1989: 44.

Newspapers:

Helwig, David. "Anger Evident at Race Theory Debate." Globe and Mail [Toronto]. 10 Feb. 1989, national ed.: A3.

MLA

Parenthetical References:

(Zuckerman and Brody 1028)

This refers to page 1028 of the article by Zuckerman and Brody listed under "Works Cited". Note that if the name of the author(s) has just been mentioned in the body of your essay or is clear from the context, only the page reference need be given.

Special Cases:

Works with no author — alphabetize by title in the List of Works Cited. In the parenthetical references you may use a shortened version of the title.

Oxford English Dictionary 2nd ed. Oxford: Oxford U P: 1989.

(OED, "artifice")

Two or more authors with the same last name — supply both first and last names in your parenthetical reference:

(Harry Johnston 197)

Multivolume works — indicate the specific volume in your parenthetical reference:

(Carson 2: 1987)

The Bible and works of drama or poetry available in numerous editions — should be cited in a way that enables the reader to check the reference in any edition:

(MV 2.3.8-13)

The parenthetical reference is to Shakespeare's *The Merchant of Venice*, Act 2, Scene 3, lines 8-13.

(Gen. 2.14)

The parenthetical reference is to *Genesis*, Chapter 2, verse 14.

All university professors, like all book publishers and all journal editors, are primarily concerned with two things when it comes to citing and documenting material: accuracy and consistency. Whatever system is recommended, a research writer must take the responsibility of following it closely — by consulting a manual or a style sheet (some professors compose their own) or, if accessible, exemplary essays. Just as audiences vary from discipline to discipline,

---

THE APA SYSTEM

Books

Two or more works by the same author:

Sadler, Doug. 1987. Reading nature's clues: A guide to the wild. Peterborough, Ontario: Broadview.

—. 1990. Winter: A natural history. Peterborough, Ontario: Broadview.

(Note the use of lower case in giving the title. Proper nouns are still capitalized, however.)

A book with two, three, four or five authors:

Houston, Susan E., and Alison Prentice. 1989. Schooling and scholars in nineteenth century Ontario. Toronto: U of Toronto P.

(The first author's appears surname first; other authors appear in their natural order.)

A book with more than six authors:

Only the first author's name is given, followed by "et al." (Latin abbreviation of "et alia" — and others).

An edited or translated book:

Rosengarten, Herbert and Jane Flick (Eds.) 1987. The Broadview reader. Peterborough, Ontario: Broadview.

Aristotle. Nichomachean ethics. Trans. Terence Irwin. 1985. Indianapolis, IN.: Hackett.

COLLABORATION: RESEARCH AND CRITICISM

so do systems of documentation; those provided by the MLA and the APA are certainly not the only ones. While their differences may at times seem trivial (professors have been known to penalize essays whose citations exhibit misplaced commas), accuracy and consistency should nevertheless be sought. This is the one facet of essay-writing that calls on a good writer to suspend his independent attitude in favour of slavish

---

Scholarly Journals: APA

Raedts, P. "The children's Crusade of 1212." Journal of medieval history 3.4 (1977): 279-325.

Parenthetical References:

(Zuckerman and Brody 1988)

> refers to the 1988 publication by those authors listed under "Works Cited". Note that no page number is required in the parenthetical reference unless you have referred to a specific section of the work or quoted it directly.

Special Cases:

Works with no author — alphabetize by title in the List of Works Cited. In the parenthetical references you may use a shortened version of the title.

Oxford English dictionary 2nd ed. Oxford: Oxford U P: 1989, "artifice".

Two or more authors with the same last name — supply both first and last names in your parenthetical reference:

(Harry Johnston 1979)

Multivolume works — indicate the specific volume in your parenthetical reference:

(Carson 2: 1989)

---

obedience and conformity.

The current systems have done away with citations at the bottoms of pages (footnotes), but they have preserved a means for writers to offer marginal explanations to their readers. Called endnotes, or simply "notes," these explanations appear immediately after the text of the essay but before the list of "Works Cited." Endnotes have one of two purposes: either to direct readers towards additional sources of information on a topic (as does Mary Dillon's second endnote); or to digress responsibly from a topic. An example of the second — of responsible digression — occurs in Neil Jumonville's article, when he first uses the term "rationalism." Aware of its abstract (and therefore changeable) nature, Jumonville inserts a superscript number "2"; this refers his readers to the corresponding note at the end of the article:

> 2 In this article I am not using rationalism in its formal philosophical sense as a doctrine that assumes innate ideas (and as opposed to empiricism). Instead I use rationalism to mean a belief in the importance, for proper analysis, of reasons and intellect rather than faith, intuition, or will.

The author has decided that such a meticulous definition, while crucial to the essay's development, might jeopardize the fluency of the paragraph to which it relates. He therefore opts for a segregated note, which allows his readers to absorb the information without perceiving an abrupt break, either stylistic or logical. In effect, the text of the essay collaborates with itself, creating brief explanatory paragraphs that enhance — from a peripheral position — the strength of the essay.

proofreading

The essay is done! The rough draft has been tidied up, all proofreading the references are in place; it's ready to hand in. Or is it? Experienced writers will at this point always embark on one more step — proofreading. Checking *once more* (proofreading should never be confused with revising from first to subsequent drafts) for logical and stylistic fluency. Checking for mechanical errors that may — however unfairly — take away from the effect of the essay as a whole. Checking the spelling. Checking the accuracy and the format of the

---

THE SAN FRANCISCO 50ers

The job of preparing the index for *The Broadview Book of Sports Anecdotes* was unusual in that the entries were keyed to the numbers that had been assigned to the anecdotes rather than to the page numbers. But it was a simple enough job, particularly given the magic of computerized alphabetization.

With the job almost done I realised I had omitted one anecdote — number 9. Again, the magic of computers precluded any sense of despair: a simple job of search and replace was all that was required. Replace all of the old 9's with 10's, all of the old 10's with 11's, and so on. In ten minutes I really *was* done, and soon the camera-ready copy went off to the printers. It wasn't until bound books were in hand some six weeks later that I saw the error of my ways. No one had told the computer to look only for the numbers of the anecdotes. I had told it to look for *any* number, and it had done its job to perfection; there they were, the Super Bowl champs, the San Francisco 50ers.

(Don LePan)

COLLABORATION: RESEARCH AND CRITICISM

references. A boring job, and yet one that brings satisfaction, for no writer is able to proofread an essay without finding things to fix, things to improve.

One final suggestion about proofing: try reading the essay aloud. Inevitably most writers feel silly at first reading aloud to themselves, but inevitably as well they catch things — a missing word, an extra letter — that even the most diligent proofing will have missed. For the few minutes it takes, it is always worth giving voice, in an entirely literal sense, to the written text.

---

computers

computers

Word-processing emphasizes the fluid and changeable nature of writing: texts are transferred, shared, and modified with unprecedented speed and frequency. In some senses the computer has revolutionized the process of writing over the past 20 years.

The advantages are obvious. No longer does the revision process require endless rewrites of the entire work; errors can be corrected, phrasing can be improved, paragraphs can be shifted around without re-writing or re-typing the whole. Moreover, even those whose spelling is (like that of Winnie the Pooh) " a little wobbly " can appear as perfect spellers through the wonders of spell-check. And yet...

Writers who have grown intimate with word-processing still often prefer to do their first draft in longhand. They know that writing directly onto the screen is more prone to wordiness, and they know as well that it can be difficult to keep the feel of the essay as a whole in mind if half a page is the most that can ever be before their eyes at one time. And once they have put the 'paper' onto disc as they have written the second draft, they remain as aware of the limitations of word-processing as they are of its virtues. They remain aware that a spell check is just that; it will not catch a substitution of "there" for "their", or of "its" for "it's", or of "poured over" for "pored over". In short, it is no substitute for old-fashioned proofreading.

criticism

The ultimate, and often most volatile, collaboration occurs when a writer faces the *criticism* and responses of a reader. For journalists, such collaboration is fairly routine, since both editors and subscribers are only too eager to correct or modify articles. The university writer also expects regular doses of criticism and advice. Professorial zeal can, however, prove to be a shock, as one student explains:

> My problem is that my essays are perfect only up until the moment I hand them in to be marked. Suddenly, the paper

undergoes a drastic transformation. Red marks appear scattered across the page. Words like "NO!" or "EXPLAIN!" appear, linked by arrows to the short forms "AWK" and "SP." Then there's the ultimate in humiliation — a red line scribbling out my sentence, and a better one written in its place.

Warding off humiliation very often depends on active response to criticism. Collaboration is, after all, a two-sided affair; no red-penned advice or correction has the power to improve a writer's skills unless that writer evaluates it independently. Questions are bound to arise ("Sure this passage is awkward, but how can I improve it?" "What's wrong with this?!"); finding satisfactory answers depends on continued dialogue and revision. When all is said and done, when all is written and submitted, competent assessors of essays — while experienced and qualified — are far from dictatorial. They look for logical coherence, not for reflections of their own beliefs; and for stylistic clarity, not for imitations of their own writing. Writers who take advantage of actually collaborating with their most demanding readers are the ones who progress most steadily.

"Getting even is one reason for writing," according to a writer named William Gass. Think about it. We use the idiom "getting even" to express the accomplishment of revenge — the settling of a score, once and for all. Surely some essay-writers (especially those coerced by writing assignments) must occasionally feel the aggressive satisfaction of having returned a volley and neutralized a threat. Commands, formats, and deadlines can, after all, become debilitating, especially when they appear clustered during a few fleeting weeks towards the close of an academic semester.

Yet another connotation is possible, though, when thinking about getting even. Look back to page 17, where Janice Lauer's notion of "a pressure to restore equilibrium" is quoted. She emphasizes, as so many practising writers do, the mental tension that often motivates worthwhile essays. Something is out of whack, not quite right, anxiously imbalanced or uneven. In this context, getting even means the writer's process of discovering what's on her mind (attitude, audience, purpose), articulating her main ideas (reading, mapping, dialogue), achieving logical and stylistic fluency, and collaborating with informed sources. Not an easy thing to do. The writing process can be awful, but it can be simultaneously daring — as Anatole Broyard explains:

> It's not that most people lack imagination: it's that they don't connect their imaginations to their speech. If they were to flush their minds and start afresh, if they didn't dress their speech in castoff clothes of worn-out imagery, their utterances might be thrillingly naked and explicit. This would be their first poetry, the sweet, pristine taste of words, the awful daring of trying to say what they mean.

The Broadview Guide is not recommending, finally, that essayists working in History 243 or Sociology 111 be thrillingly naked and explicit. Nevertheless, Broyard's dramatic and idealistic phrases capture a sense of excitement that is within the grasp of all writers who care, at all, about what they are doing. The awful dare of writing enables people to come to grips with the intricate swirls of thought that might otherwise go undetected — or at least undernourished — inside their minds.

SAMPLE ESSAY

RESEARCH OR RACISM: A QUESTION OF ACADEMIC FREEDOM

Mary C. Dillon

Prof. K.D. Smith

Humanities 105

SAMPLE ESSAY

text is

double spaced

1

title of article

(book titles
should be
underlined)

thesis statement
at end of first
paragraph

2

Universities are forums for the exchange of ideas, which
are often new, radical and controversial. Some of these
ideas cause small ripples, others cause stirs. Recently,
however, a professor at the University of Western Ontario
unleashed a tidal wave: Philippe Rushton published and
presented "Race Differences in Behaviour: A Review and
Evolutionary Analysis" (Rushton 1009), in which he
concluded, among other things, that orientals are more
intelligent and more sexually restrained than whites, who
are, in turn, more intelligent and restrained than
blacks. Not surprisingly, these results set off a flurry
of discussion and debate, centring on two main issues,
namely, the adequacy of Rushton's science, and the extent
to which he is protected by academic freedom. Evaluation
of Rushton's work and its impact reveals that his
research is faulty, and to support his rights using
academic freedom ignores the rights of students and the
interests of the public.

    Controversial work is unlikely to go unnoticed or
unchallenged, and Rushton's research was no exception.
Much of the initial response to his work was nothing more
than emotionally-charged denial of repugnant ideas, and
the media freely reported the reactions of people who had
not actually examined Rushton's reports. Curiously,

1

SAMPLE ESSAY

while the press furiously covered the story, Rushton's colleagues were generally quiet. Perhaps he was not quickly refuted by the scientific community because his peers found it hard to respond to such ludicrous ideas. University of Western Ontario geneticist Joseph Cummings remarked that "if it wasn't as serious as it is, it would be truly hilarious. Some of Rushton's theories are totally bizarre" (Dolphin 44). Fortunately there were those who took the time to evaluate the scientific merit of Rushton's work, and the general conclusions were that he misrepresents, misapplies and ignorantly use the data (Ingram) and that his logic is flawed, his data selection and analysis are biased, and his consideration of diversity within races that may exceed differences between races poor (Zuckerman and Brody 1028). In short, no academic who evaluated Rushton's work found it to be scientifically acceptable.

quotation integrated into structure of sentence

Given that Rushton's work is so flawed, one wonders whether the principles of academic freedom, which allow such research to get funded and published, are sufficient. Academic freedom, the central issue here, is the "principle that academics are free to espouse views that might be offensive or unpopular without threats from outside the university" (Ingram).[1] It is a freedom that academics hold almost as dearly as the basic freedom of expression; for this reason, those who support Rushton's right to research, although recognizing his work as

parenthetical reference (MLA style)

3

2

profoundly distasteful and offensive, say that "the
offensiveness of an idea says nothing about its truth or
falsehood," and that to silence him "would serve neither
the cause of academic freedom nor the advancement of
knowledge" (Horn A7). Citing academic freedom as the
justification, University of Western Ontario president
George Pedersen made it clear that the university would
defend the right of Rushton to pursue his research
(Platiel A3).

4

paragraphs

indented

While it is true that ideas should not be silenced
because of their likely unpopularity, it is an abuse of
academic freedom to use that right to support bad
science. Academic freedom is not a licence to say
anything and everything one wants; a carte blanche is not
equated with Ph.D. A more complete definition of this
central freedom, provided by McGill ethics professor
David Roy (quoted in Ingram), says that "academic freedom
means liberty from outside interference and influences
that would restrict solid, competent, methodologically
rigorous scientific, humanistic, philosophical and
academic work"; it is here, in the requirement for sound
methodology, that Rushton's work clearly falls beyond
what can be protected by academic freedom,[2] and therefore,
it should not be supported or defended by the University
of Western Ontario.

5

Yet the principles of academic freedom have been
used to support this methodologically unsound research,

pages

numbered

3

SAMPLE ESSAY

and this is a tremendous disservice not only to students at the University of Western Ontario but also to society at large. Scientists do not research in isolation, and their work can have profound effects. This is why research must be carefully examined for scientific merit, and in the case of explosive topics such as racial differences, one expects special caution to be exercised; with Dr. Rushton this was not the case. Academic freedom, while supporting Rushton, is allowing harm to others. The fallout from Rushton's bombshell reached far beyond the walls of academia. One poignant example was given by a man who was asked by his son, the only non-white in his grade five class: "Daddy, does Rushton's work mean that I am the dumbest person in my class?" (Helwig A3); the psychological effects are obvious. Less obvious, but equally disturbing, are the effects this work could have in places like Toronto, where -- after the shooting of black youths -- policemen are being accused of valuing the lives of blacks less than whites. In the midst of this controversy, Rushton asserts that black people are worth less because they mature faster, don't live as long, have more children, and invest less parental care.[3] The effect of his work can only be reinforcement of stereotypes that are detrimental to society.

The negative impact of this work will continue when Rushton returns to the classroom to teach his theories.

quotation introduced by colon

- - used for dash

superscript refers reader to explanatory note

6

SAMPLE ESSAY

It is reasonable to expect harmful effects on students, as it is hard to imagine any black student feeling comfortable in a classroom where the professor has said, "Let's face it, that's what blacks do (ask for special treatment). We've had to change everything in educational systems and professional schools to make sure that blacks do not fail in large numbers" (Platiel A3). Hopefully, before he returns to the classroom, the University of Western Ontario administration will realize that Rushton has gone beyond the protection of academic freedom, and that students deserve better than to be subjected to such outrageous views.

7

conclusion reiterates main points and introduces an additional argument

The emotional, sensitive, and contentious case of Professor Rushton is an issue of freedom, but this freedom does not apply only to scientists; rather, academic freedom is the freedom of students to study in an environment which does not discriminate against them because of race, gender, or any other characteristic, and it is the freedom of all taxpayers to know that public money is not used to support researchers who do faulty work to perpetuate cancerous myths that spread through our society, causing nothing but harm. It is imperative that academic freedom not be allowed to supersede academic competence and responsibility.

5

SAMPLE ESSAY

ENDNOTES

1 From a tape recording of the CBC radio programme "Quirks and Quarks." See "Works Cited" for complete reference.

2 See also: Suzuki, David. "Defence of Rushton 'right' is propping up faulty work." The Globe and Mail. 11 February 1989: D4 ; Ziegler, David et al. "Is science too eager to stake its claims?" The Globe and Mail. 3 February 1989: A7.

3 See Rushton 1018-21 for his discussion of r/K reproductive strategies.

SAMPLE ESSAY

WORKS CITED

Dolphin, Ric. "Race and Behavior: A Theory Outrages
    Ethnic and Other Critics." <u>Maclean's</u> 13 February
    1989: 44.

Helwig, David. "Anger Evident at Race Theory Debate." <u>The
    Globe and Mail</u>. 10 February 1989, national ed.: A3.

Horn, Micheal. "Academic Freedom: It May Protect
    Crackpots But It's Not Expendable." <u>The Globe and
    Mail</u>. 13 February 1989, national ed.: A7.

Ingram, Jay. "Quirks and Quarks." <u>Canadian Broadcast
    Corp</u>. 11 February 1989.

Platiel, Rudy. "University Chief Defends Professor's
    Right to Voice Racial Theory." <u>The Globe and Mail</u>. 4
    February 1989, national ed.: A3.

Rushton, J. Philippe. "Race Differences in Behaviour: A
    Review and Evolutionary Analysis." <u>Personality and
    Individual Differences</u> 9 (1988): 1009-24.

Zuckerman, Marvin and Nathan Brody. "Oysters, Rabbits and
    People: A Critique of 'Race Differences in
    Behaviour' by J.P. Rushton." <u>Personality and
    Individual Differences</u> 9 (1988): 1025-33.

note the placing of
punctuation

edition specified

two authors: only the
first name is reversed

SAMPLE ESSAY

GRAMMAR AND USAGE

BASIC GRAMMAR: A Reference Guide

PARTS OF SPEECH

NOUNS

Nouns are words that name people, things, places or qualities. Some examples follow:

boy
John   names of people
parent

hat
spaghetti   names of things
fish

Saskatoon
Zambia   names of places
New York

silence
intelligence   names of qualities
anger

Nouns can be used to fill the gaps in sentences like these:

I saw_____at the market yesterday.

He dropped the _____into the gutter.

Has she lost a lot of _____?

Hamilton is a _____with several hundred thousand _____living in it.

PRONOUNS

Pronouns replace or stand for nouns. For example, instead of saying, "The man slipped on a banana peel" or "George slipped on a banana peel", we can replace the noun *man* (or the noun *George*) with the pronoun *he* and say "He slipped on a banana peel".

Definite and Indefinite Pronouns: Whereas a pronoun such as "he" refers to a definite person, the words *each, every, either, neither,* *one, another,* and *much* are indefinite. They may be used as pronouns or as adjectives; in either case, a *singular* verb is needed.

Each player wants to do his best.
(Here the word *each* is an adjective, describing the noun *player*.)

Each wants to do his best.
(Here the word *each* is a pronoun, acting as the subject of the sentence.)

Each of the players wants to do his best.
(The word *each* is still a pronoun, this time followed by the phrase *of the players.* But it is the pronoun *each* that is the subject of the sentence; the verb must be the singular *wants.*)

Possessive Pronouns and Adjectives: See under *adjectives* below (123).

Relative Pronouns: These pronouns relate back to a noun that has been used earlier in the same sentence. Look at how repetitious these sentences sound:

I talked to the man. The man wore a red hat.

We could of course replace the second *man* with *he.* Even better, though, is to relate or connect the second idea to the first by using a relative pronoun:

I talked to the man who wore a red hat.

I found the pencil. I had lost the pencil.

I found the pencil that I had lost.

The following are all relative pronouns:

who	whose (has other uses too)
which	that (has other uses too)
whom	

Try replacing the second noun in these pairs of sentences with a relative pronoun, so as to make only one sentence out of each pair:

1) I polished the table. I had built the table.

2) Premier Rae is vacationing this week in Quebec's Eastern Townships. The Premier cancelled a planned holiday last fall.

3) The word "other" has developed a special cachet among

literary theorists. "Other," incidentally, is usually put in quotation marks when so used.

Pronouns Acting as Subject and as Object

We use different personal pronouns depending on whether we are using them as the subject or the object (128).

Subject Pronouns

I	we
you	you
he/she/it	they
who, what, which	who, what, which (interrogative)

Object Pronouns

me	us
you	you
him/her/it	them
whom, what, which	who, what, which (interrogative)

He shot the sherrif.
(Here the pronoun *he* is the subject of the sentence.)

The sherrif shot him.
(Here the word *him* is the object; *the sherrif* is the subject.)

That's the man who shot the sherrif.
(Here the pronoun *who* is the subject of the clause "who shot the sherrif".)

That's the man whom the sherrif shot.
(Here the pronoun *whom* is the object; *the sherrif* is the subject.)

The distinctions between *I* and *me* and between *who* and *whom* are treated more fully below (202).

Articles

These are words used to introduce nouns. There are only three of them- *a*, *an* and *the*. Articles show whether or not one is drawing attention to a <u>particular</u> person or thing.

For example, we would say "I stood beside a house" if we did not

articles

want to draw attention to that particular house, but "I stood beside the house that the Taylors used to live in" if we did want to draw attention to the particular house. *A* (or *an* if the noun following begins with a vowel) is an <u>indefinite</u> article – used when you do not wish to be definite or specific about which thing or person you are referring to. *The* is a <u>definite</u> article, used when you do wish to call attention to the particular thing or person. Remember that if you use *the*, you are suggesting that there can only be <u>one</u> of what you are referring to.

Choose the appropriate article ("a", "an" or "the"):

1) _____ moon shone brightly last night.

2) She had _____ long conversation with _____ friend of hers.

3) Have you ever driven _____ car?

4) Have you driven _____ car that your wife bought on Monday?

Adjectives

adjectives

Adjectives are words used to tell us more about (describe or modify) nouns or pronouns. Here are some examples of adjectives:

big	good	heavy
small	bad	expensive
pretty	careful	fat
quick	slow	thin

e.g. The fat man girl lifted the heavy table.
(Here the adjective *fat* describes or tells us more about the noun *man*, and the adjective *heavy* describes the noun *table*.)

e.g. The fast runner finished ahead of the slow one.
(*fast* describes *runner* and *slow* describes *one*)

Notice that adjectives usually come before the nouns that they describe. This is not always the case, however; when the verb *to be* is used, adjectives often come after the noun or pronoun, and after the verb:

e.g. That woman is particularly careful about her finances.
(*careful* describes *woman*)

e.g.   It is too difficult for me to do.
             (*difficult* describes *it*)

Adjectives can be used to fill the gaps in sentences like these:

1) This _____sweater was knitted by hand.
2) As soon as we entered the _____house we heard a
   _____ clap of thunder.
3) Those shoes are very _____.
4) Derrida's argument at this point could fairly be described
   as _____.

Some words can be either adjectives or pronouns, depending on how
they are used. That is the case with the indefinite pronouns (see above),
and also with certain possessives (words that show possession):

Possessive Adjectives
  my   our
  your   your
  his/her   their

  whose   whose

Possessive Pronouns
  mine   ours
  yours   yours
  his/hers   theirs

  whose   whose

             I have my cup, and he has his.
(Here the word *his* is a pronoun, used in place of the noun *cup*.)
                  He has his cup.
(Here the word *his* is an adjective , describing the noun *cup*.)

              Whose book is this?
(Here the word *whose* is a possessive adjective, describing the
                  noun *book*.)
              Whose is this?
(Here the word *whose* is a possessive pronoun, acting as the
              subject of the sentence.)

Verbs

verbs

Verbs are words that express actions or states of affairs. Most verbs can be conveniently thought of as *doing* words (e.g. *open, feel, do, carry, see, think, combine, send*), but a few verbs do not fit into this category. Indeed, the most common verb of all — *be* — expresses a state of affairs, not a particular action that is done.

Verbs are used to fill gaps in sentences like these:

1) I _____ very quickly, but I _____ not _____ up with my brother.

2) She usually _____ to sleep at 9:30.

3) Stephen _____ his breakfast very quickly.

4) They _____ a large farm near Newcastle.

5) There _____ many different languages that people in India _____ .

One thing that makes verbs different from other parts of speech is that verbs have <u>tenses</u>; in other words, they change their form depending on the time you are talking about. For example, the present tense of the verb *to be* is *I am, you are, he is*, etc., while the past tense is *I was, you were, he was*, etc. If unsure whether or not a particular word is a verb, one way to check is to ask if it has different tenses. For example, if one thought that perhaps the word *football* might be a verb, one need only ask oneself if it would be correct to say, *I footballed, I am footballing, I will football* and so on. Obviously it would not be, so one knows that *football* is the noun that names the game, not a verb that expresses an action. See the next chapter for a discussion of verb tenses.

Adverbs

These words are usually used to tell us more about (describe or modify) verbs, although they can also be used to tell us more about adjectives or about other adverbs. They answer questions like "How...?", "When...?", and "To what extent...?", and often they end with the letters *ly*. Here are a few examples, with the adjectives also listed for comparison.

adverbs

ADJECTIVE	ADVERB
careful	carefully
beautiful	beautifully
thorough	thoroughly
sudden	suddenly
slow	slowly
easy	easily
good	well
	today
	often
	very

He walked carefully.
(The adverb *carefully* tells us <u>how</u> he walked; it describes the verb, *walked*.)

He is a careful boy.
(The adjective *careful* describes the noun *boy*.)

My grandfather died suddenly last week.
(The adverb *suddenly* tells <u>how</u> he died; it describes the verb *died*.)

We were upset by the sudden death of my grandfather.
(The adjective *sudden* describes the noun *death*.)

She plays the game very well.

(The adverb *well* tells us h̲o̲w̲ she plays; it describes the verb *plays*. The adverb *very* describes the adverb *well*.)

She played a good game this afternoon.
(The adjective *good* describes the noun *game*.)

She played a very good game.
(The adverb *very* describes the adjective *good*, telling us h̲o̲w̲ good it was.)

According to his Press Secretary, Bush will meet Gorbachev soon.
(The adverb *soon* describes the verb *will meet*, telling w̲h̲e̲n̲ the action will happen.)

Choose adverbs to fill the gaps in these sentences:

1) Ralph writes very _____.

2) The Judge spoke _____ to Milken after he had been convicted on six counts of stock manipulation and fraud.

3) They were _____ late for the meeting this morning.

Prepositions

prepositions

Prepositions are joining words, normally used before nouns or pronouns. Some of the most common prepositions are as follows:

after	from	off
across	in	over
at	into	to
before	of	until
for	on	with

Choose prepositions to fill the gaps in these sentences:

1) I will tell you _____ it _____ the morning.

2) Please try to arrive _____ eight o'clock.

3) He did not come back _____ Toronto _____ yesterday.

4) I received a letter _____ my sister.

Conjunctions

Conjunctions are normally used to join groups of words together, and in particular join clauses together. Some examples:

conjunctions

because	unless	after
although	until	if
and	since	or
as	before	that

> They stopped playing because they were tired.

(The conjunction *because* joins the group of words "because they were tired" to the group of words, "They stopped playing")

> I will give her your message if I see her.

(The conjunction *if* introduces the second group of words and joins it to the first.)

Many conjunctions can also act as other parts of speech, depending on how they are used. Notice the difference in each of these pairs of sentences:

> He will not do anything about it until the morning.

(Here *until* is a preposition joining the noun *morning* to the rest of the sentence.)

> He will not do anything about it until he has discussed it with his wife.

(Here *until* is a conjunction introducing the clause "until he has discussed it with his wife".)

> I slept for half an hour after dinner.

(Here *after* is a preposition joining the noun *dinner* to the rest of the sentence.)

> I slept for half an hour after they had gone home.

(Here *after* is a conjunction introducing the clause "after they had gone home.")

> She wants to buy that dress.

(Here *that* is an adjective describing the noun *dress*: "Which dress?", "That dress!")

> George said that he was unhappy.

(Here *that* is a conjunction introducing the clause, "that he was unhappy".)

Choose conjunctions to fill the gaps in the following sentences:

1) We believed _____ we would win.

2) They sat down in the shade _____ it was hot.

3) My father did not speak to me _____ he left.

PARTS OF SENTENCES

Subject

subject

The subject is the thing, person, or quality about which something is said in a clause. The subject is usually a noun or pronoun.

> The man went to town.
> (The sentence is about the man, not about the town; thus the noun *man* is the subject.)

> Groundnuts are an important crop in Nigeria.
> (The sentence is about groundnuts, not about crops or about Nigeria; thus the noun *groundnuts* is the subject.)

> Nigeria is the most populous country in Africa.
> (The sentence is about Nigeria, not about countries or about Africa; thus the noun *Nigeria* is the subject.)

> He followed me wherever I went.
> (The pronoun *He* is the subject.)

Core Subject: The core subject is the single noun or pronoun that forms the subject.

Complete Subject: The complete subject is the subject together with any adjectives or adjectival phrases modifying it.

> The lady in the huge hat went to the market to buy groceries.

The core subject is *the lady* and the complete subject is *the lady in the huge hat*.

Object

object

An object is something or someone towards which an action or feeling is directed. In grammar an object is the thing, person or quality affected by the action of the verb. (To put it another way, it receives the action of the verb.) Like a subject, an object normally is made up of a noun or pronoun.

Direct object: The direct object is the thing, person, or quality <u>directly</u> affected by the action of the verb. A direct object usually answers the question, "What...?" or "Who...?".

Indirect object: The indirect object is the thing, person, or quality that is <u>indirectly</u> affected by the action of the verb. All indirect objects *could be* expressed differently by making them the objects of the prepositions *to* or *for*. Instead, the prepositions have been omitted. Indirect objects answer the questions, "To whom?", "For whom?".

McGriff hit the ball a long way.
(<u>What</u> did he hit? The ball. *The ball* is the direct object of the verb *hit*.)

She threw me her hat.
(<u>What</u> did she throw? Her hat. *Her hat* is the direct object. <u>To whom</u> did she throw it? To me. *Me* is the indirect object. Note that the sentence could be rephrased, "She threw her hat to me.")

They gave their father a watch to their father for Christmas.
(direct object is *watch*; indirect object *father*)

Predicate

predicate

The predicate is everything that is said about the subject. In the above example, "went to the market to buy groceries" is the predicate. A predicate <u>always</u> includes a verb.

Clause

clause

A distinct group of words that includes both a subject and a predicate. Thus a clause always includes a verb.

Phrase

phrases

A distinct group of words that does <u>not</u> include both a subject and a verb. Examples:

CLAUSES	PHRASES
because he is strong	because of his strength (no verb)
before she comes home	before the meeting (no verb)
The professor likes me	from Halifax
A tree fell down	at lunch
who came to dinner	in the evening

TYPES OF CLAUSES

Main clause

main clauses

A main clause is a group of words which is, <u>or could be</u> a sentence on its own.

Subordinate clause

subordinates

A subordinate clause is a clause which could <u>not</u> form a complete sentence on its own.

Except for *and*, *but*, and *or*, conjunctions do not introduce main clauses, so if a clause begins with a word such as *because*, *although*, *after* or *if*, you can be confident it is a subordinate clause. Similarly, relative pronouns introduce subordinate clauses — never main clauses.

She lives near Pittsburgh.
(one main clause forming a complete sentence; the pronoun
She is the subject, *lives* is the verb, and the preposition *near*
and the noun *Pittsburgh* together form a phrase)

He danced in the street because he was feeling happy.

main clause: He danced in the street

subject:_____

verb:_____

subordinate clause: because he was feeling happy

subject:_____

verb:_____

Mavis has married a man who is older than her father.

main clause: Mavis has married a man

subject:_____

verb:_____

subordinate clause: who is older than her father

subject: who

verb: _____

TYPES OF SUBORDINATE CLAUSES

Adjectival subordinate clause: a subordinate clause that tells us more about a noun or pronoun. Adjectival clauses begin with relative pronouns such as *who, whom, whose, which,* and *that.*

clause types

Adverbial subordinate clause: a subordinate clause that tells us more about the action of the verb—telling how, when, why or where the action occurred.

Noun subordinate clause: a clause that acts like a noun to form the subject or object of a sentence.

Examples:

He talked at length to his cousin, who quickly became bored.

("who quickly became bored" is an adjectival subordinate clause, telling us more about the noun *cousin*)

subject of subordinate clause: the pronoun *who*

verb in subordinate clause:_____

subject of main clause: the pronoun *He*

verb of main clause:_____

> My husband did not like the gift that I gave him.

("that I gave him" is an adjectival subordinate clause telling us more about the noun *gift*)

subject of subordinate clause: the pronoun *I*

verb in subordinate clause:_____

subject of main clause:_____

verb in main clause:_____

> The boy whom she wants to marry is very poor.

("whom she wants to marry" is an adjectival subordinate clause telling us more about the noun *boy*. Notice that here the subordinate clause appears in the middle of the main clause, "The boy is very poor".)

subject of subordinate clause:_____

verb in subordinate clause:_____

subject of main clause:_____

verb of main clause:_____

> I felt worse after I had been to the doctor.

("after I had been to the doctor" is an adverbial subordinate clause telling you when I felt worse)

> He could not attend because he had broken his leg.

("because he had broken his leg" is an adverbial subordinate clause telling you why he could not attend.)

> She looked as if she had seen a ghost.

("as if she had seen a ghost" is an adverbial subordinate clause telling you how she looked.)

> What he said was very interesting.

("What he said" is a noun clause acting as the subject of the sentence, in the same way that the noun *conversation* acts as the subject in "The conversation was very interesting.")

> Sue-Ellen told me that she wanted to become a lawyer.

("That she wanted to become a lawyer" is a noun clause acting as the object, in the same way that the noun *plans* acts as the object in "Sue-Ellen told me her plans.")

Types of Phrases

Adjectival phrase: a phrase that tells us more about a noun or pronoun.

phrase types

Adverbial phrase: a phrase that tells us more about the action of a verb, answering questions such as "When...?", "Where...?". "How...?" and "Why...?".

The boy in the new jacket got into the car.
("In the new jacket" is an adjectival phrase telling us more about the noun *boy*.)

I drank from the cup with a broken handle.
("With a broken handle" is a phrase telling us more about the noun *cup*.)

We went to the park.
("To the park" is an adverbial phrase telling where we went.)

They arrived after breakfast.
("After breakfast" is an adverbial phrase telling when they arrived.)

Phrases and Clauses

They were late because of the weather.
("Because of the weather" is an adverbial _____ telling us why they were late. It has no verb.)

They were late because the weather was bad.
("Because the weather was bad" is an adverbial _____ telling us why they were late. Subject:_____ Verb:_____)

The man at the corner appeared to be drunk.
("At the corner" is an adjectival _____ telling us more about the noun _____.)

The man who stood at the corner appeared to be drunk.
("who stood at the corner" is an _____, telling us more about the noun _____.
Subject:_____

Verb:_____

Parts of Speech and Parts of the Sentence

Example: After the generous man with the big ears has bought presents, he will quickly give them to his friends.

Parts of speech:

after: conjunction
generous:_____
with: _____
big: _____
has brought:_____
he:_____
quickly:_____
to:_____
friends:_____

the: article
man:_____
the:_____
ears: _____
presents:_____
will give:_____
them:_____
his:_____

Parts of the sentence:

Main clause: He will quickly give them to his friends.

subject:_____

predicate:_____

verb:_____

direct object:_____

indirect object:_____

Subordinate clause: After the generous man with the big ears
    Is this an adjectival or an adverbial subordinate clause?
Core subject: the noun _____

Complete subject:_____

Adjectival phrase: with the big ears

This phrase tells us more about the noun: _____

predicate:_____

direct object:_____

VERBS AND VERB DIFFICULTIES

The Infinitive

Although not properly speaking a verb tense, the infinitive is the starting point for building a knowledge of verb tenses; the infinitive is the most basic form of the verb. Some examples of infinitives are *to go, to be, to do, to begin, to come, to investigate.* The infinitive form remains the same, of course, whether the action referred to happens in the past, the present, or the future.

infinitives

1. **Split infinitives**: The most commonly made mistake involving infinitives is undoubtedly the slang substitution of *and* for *to,* especially in the expression *try and do it* for *try to do it* (see under *Usage* for a fuller treatment). The great issue in this area among grammarians, however, is the split infinitive — the infinitive which has another word or words inserted between *to* and the verb:

worth checking   The time has come to once again go to the polls. Economic conditions are likely to greatly influence the outcome, and the Prime Minister has promised to forcefully speak out in defence of the government's fiscal record.

With re-united infinitives, the same passage looks like this:

revised   The time has come to go once again to the polls, Economic conditions are likely to influence greatly the outcome, and the Prime Minister has promised to speak forcefully in defence of the government's fiscal record.

On what grounds can the second passage be considered better? It comes down to a matter of sound and rhythm. To most ears *to go once again* and *to speak out forcefully* are preferable to the split alternatives, but *to influence greatly* seems more awkward than *to greatly influence.* Happily most authorities are now agreed that it is not a grievous sin to split an infinitive; Philip Howard, editor of *The Times of London*, calls the split infinitive "the great Shibboleth of English syntax," and even the traditionalist H.W. Fowler allows that while "the split infinitive is an ugly thing, we must warn the novice against the curious superstition that splitting or not splitting makes the difference between a good and a bad writer."

This is not to say that the splitting of infinitives should be encouraged. In many cases a split infinitive is a sign of wordiness; in cases such as the following it is better to drop the adverb entirely:

Poor	The Chairman said it was important to really investigate the matter thoroughly.
Better	The Chairman said it was important to investigate the matter thoroughly.

Like all verb forms, infinitives have both an <u>active</u> and a <u>passive</u> voice. The active, which is more common, is used when the subject of the verb is doing the action, whereas the passive is used when the subject of the verb is receiving the action, or being acted <u>on</u>. *To do, to hit, to write* are examples of infinitives in the active voice, while *to be done, to be hit, to be written* are examples of infinitives in the passive voice.

EXERCISE:
Split Infinitives

Change the following split infinitives:

1) They did not want to quickly decide the issue.
2) We were asked to patiently await the decision.
3) The contractor said that they would have to carefully restore the house.
4) Their policy was to perpetually maintain a state of economic equilibrium.
5) The choir began to loudly sing the anthem.

The Simple Present Tense

	singular	plural
1st person	I say	we say
2nd person	you say	you say
3rd person	he, she, it says	they say

simple present

2. **Subject-verb agreement**: The simple present tense seems *agreement* entirely straightforward, and usually it is. Most of us have no difficulty with the first person or the second person. But almost all of us occasionally have problems in writing the third person correctly. All too often the letter *s* at the end of the third person singular is left out. The simple rule to remember is that whenever you use a verb in the third person singular of the simple present tense, it <u>*must*</u> end in *s*.

worth checking	He go to Vancouver at least once a month.
revised	He goes to Vancouver at least once a month.
worth checking	The litmus paper change colour when the solution is poured into the beaker.
revised	The litmus paper changes colour when the solution is poured into the beaker.

(*paper*, which is the subject, is an it, and therefore third person singular)

It is not particularly difficult to ensure that the subject agrees with the verb in the above examples, but even professional writers often have trouble with more complex sentences. Here are two common causes of subject-verb agreement errors:

(a) The subject and verb are separated by a long phrase or clause.

worth checking	The state of Afghanistan's roads reflect the chaotic situation. (*Toronto Star*, Nov. 1986)
revised	The state of Afghanistan's roads reflects the chaotic situation.

Here the writer has made the mental error of thinking of *roads* as the subject of the verb reflect, whereas in fact the subject is the singular noun state. *The state reflect...* would immediately strike

VERBS AND VERB DIFFICULTIES

most people as wrong, but the intervening words have in this case caused grammatical confusion.

worth checking   Airlines and travel industry representatives have long been complaining with increasing urgency about congestion at the airport, where the number of flights and passengers have long outstripped the airport's capabilities.
(*The Globe and Mail*, Nov. 29, 1988)

revised   Airlines and travel industry representatives have long been complaining with increasing urgency about congestion at the airport, where the number of flights and passengers **has** long outstripped the airport's capabilities.

The subject is the singular noun *number*, so the verb must be has rather than have.

worth checking   The real price of tea and jute are only about 1/3 of their value of 20 years ago.
(Prof. Charles Weitz at a paper given at a 1985 conference)

revised   The real prices of tea and jute are only about 1/3 of their value of twenty years ago.

Sometimes a long sentence can in itself throw off a writer's sense of subject-verb agreement, even if subject and verb are close together. In the following example the close proximity of the subject *simplifications* to the verb has not prevented error:

worth checking   The decline in the quality of American leadership is mirrored in the crude simplifications which characterises the average American's view of the world.
(*The Guardian*, April 19, 1987)

revised   The decline in the quality of American leadership is mirrored in the crude simplifications which characterise the average American's view of the world.

(b) The error of using *there is* instead of *there are* when the subject is plural has become more and more frequent in writing as well as speech. When these two expressions are used, remember that the subject comes after the verb; use *is* or *are* depending on whether the subject is singular or plural.

worth checking There's more Stars with our Stripes.
(Advertisement for the Sentinel Equity Fund, June 1987)
revised There are more Stars with our Stripes.

3. **Habitual action:** the simple present tense is often used to express what is called *habitual* action – the way an action often or ordinarily, or habitually occurs. The simple present tense is used to name such action *even if* the main verb of the sentence is in the past or future tense.

worth checking The professor told us that Jupiter was the largest planet.

revised The professor told us that Jupiter is the largest planet.

(Jupiter has not stopped being the largest since he spoke.)

EXERCISE: **Simple Present Tense**

Fill in the correct tense of the verb:

1) Every day the sun _____ *[to rise]* in the east and _____ *[to set]* in the west. Because of this, some people _____ *[to think]* that the sun _____ *[to revolve]* around the earth. In fact, the opposite _____ *[to be]* true; the earth _____ *[to circle]* the sun once every day. While the sun _____ *[to shine]* on one side of the earth, it _____ *[to be]* night on the other side.

2) This year she _____ *[to follow]* the same pattern of teaching in many lessons. As soon as she _____ *[to come]* into the class she _____ *[to ask]* several questions on the previous day's work. Then she usually _____ *[to introduce]* a new topic, and _____ *[to talk]* to us about it for several minutes. More often than not she then _____ *[to assign]* a written exercise to do in class.

EXERCISE: **Simple Present Tense**

Add an *s* where necessary to plural nouns, third person singular verbs, etc.

1) Train in Burma usually run on time, although it sometime take many hours to get from one place to another. The trip from Belowa to Rangoon, for example, last about eleven hour. The Railway Corporation use several different type of locomotive- steam, electric,

and diesel. The newest are the electric locomotive that travel between Rangoon and Mutisa.

2) Most of the electricity that the State need come from the dam. When the water flow over the large turbine, it turn them and this produce large amount of electricity.

3) In politic as in everyday life the variation that interest us occur in two dimension. Sometime political scientist are curious about variation over time. For instance, they may ask why the number of vote received by the various parties fluctuate so much from one election to the next. At other time political scientist concentrate their attention on variation over space. They may be interested, for example, in why one nation government seem to enjoy more success than it neighbour in combatting inflation, or protecting human right.

The Present Progressive (or Continuous) Tense

present progressive

	singular	plural
1st person	I am saying	we are saying
2nd person	you are saying	you are saying
3rd person	he, she, it is saying	they are saying

4.   **Verbs not normally used in the continuous tenses:** In English the continuous tenses are not normally used with many verbs which have to do with feelings, emotions, or senses. Some of these verbs are *to see, to hear, to understand, to believe, to hope, to know, to think* (meaning *believe*), *to trust, to comprehend, to mean, to doubt, to suppose, to wish, to want, to love, to desire, to prefer, to dislike, to hate.*

worth checking   He was not understanding what I meant.

revised   He did not understand what I meant.

The Simple Past Tense

simple past

	singular	**plural**
1st person	I finished	we finished
2nd person	you finished	you finished
3rd person	he, she, it finished	they finished

5.   The occasional problems that crop up with the simple past

VERBS AND VERB DIFFICULTIES

tense usually involve irregular verbs. *May, might* is a good example:

worth checking   Bands such as U2 and Simple Minds gained a
foothold in North America through campus radio;
without it they may not have broken through.

revised   Bands such as U2 and Simple Minds gained a
foothold in North America through campus radio;
without it they **might** not have broken through.

6. **Tense errors when writing about literature:** The simple   literature & tense
past tense is of course used to name actions which happened in
the past. One exception to this practice deserves mention; when
writing about what happens in a work of literature, convention
decrees that we use the simple present tense. This should be
done regardless of whether we are speaking about the way the
book is written or recounting the events in the story, and
regardless of whether the story takes place in 1987 or in 1543.

worth checking   Romeo fell in love with Juliet as soon as he saw her.

revised   Romeo falls in love with Juliet as soon as he sees her.

worth checking   In her short stories Alice Munro explored both
the outer and the inner worlds of small town life
with a deceptively simple style.

revised   In her short stories Alice Munro explores both
the outer and the inner worlds of small town life
with a deceptively simple style.

If literature in its historical context is being discussed, however,
the simple past tense is often more appropriate.

worth checking   Marlowe writes *Doctor Faustus* when he is only
twenty-nine.

revised   Marlowe wrote *Doctor Faustus* when he was
only twenty-nine.

Often the context may require shifting back and forth between
the past and present tenses in an essay about literature. In such
cases one is very likely to make mistakes during the writing of the
first draft; even experienced writers have to think carefully during
the revision process about the tense of each verb.

VERBS AND VERB DIFFICULTIES

worth checking In *The Two Gentlemen of Verona*, then, Shakespeare exhibited a degree and a variety of technical accomplishment unprecedented in the English drama. He still of course had much to learn as a dramatist and as a poet; in its wit or its power to move us emotionally *The Two Gentleman* was at an enormous remove from the great works of a few years later. But already, in 1592, Shakespeare had mastered all the basic techniques of plot construction that were to sustain the structures of the great plays.

revised In *The Two Gentlemen of Verona*, then, Shakespeare exhibits a degree and a variety of technical accomplishment unprecedented in the English drama. He still of course had much to learn as a dramatist and as a poet; in its wit or its power to move us emotionally *The Two Gentleman* is at an enormous remove from the great works of a few years later. But already, in 1592, Shakespeare had mastered all the basic techniques of plot construction that were to sustain the structures of the great plays.

The Past Progressive (or Continuous) Tense

past progressive

	singular	plural
1st person	I was leaving	we were leaving
2nd person	you were leaving	you were leaving
3rd person	he, she, it was leaving	they were leaving

The problems that sometimes occur with the past continuous tense are the same as those that occur with the present continuous (see above, number 4). Remember to avoid these tenses when using verbs having to do with the feelings, emotions, or senses (e.g. *see, hear, understand, believe, hope, know, think, trust, comprehend*) and when using the verb to have to mean own, possess, or suffer from.

worth checking At that time he was believing that everything on earth was created within one week.

revised At that time he believed that everything on earth was created within one week.

VERBS AND VERB DIFFICULTIES

The Simple Future Tense

	singular	plural
1st person	I will arrive	we will arrive
2nd person	you will arrive	you will arrive
3rd person	he, she, it will arrive	they will arrive

The only significant difficulty in using the simple future tense occurs over the issue of when to use *shall*, which has for the most part given way to *will* in ordinary usage. But it shall never disappear; most of us who would never dream of wading through the pages and pages many authorities offer on when to use *will* and when to use *shall* nevertheless sense instinctively moments when *shall* lends the resonance of added conviction to a verb.

milder	We will not fail.
more determined	We shall not fail.

The Future Progressive (or Continuous) Tense

	singular	plural
1st person	I will be finding	we will be finding
2nd person	you will be finding	you will be finding
3rd person	he, she, it will be finding	they will be finding

The Perfect Tenses

As used to refer to the perfect tenses, the word *perfect* means *completed*; as you might expect, then, the perfect tenses are often (though not always) used to speak of actions that have been completed. They are formed by combining some form of the verb *to have* with a past participle (e.g. *opened, finished, believed, done*).

The Present Perfect Tense

	singular	plural
1st person	I have worked	we have worked
2nd person	you have worked	you have worked
3rd person	he, she, it has worked	they have worked

7.   One way in which this tense is used is to speak of past actions which may continue into the present, or be repeated in the present or future. In the sentence, "Margaret Atwood has written a number of books," for example, the form of the verb shows that she will probably write more; she has neither died nor given up writing.)

A simple enough practice in normal usage, but in the long sentences often attempted as part of academic writing it is easy to become confused:

worth checking   Since it called the First World Food Congress in 1963, the Food and Agriculture Organization has said clearly that the world, with the science and technology then known, had enough knowledge to ensure man's freedom from hunger. Successive world congresses and conferences have repeated this contention.
(from a paper given by a distinguished professor at a 1985 academic conference)

Here the writer has evidently chosen the present perfect, thinking that he is referring to a situation which has continued on into the present. But when he refers to the *science and technology then known* and to *successive world congresses and conferences* he has cut off the 1963 conference from any grammatical connection with the present. This is again the sort of mistake that most writers can only catch during the revision process.

revised   When it called the First World Food Congress in 1963, the Food and Agriculture Organization said clearly that the world, with the science and technology then known, had enough knowledge to ensure man's freedom from hunger. Successive world congresses and conferences have repeated this contention.

The Past Perfect Tense

past perfect

		singular	plural
	1st person	I had believed	we had believed
	2nd person	you had believed	you had believed
	3rd person	he, she, it had believed	they had believed

VERBS AND VERB DIFFICULTIES

Since the verb remains unchanged in all these forms, the past perfect is one of the easiest tenses to remember. What is difficult is learning how and when to use it. In English, however, there are quite definite rules about when the past perfect tense should be used. Its chief use is to show that one action in the past was completed before another action in the past began. Here are some examples:

> I told my parents what <u>had happened</u>.
> (The happening occurred before the telling.)

> By the time the group of tourists left Zimbabwe, they <u>had formed</u> a very favourable impression of the country.
> (The forming occurred before the leaving.)

> When he had gone I thought very seriously about what he <u>had said</u>.
> (Both the going and the saying occurred before the thinking.)

The usefulness of the past perfect tense can be clearly seen in passages in which the writer wishes to *flashback*, or move backwards in time. If you compare the following passages, you will see that the use of the past perfect tense in the second passage removes any confusion about the order in which the events happened. In the example below, when only the simple past tense is used, it sounds as if the dead snake is able to crawl.

worth checking The tail was still moving, but the snake itself it was quite dead. It crawled out froum under a rock and slowly moved towards me as I was lowering the canoe at the end of the portage.

revised The tail was still moving, but the snake itself it was quite dead. It had crawled out from under a rock and had moved slowly towards me as I had been lowering the canoe at the end of the portage.

In the second passage it is clear that the snake approached this person <u>before</u> it died, and not afterwards.

Perhaps the most common occasions in which we use the past perfect tense are when we are using indirect speech:

> She said that she had knocked on my door in the morning, but that there had been no answer.
> (The knocking happened before the saying.)

VERBS AND VERB DIFFICULTIES

The Committee Chairman repeatedly asked Col. North when the President had known of the diversion of funds to the Contras. (The knowing happened before the asking.)

In a few cases it is possible to correctly speak of two actions which happened one after the other in the past by using the simple past tense for both actions. The use of the word *after*, for example, often makes it clear that the first action was completed before the other began.

8.   Writers often neglect to use the past perfect to name the earlier action when they are speaking of two (or more) actions that happened at different times in the past.

worth checking	He asked me if I talked to his secretary before coming to him.
revised	He asked me if I had talked to his secretary before coming to him.
worth checking	By the time the Allies decided to resist Hitler, the Nazis built up a huge military machine.
revised	By the time the Allies decided to resist Hitler, the Nazis had built up a huge military machine.
worth checking	Johnson's girlfriend, Marsha Dianne Blaylock,

> said she knew Williams since October 1984,
> when she and Johnson began their relationship.
> (news report, *Chattanooga Times*, Aug. 9, 1985)

revised
> Johnson's girlfriend, Marsha Dianne Blaylock,
> said she had known Williams since October
> 1984, when she and Johnson began their
> relationship.

Note that like the present perfect, the past perfect is very frequently required with *since* or *for*.

The past perfect is also used to indicate that a past action occurred over a prolonged period:

> In the late 1960s Tom Hayden was a disheveled student radical; by the late 1980s he had become a respected state legislator leading the campaign for 'Big Green', the comprehensive set of California environment proposals.

worth checking
> In 1970, 10 per cent of Chile's families did not have sufficient income to satisfy the minimum food requirements recommended by international organizations; in 1983 the figure grew to 32 per cent.
> (*New York Review of Books*, May, 1988)

revised
> In 1970, 10 per cent of Chile's families did not have sufficient income to satisfy the minimum food requirements recommended by international organizations; by 1983 the figure had grown to 32 per cent.

revised
> ...in 1983 the figure was 32 per cent.

The original suggests that the figure had remained at 10 per cent in every year from 1970 to 1983, and then jumped in the course of one year to 32 per cent.

The Future Perfect Tense

	singular	**plural**	
1st person	I will have gone	we will have gone	future perfect
2nd person	you will have gone	you will have gone	
3rd person	he, she, it will have gone	they will have gone	

The Conditional Tense

	singular	plural
1st person	I would go	we would go
2nd person	you would go	you would go
3rd person	he, she, it would go	they would go

The conditional tense is used when we are speaking of actions which would happen _if_ certain conditions were fulfilled. Here are some examples:

If I <u>wanted</u> to go to Australia, I <u>would have</u> to fly.

If I <u>drank</u> a lot of gin, I <u>would be</u> very sick.

I <u>would lend</u> Joe the money he wants if I <u>trusted</u> him.

Notice that each of these sentences is made up of a main clause, in which the conditional tense _would have_, _would be_, etc. is used, and a subordinate clause beginning with _if_, with a verb in the simple past tense (_wanted, drank, trusted_, etc.). In all cases the action named in the _if_ clause is considered by the speaker to be unlikely to happen, or quite impossible. The speaker does not really want to go to Australia: she is just speculating about what she would have to do if she did. Similarly the second speaker does not expect to drink a lot of gin: if he <u>did</u>, he <u>would be</u> sick, but he does not plan to. In the same way, the speaker of the third sentence does <u>not</u> trust Joe: he is speaking about what the situation <u>would be</u> if he <u>did</u> trust Joe. Situations like these which are not happening and which we do not expect to happen are called _hypothetical situations_: we speculate on what <u>would</u> happen _if_... but we do not expect the _if_... to come true.

If we think the _if_... <u>is</u> likely to come true, then we use the future tense instead of the conditional in the main clause, and the present tense in the subordinate _if_ clause, as in these examples:

If I drink a lot of gin, I will be very sick.
(Here the speaker thinks that it is very possible or likely that he <u>will</u> drink a lot of gin)

If I want to go to Australia, I will have to fly.
(Here the speaker thinks that she may really want to go)

Notice the difference between the following two sentences:

If an NDP government is elected, the American administration

will not be pleased.
(Here the writer thinks that it is quite possible or likely that the NDP will be elected.)

If an NDP government were elected, the American administration would not be pleased.
(Here the writer is assuming that the NDP probably will <u>not</u> be elected.)

9. **The subjunctive**: Notice in the above example that *were* is used instead of *was*. This is what is known as the subjunctive mood, used in certain cases to denote actions that are wished for or imagined. Years ago there were many more types of sentence in which the subjunctive was used than there are now, but it has by no means disappeared.

subjunctive mood

If we can't even get this much done, God help us. [not *God helps us*]

If I were you, I'd do what she says. [not *if I was you*]

Suffice it to say that the subject is a controversial one. [not *suffices it...*]

Be that as it may, the central assertion of Smith's book is irrefutable. [not *is that...*]

The doctor advises that he stop smoking immediately. [not *that he stops*]

worth checking If a bank was willing to lend new businesses very large amounts without proper guarantees, it would go bankrupt very quickly.

revised If a bank <u>were</u> willing to lend new businesses very large amounts without proper guarantees, it would go bankrupt very quickly.

10. Some writers mistakenly use the conditional tense or the present tense (instead of the past tense) in the *if* clause when they are using the conditional tense in the main clause.

worth checking If I want to buy a car, I would look carefully at all the models available.

revised If I <u>wanted</u> to buy a car, I would look carefully at all the models available.
(The speaker does not want to buy a car.)

or If I <u>want</u> to buy a car, I will look carefully at all

VERBS AND VERB DIFFICULTIES

the models available.
(The speaker may really want to buy a car.)

worth checking   If television networks would produce fewer
series about violent crime, parents would allow
their children to watch even more television
than they do now.

revised   If television networks produced fewer series
about violent crime, parents would allow their
children to watch even more television than
they do now.

Remember that the <u>past</u> tense (or with the verb *to be* the subjunctive) is used in the *if* clause whenever the conditional tense is being used in the main clause.

The Past Conditional Tense

past conditional

	singular	plural
1st person	I would have gone	we would have gone
2nd person	you would have gone	you would have gone
3rd person	he, she, it would have gone	they would have gone

This tense is used in conditional sentences in which we are speaking of actions which never happened. It is used in the main clause, with the past perfect tense being used in the *if* clause.

If I had studied harder, I would have passed.
(meaning that in fact I did not study very hard, and did not pass)

If Kitchener had arrived at Khartoum a day earlier, he would
have saved Gordon and the rest of the British garrison force.
(meaning that Kitchener did not come early enough, and was
not able to prevent the 1885 massacre at Khartoum)

11.   Some students mistakenly use the past conditional tense in both clauses of sentences such as these. Remember that the past conditional should be used only in the main clause; use the past perfect in the *if* clause.

worth checking   If the Titanic would have carried more lifeboats,
hundreds of lives would have been saved.

revised   If the Titanic had carried more lifeboats,
hundreds of lives would have been saved.

VERBS AND VERB DIFFICULTIES

worth checking	If the Conservatives under Robert Stanfield would have won two more seats in the 1972 election, the course of Canadian politics in the seventies would have been very different.
revised	If the Conservatives under Robert Stanfield had won two more seats in the 1972 election, the course of Canadian politics in the seventies would have been very different.

EXERCISE: Conditional Sentences

Fill in the missing verbs.

1) He _____*[to supply]* our company with what we need if we _____*[pay]* him $50,000. However, we only _____*[to have]* $30,000 in liquid assets.

2) If he _____*[to reply]* to me quickly, as I think he will, I _____*[to be able]* to make reservations for our holiday.

3) If she _____*[to believe]* in God she _____*[to go]* to church. However, she _____*[to be]* an atheist.

4) My friend and I are thinking of going to the game this afternoon. If we _____*[to go]* we probably _____*[to take]* our wives with us.

5) If we _____*[to arrive]* sooner, we would have been able to help him.

6) If Montcalm's most important officer _____not_____*[to be hiding]* away with his mistress, the French troops _____*[to be assembled]* earlier and the British _____*[to lose]* the battle on the Plains of Abraham.

7) We would have been better off if we _____*[to plant]* wheat instead of cotton.

8) If you had spoken to me about it, I _____*[to do]* something sooner.

9) I would have told them the truth if they _____*[to ask]* me.

10) The Titanic _____probably not _____*[to sink]* if it had struck the iceberg head on.

Complete the following sentences in any appropriate way.

1)   If I wore no clothes at all...

2)   If South Africa eliminates apartheid...

3) He would buy a truck if...
4) He will buy a truck if...
5) If an election is held next month...
6) She will win if...
7) She would win if...
8) If money were abolished...
9) Local farms would be more productive if...
10) If he sends me the money in time...

Other Tenses

The present perfect continuous tense — I have been running, you have been working, etc.

The past perfect continuous tense — I have been looking, you have been following, etc.

The future perfect continuous tense — I will have been sleeping, they will have been studying, etc.

The conditional continuous tense — I would be bringing, she would be starting, etc.

The past conditional continuous tense — I would have been working, he would have been driving, etc.

EXERCISE: Verb Tenses

Fill in the correct tenses of the verbs.

1) This train always _____ [to leave] at exactly five o'clock.

2) As he _____ [to climb] the mountain he _____ [to lose] his grip and _____ [to plunge] five hundred feet to his death.

3) After we _____ [to make] our way through the forest, we sat down to rest.

4) This machinery _____ [to be] very reliable. It almost never _____ [to break] down and it _____ [to need] very little maintenance.

5) He _____ [to tell] me before the meeting yesterday that they _____ [to reach] a decision already.

6) The Cleveland Indians _____ [to improve] at the moment, but I _____ [to not think] that they _____ [to be] as good as the Red Sox yet.

7) The government of El Salvador _____ [to oppress] the Chilean people for many years. I _____ [to hope] that it _____ [to be] overthrown soon.

8) _____ you ever _____ [to see] a flying saucer?

9) I _____ _____ [to tell] him what I knew if I _____ [to trust] him. Unfortunately, I don't trust him.

10) She _____ [to not eat] much before the party began.

11) He said that he _____ *[to not understand]* me.

12) There _____ *[to be]* fifty stars in the American flag—one for every state.

13) Mrs. Morris discovered that her students _____ *[to not do]* the assigned work.

14) If he _____ *[to find out]* about this he _____ *[to be]* very angry, but I am sure he will not find out.

15) Greene's greatest novel _____ *[to recount]* the story of an alcoholic Mexican priest during a period in which the government _____ *[to suppress]* organized religion.

16) Shylock _____ *[to be]* the most important character in Shakespeare's *The Merchant of Venice*. We _____ *[to sympathize]* with him despite his streak of cruelty, because we_____ *[to be made]* to understand his resentment against the Christians. When Shylock _____ *[to accuse]* Antonio in Act One of having sworn at him and spat on him merely because of his religion, Antonio—far from denying the charges—_____ *[to say]* that he would do the same again. Moreover, Antonio's prejudice against Jews _____ *[to seem]* to be shared by all the Christian characters in the play.

DANGLING CONSTRUCTIONS

Dangling Participles and Infinitives

A present participle is an *-ing* word (*going, thinking* etc.). When combined with a form of the verb *to be*, participles form part of a complete verb. They can also be used in a number of ways on their own, however:

> The President felt that visiting China would be unwise at that time.
> (Here *visiting China* acts as a noun phrase.)

> Having taken into account the various reports, the Committee decided to delay the project for a year.
> (Here *having taken into account the various reports* acts as an adjectival phrase modifying the noun *Committee*.)

1. **Dangling present participles or participial phrases**: The danger of dangling occurs with sentences such as the second example above. If the writer does not take care that the participial phrase refers to the subject of the main clause, some absurd sentences can result:

worth checking   Waiting for a bus, a brick fell on my head.

	(Bricks do not normally wait for buses.)
revised	While I was waiting for a bus, a brick fell on my head.
worth checking	Leaving the room, the lights must be turned off.
	(Lights do not normally leave the room.)
revised	When you leave the room you must turn the lights off.

In sentences such as these the amusing error is relatively easy to notice; it can be much more difficult with longer and more complex sentences. Experienced writers are especially alert to this pitfall if they begin a sentence with a participle or participial phrase that describes a mental operation; they are wary of beginning by *considering, believing, taking into account remembering, turning for a moment* or *regarding.*

worth checking	Believing that he had done no wrong, the fact of being accused of dishonesty infuriated Col. North.
revised	Believing that he had done no wrong, Col. North was infuriated at being accused of dishonesty.
or	Col. North was infuriated at being accused of dishonesty; he believed he had done no wrong.
worth checking	Considering all of the above-mentioned studies, the evidence shows conclusively that smoking can cause cancer.
revised	Considering all of the above-mentioned studies, we conclude that smoking causes cancer.
Better	These studies show conclusively that smoking can cause cancer.
worth checking	Turning for a moment to the thorny question of Joyce's style, the stream of consciousness technique realistically depicts the workings of the human mind.
revised	Turning for a moment to the thorny question of Joyce's style, we may observe that his stream of consciousness technique realistically depicts the workings of the human mind.
Better	Joyce's style does not make Ulysses easy to read, but his stream of consciousness

DANGLING CONSTRUCTIONS

technique realistically depicts the workings of the human mind.

worth checking	Taking into account the uncertainty as to the initial temperature of the beaker, the results are not conclusive.
Poor	Taking into account the uncertainty as to the initial temperature of the beaker necessitates that the results be deemed inconclusive.
Better	Since the initial temperature of the beaker was not recorded, the results are inconclusive.

Notice that in each case the best way to eliminate the problem is to dispense with the participial phrase entirely. More often than not one's writing is improved by using active verbs rather than participial phrases. Many students and not a few professors seem to feel that writing which is filled with participial phrases somehow sounds more important; in fact, such phrases tend to obscure the writer's meaning under unnecessary padding. This is true even when the participles are not dangling:

worth checking	Another significant characteristic having a significant impact on animal populations is the extreme diurnal temperature range on the desert surface.
	(Can a characteristic have an impact? A small point is here buried in a morass of meaningless abstraction.)
Better	The extreme diurnal temperature range on the desert surface also affects animal populations.
worth checking	Referring generally to the social stratification systems of the city as a whole, we can see clearly that types of accommodation, varying throughout in accordance with income levels and other socio-economic factors, display an extraordinary diversity.
	(Is there anything either clear or extraordinary about this?)
Better	In this city rich people and poor people live in different neighborhoods and rich people live in larger houses than poor people.

By cutting out the padding in this way the writer may occasionally find to his surprise that instead of saying something rather weighty and important as he had thought he was doing he is in fact saying

DANGLING CONSTRUCTIONS

little or nothing. But he should not be discouraged if this happens; the same is true for all writers. The best response is simply to chuckle and scratch out the sentence!

2. **Dangling past participles** (e.g. *considered, developed, regarded*): The same sorts of problems that occur with present participles are frequent with past participles as well:

worth checking Considered from a cost point of view, Dome Petroleum could not really afford to purchase Hudson Bay Oil and Gas.
(Dome is not being considered; the purchase is.)

Poor Considered from the point of view of cost, the purchase of Hudson Bay Oil and Gas was not a wise move by Dome Petroleum.

Better Dome Petroleum could not really afford to buy Hudson Bay Oil and Gas.

worth checking Regarded by many as a public relations ploy, nonetheless through a Freedom from Hunger campaign launched in 1960 the Organization's Director forced debate and concern for the issues of underdevelopment, hunger, malnutrition, population, and transfer of technology and resources.
(A person cannot be a ploy.)

Poor Regarded by many as a public relations ploy, the Freedom from Hunger campaign launched in 1960 by the Organization's Director nonetheless forced debate and concern for the issues of underdevelopment, hunger, malnutrition, population, and transfer of technology and resources.

Better In 1960 the Organization's Director launched a Freedom from Hunger campaign. Though many regarded it as a public relations ploy, the Campaign did provoke debate on the issues of underdevelopment.

3. **Dangling infinitive phrases:**

infinitive phrases

worth checking To conclude this essay, the French Revolution was a product of many interacting causes.
(The French Revolution concluded no essays.)

DANGLING CONSTRUCTIONS

Poor	To conclude this essay, let me say that the French Revolution was a product of many causes.
Better	The explanations given for the French Revolution, then, are not mutually exclusive; it was a product of many interacting causes.

[A good writer does not normally need to tell her readers that she is concluding an essay; they can see the space at the bottom of the page. A little word such as *then*, set off by commas, is more than enough to signal that this is a summing-up.]

worth checking	To receive a complimentary copy, the business reply card should be returned before June 30. (The card will not receive anything.)
revised	To receive a complimentary copy, you should return the business reply card before June 30.
worth checking	To appreciate the full significance of the Meech Lake Accord, a range of factors need to be considered. (A factor cannot appreciate.)
Poor	To appreciate the full significance of the Meech Lake Accord, we need to consider many things.
Better	The Meech Lake Accord was important in many ways.

4. **Dangling gerund** *(of going, in doing, etc.)* **phrases:**

gerund phrases

worth checking	In reviewing the evidence, one point stands out plainly. (A point cannot review evidence.)
Poor	In reviewing the evidence, we can see one point standing out plainly.
Better	One point stands out plainly from this evidence.
worth checking	When analyzing the figures, ways to achieve substantial savings can be discerned. (The ways cannot analyse.)
Poor	When we analyze the figures we can see ways to achieve substantial savings.
Better	The figures suggest that we can greatly reduce our expenses.

DANGLING CONSTRUCTIONS

Other sorts of phrases can be caught dangling too. But almost all writers are capable of attaching them properly if they re-read and revise their work carefully.

worth checking   On behalf of City Council and the people of Windsor, it gives me great pleasure to welcome you to our city.

(Mayor David A Burr, *Windsor Guide*, Winter 1988)

(The Mayor, not a faceless *it*, is acting on behalf of the others.)

revised   On behalf of City Council and the people of Windsor, I am pleased to welcome you to our city.

EXERCISE: Dangling Constructions

Correct the following sentences:

1) Riding the bus to work, his wife waved at him from the sidewalk.

2) When covered with aluminum siding, we will have a much more salable house.

3) Regarding the fiscal requirements of the government, an increase in taxes will be required if the deficit is to be reduced.

4) Looking for a moment at the implications of Smith's argument, he allows us to justify our selfish behavior.

5) Having covered the issue of stratification, the means of redistributing income will be dealt with next.

6) To obtain a sense of the density of structuralist prose, a few examples should suffice.

7) We have asked for a survey of the attitudes of consumers carried out randomly.

8) Considering all of this evidence, there is no doubt that an increased awareness of the usefulness of uniform and objectively-defined time led to the spread of clocks, and not the other way round.

9) Widely regarded as a failure by observers at the time, we can now see that Truman was a remarkably successful president.

10) To begin this essay, Faulkner's novel is written from several points of view.

11) To obtain a refund, any copies damaged in shipment must be returned promptly.

12) Having settled the issue of independence, questions of economic growth came to the fore in the public consciousness.

SEQUENCE OF TENSES

If the main verb of a sentence is in the past tense, other verbs must also express a past viewpoint (except when a general truth is being expressed — see above, p.137). Some writers have trouble keeping the verb tenses they use in agreement, particularly when indirect speech is involved, or when a quotation is incorporated into a sentence:

Agreement of tenses - indirect speech:

agreement of tense

worth checking   He said that he will fix the engine before the end of 1986.

revised   He said that he would fix the engine before the end of 1986.

2.   **Agreement of tenses - quoted material:**

worth checking   The President admitted that "such a policy is not without its drawbacks."

(The past tense *admitted* and the present tense *is* do not agree.)

There are two ways of dealing with a difficulty such as this:

(a) Change the sentence so as to set off the quotation without using the connecting word, *that*. Usually this can be done with a colon. In this case the tense you use does not have to agree with the tense used in the quotation. The words before the colon, though, must be able to act as a complete sentence in themselves.

(b) Use only that part of the quotation that can be used in agreement with the tense of the main verb.

revised   The President did not claim perfection: "such a policy is not without its drawbacks," he admitted.

or   The President admitted that such a policy was

"not without its drawbacks."

Here are some other examples:

worth checking	Churchill promised that "we shall fight on the beaches,...we shall fight in the fields and in the streets, we shall fight in the hills; we shall never surrender."

(This suggests that you, the writer, will be among those fighting.)

revised	Churchill made the following promise: "we shall fight on the beaches,...we shall fight in the fields and in the streets, we shall fight in the hills; we shall never surrender."

(Notice that the word *that* is now removed.)

or	Churchill promised that the British people would "fight on the beaches,...in the fields and in the streets,... in the hills", and that they would "never surrender."

worth checking	In the 1974 election campaign the Liberals' claimed that "the Land is strong."
revised	In the 1974 election campaign the Liberals' slogan was, "The Land is Strong."
or	In the 1974 election campaign the Liberals' asserted that the Land was strong.

literary tenses   3.   When writing about history or politics – in the <u>past</u> tense – one is likely to find difficulty with quotations in the <u>present</u> or <u>future</u> tenses. When writing about literature the problem is the reverse; one is writing in the <u>present</u> tense, but many of the quotations one usually wishes to use are in the <u>past</u> tense.

worth checking	Emma Bovary lives largely through memory and fantasy. She daydreams frequently, and as she reads, "the memory of the Vicomte kept her happy."
revised	Emma Bovary lives largely through memory and fantasy. She daydreams frequently, and as she reads "the memory of the Vicomte" keeps her happy.
or	Emma Bovary lives largely through memory and fantasy. She daydreams frequently, and blends fiction and memory in her imaginings:

SEQUENCE OF TENSES

"Always, as she read, the memory of the Vicomte kept her happy. She established a connexion between him and the characters of her favourite fiction."

worth checking   In *The Mayor of Casterbridge* the strength of Henchard's personality is felt even after his death. The extraordinary series of requests he writes as he is dying, "was respected as far as practicable by Elizabeth-Jane...from her independent knowledge that the man who wrote them meant what he said."

revised   In *The Mayor of Casterbridge* the strength of Henchard's personality is felt even after his death. The extraordinary series of requests he writes as he is dying is "respected as far as practicable" by Elizabeth-Jane, who realizes that Henchard means what he has said.

or   In *The Mayor of Casterbridge* the strength of Henchard's personality is felt even after his death: "What Henchard had written in the anguish of his dying was respected as far as practicable by Elizabeth-Jane, though less from a sense of the sacredness of last words, as such, than from her independent knowledge that the man who wrote them meant what he said."

EXERCISE 16:   Agreement of Tenses — Direct and Indirect Speech

Correct the following sentences:

1) The Vice President said that "We will have to improve our productivity.

2) Tennyson's Ulysses says that "I have suffered greatly, both with those/That loved me, and alone.

3) Churchill claimed that "This is our finest hour."

4) Johnson at first believed that the war will be over before the 1968 election.

SEQUENCE OF TENSES

IRREGULAR OR DIFFICULT VERBS

irregular or difficult verbs

The majority of verbs in English follow a regular pattern - *I open* in the simple present tense, *I opened* in the simple past tense, *I have opened* in the present perfect tense, and so forth. However, most of the more frequently used verbs are in some way or another irregular. To pick an obvious example, we say *I went* instead of *I goed*, and *I have gone* instead of *I have goed*. What follows is a list of the main irregular or difficult verbs in English. The past participle (column 3) is used in tenses such as the present perfect (e.g. *I have grown, He has found*) and the past perfect (*I had grown, I had found*).

The verbs that most frequently cause problems are given special treatment in the following list.

Note: In both regular and irregular verbs, the present tense is formed by using the infinitive without the preposition *to*.

Present and infinitive	Simple past	Past participle
1. arise	arose	arisen
worth checking	A problem had arose even before the discussion began.	
revised	A problem had arisen even before the discussion began.	
awake	awoke/awaked (passive: was awakened)	awoken/awaked/woken
be	was/were	been
2. bear	bore	borne
worth checking	It was heartbreaking for her to lose the child after having bore it for so long.	
revised	It was heartbreaking for her to lose the child after having borne it for so long.	
3. beat	beat	beaten
worth checking	The Yankees were badly beat by the Blue Jays.	

revised	The Yankees were badly beaten by the Blue Jays.	
	become	became	become

4. begin   began   begun

worth checking   He had already began treatment when I met him.

revised   He had already begun treatment when I met him.

bend	bent	bent
bite	bit	bitten
bleed	bled	bled
blow	blew	blown
break	broke	broken
bring	brought	brought
build	built	built
burn	burned/burnt	burned/ burnt

5. burst   burst   burst

worth checking   The pipes bursted while we were on holiday.

revised   The pipes burst while we were on holiday.

buy	bought	bought
can	could	been able
catch	caught	caught

6. choose   chose   chosen

worth checking   In 1949 Newfoundlanders choose to join Confederation.

revised   In 1949 Newfoundlanders chose to join Confederation.

cling	clung	clung
come	came	come
cost	cost	cost
dig	dug	dug
do	did	done

7. dive   dived   dived

worth checking   He dove into the shallow water.

revised   He dived into the shallow water.

8. drag   dragged   dragged

worth checking   The newspapers drug up a lot of scandal about her.

revised   The newspapers dragged up a lot of scandal about her.

IRREGULAR OR DIFFICULT VERBS

draw	drew	drawn
dream	dreamed/dreamt	dreamed/dreamt

Habs Should Have Drank A Toast To Discipline
(headline, *The Globe and Mail*, Dec. 19, 1990)

Short on Education
(letters to the editor, *The Globe and Mail*, Dec. 27, 1990)

Re Habs Should Have Drank A Toast To Discipline (Dec. 19):
Whoever wrote this headline should have went to school longer.

Simon Farrow, North Vancouver

---

9. | drink | drank | drunk |
|---|---|---|

worth checking He has drank more than is good for him.

revised He has drunk more than is good for him.

drive	drove	driven
eat	ate	eaten
fall	fell	fallen
feel	felt	felt
fight	fought	fought
find	found	found

10. | fit | fitted or fit (US) | fitted |
|---|---|---|

worth checking That dress has fit her since she was married.

revised That dress has fitted her since she was married.

flee	fled	fled

11. | fling | flung | flung |
|---|---|---|

worth checking George flinged his plate across the room.

revised George flung his plate across the room.

fly	flew	flown

12. | forbid | forbade | forbidden |
|---|---|---|

worth checking Yesterday he forbid us to climb the fence.

revised Yesterday he forbade us to climb the fence.

IRREGULAR OR DIFFICULT VERBS

13.   forecast   forecast   forecast

worth checking   The Weather Office has forecasted more rain.

revised   The Weather Office has forecast more rain.

forget	forgot	forgotten
forgive	forgave	forgiven
freeze	froze	frozen
get	got	got
give	gave	given
go	went	gone
grind	ground	ground
	(e.g., I have ground the coffee.)	
grow	grew	grown

14.   hang   hanged/hung   hanged/hung

Note: *Hanged* is used only when you are referring to a person being killed by hanging. Say, "The criminal has been hanged", but "We have hung the picture on the wall."

worth checking   No one has been hung in Canada since 1962.

revised   No one has been hanged in Canada since 1962.

have	had	had
hear	heard	heard
hide	hid	hidden
hit	hit	hit
hold	held	held
hurt	hurt	hurt
keep	kept	kept
kneel	knelt	knelt
know	knew	known

15.   lay   laid   laid

Note: Do not confuse *lay* with *lie*; you *lay* something on a table, and a hen *lays* eggs, but you *lie* down to sleep.

worth checking   The government has lain the issue to one side for the moment.

revised   The government has laid the issue to one side for the moment.

lead	led	led
lean	leaned/leant	leaned/leant
leap	leaped/leapt	leaped/leapt
learn	learned/learnt	learned/learnt
leave	left	left
lend	lent	lent
let	let	let

16.   lie   lay   lain

     worth checking   He asked if I would like to lay down and rest.

     revised   He asked if I would like to lie down and rest.

light	lighted/lit	lighted/lit
lose	lost	lost
make	made	made
may	might	
mean	meant	meant
meet	met	met
must	had to	
pay	paid	paid

17.   prove   proved   proven

     worth checking   We have proved the hypothesis to be correct.

     revised   We have proven the hypothesis to be correct.

put	put	put
read	read	read

18.   ride   rode   ridden

     worth checking   The actor had never rode a horse before.

     revised   The actor had never ridden a horse before.

19.   ring   rang   rung

     worth checking   I rung the bell three times, but no one answered.

     revised   I rang the bell three times, but no one answered.

rise	rose	risen
run	ran	run
saw	sawed	sawed/sawn
say	said	said
see	saw	seen
seek	sought	sought
sell	sold	sold
send	sent	sent
sew	sewed	sewed/sewn
shake	shook	shaken
shall	should	

20.   shine   shone   shone

     worth checking   The moon shined almost as brightly as the sun.

     revised   The moon shone almost as brightly as the sun.

shoot	shot	shot
show	showed	showed/shown

21.   shrink   shrank   shrunk

IRREGULAR OR DIFFICULT VERBS

worth checking	The Government's majority shrunk in the election.	
revised	The Government's majority shrank in the election.	

shut	shut	shut
sing	sang	sung

22. sink — sank — sunk

worth checking	The *Edmund Fitzgerald* sunk on Lake Superior.	
revised	The *Edmund Fitzgerald* sank on Lake Superior.	

sit	sat	sat
sleep	slept	slept
slide	slid	slid
smell	smelled/smelt	smelled/smelt
sow	sowed	sowed/sown
speak	spoke	spoken
speed	speeded/sped	speeded/sped
spell	spelled/spelt	spelled/spelt
spend	spent	spent
spill	spilled/spilt	spilled/spilt
spin	spun	spun
spit	spat	spat
split	split	split
spread	spread	spread

23. spring — sprang — sprung

worth checking	The soldiers hurriedly sprung to their feet.	
revised	The soldiers hurriedly sprang to their feet.	

stand	stood	stood
steal	stole	stolen
stick	stuck	stuck
sting	stung	stung
strike	struck	struck
swear	swore	sworn
sweep	swept	swept

24. swim — swam — swum

worth checking	Pictures were taken while the royal couple swum in what they thought was a private cove.	
revised	Pictures were taken while the royal couple swam in what they had thought was a private cove.	

swing	swung	swung
take	took	taken
teach	taught	taught
tear	tore	torn

IRREGULAR OR DIFFICULT VERBS

tell	told	told
think	thought	thought
throw	threw	thrown
tread	trod	trodden/trod
understand	understood	understood
wake	waked/woke	waked/woken
wear	wore	worn
weep	wept	wept
win	won	won
wind	wound	wound
wring	wrung	wrung

e.g.   She wrings out her clothes if they are wet.

write	wrote	written

TO BE, NOT TO BE, OR BEING?

INFINITIVES, GERUNDS AND DIRECT OBJECTS

There are no rules in English to explain why some words must be followed by an infinitive (*to go, to do, to be,* etc.), while others must be followed by a gerund (*of going, in doing,* etc.), and still others by a direct object. Here are some of the words with which difficulties of this sort most often arise.

infinitives, gerunds, direct objects

---

1. **accept** something (<u>not</u> accept to do something) — needs a direct object

worth checking	Michael Warren accepted to try to improve the quality of the postal service.
revised	Michael Warren accepted the task of trying to improve the postal service.
or	Michael Warren agreed to try to improve the postal service.

---

2. **accuse** someone <u>of doing</u> something (<u>not</u> to do).

worth checking	Klaus Barbie was accused to have killed thousands of innocent civilians in WW II.
revised	Klaus Barbie was accused of having killed thousands of innocent civilians in WW II.

---

3. **appreciate** something: When used to mean *be grateful*, this verb requires a direct object.

worth checking	I would appreciate if you could respond quickly.
revised	I would appreciate <u>it</u> if you could respond quickly.
or	I would appreciate a quick response.

(The verb *appreciate* without an object means <u>*increase in value.*</u>)

---

4. **assist** <u>in doing</u> something (<u>not</u> to do)

worth checking	He assisted me to solve the problem.
revised	He assisted me in solving the problem.
or	He helped me to solve the problem.

---

5. **capable** <u>of doing</u> something (<u>not</u> to do)

worth checking	He is capable to run 1500 metres in under four minutes.
revised	He is capable of running 1500 metres in under four minutes.
or	He is able to run 1500 metres in under four minutes.

---

6. **confident** <u>of doing</u> something

worth checking	She is confident to be able to finish the job before dusk.
revised	She is confident of being able to finish the job before dusk.
or	She is confident that she will finish the job before dusk.

---

7. **consider** something or someone to be something <u>or</u> consider them something (<u>not</u> as something)

worth checking	According to a recent policy paper, the Party now considers a guaranteed annual income as a good idea.
revised	According to a recent policy paper, the Party now considers a guaranteed annual income to be a good idea.
or	According to a recent policy paper, the Party now regards a guaranteed annual income as a good idea.

---

8. **discourage** someone <u>from doing</u> something (<u>not</u> to do).

worth checking	The new Immigration Act is intended to discourage anyone who wants to come to Canada to enter the country illegally.
revised	The new Immigration Act is intended to discourage anyone who wants to come to Canada from entering the country illegally.

---

9. **forbid** someone <u>to do</u> something (<u>not</u> from doing)

TO BE, NOT TO BE, OR BEING?

worth checking	The witnesses were forbidden from leaving the scene of the crime until the police had completed their preliminary investigation.
revised	The witnesses were forbidden to leave the scene of the crime until the police had completed their preliminary investigation.

10. **insist** <u>on doing</u> something *or* insist <u>that something be done</u> (but <u>not</u> insist to do)

worth checking	The customer has insisted to wait in the front office until she receives a refund.
revised	The customer has insisted on waiting in the front office until she receives a refund.

11. **intention:** <u>have</u> an intention <u>of doing</u> something *but* someone's intention is/was to do something

worth checking	Hitler had no intention to keep his word.
revised	Hitler had no intention of keeping his word.
or	Hitler did not intend to keep his word.
or	Hitler's intention was to break the treaty.

12. **justified** <u>in doing</u> something (<u>not</u> to do something)

worth checking	He is not justified to make these allegations.
revised	He is not justified in making these allegations.

13. **look** forward <u>to doing</u> something (<u>not</u> to do something)

TO BE, NOT TO BE, OR BEING?

worth checking	I am looking forward to receive your reply.
revised	I am looking forward to receiving your reply.

---

14. **opposed** <u>to doing</u> something (<u>not</u> to do something)

worth checking	He was opposed to set up a dictatorship.
revised	He was opposed to setting up a dictatorship.
or	He was opposed to the idea of setting up a dictatorship.

---

15. **organize** <u>something</u> (<u>not</u> organize to do something)

worth checking	We organized to meet at ten the next morning.
revised	We organized a meeting for ten the next morning.
or	We arranged to meet at ten the next morning.

---

16. **persist** <u>in doing</u> something (<u>not</u> to do something)

worth checking	Despite international disapproval and the will of Congress the American administration persisted to help the contras in Nicaragua.
revised	Despite international disapproval and the will of Congress the American administration persisted in helping the contras in Nicaragua.

---

17. **plan** to do (<u>not</u> on doing)

worth checking	They planned on closing the factory in Windsor.
revised	They planned to close the factory in Windsor.

---

18. **prohibit** someone <u>from doing</u> something.

worth checking	Members of the public were prohibited to feed the animals.
revised	Members of the public were prohibited from feeding the animals.

---

19. **regarded** <u>as</u> (<u>not</u> regarded to be)

worth checking	He is commonly regarded to be one of Canada's best musicians.
revised	He is commonly regarded as one of Canada's best musicians.

---

20. **responsible** <u>for doing</u> (<u>not</u> to do)

worth checking	Mr Dumphy is responsible to market the full line of the company's pharmaceutical products.

TO BE, NOT TO BE, OR BEING?

revised	Mr Dumphy is responsible for marketing the full line of the company's pharmaceutical products.

21.　**sacrifice** <u>something</u>: The use of *sacrifice* without a direct object may have crept into the language through the use of the verb as a baseball term (*Olerud sacrificed in the ninth to bring home Gruber.*).

worth checking	He sacrificed to work in an isolated community with no electricity or running water.
revised	He sacrificed himself to work in an isolated community with no electricity or running water.
or	He sacrificed a good deal; the isolated community he now works in has no electricity or running water.

22.　**seem** <u>to be</u> (<u>not</u> as if)

worth checking	The patient seemed as if he was in shock.
revised	The patient seemed to be in shock.

　　Exception: When the subject is *it*, *seem* can be followed by *as* (e.g. It seemed as if he was sick, so we called the doctor.)

23.　**suspect** someone <u>of doing</u> something (<u>not</u> to do)

worth checking	His wife suspected him to have committed adultery.
revised	His wife suspected him of committing adultery.
or	His wife suspected that he had committed adultery.

24.　**tendency** <u>to do</u> something (<u>not</u> of doing).

worth checking	Some Buick engines have a tendency of over-revving.
revised	Some Buick engines have a tendency to over-rev.
or	The engine has a habit of over-revving.

EXERCISE:　　Infinitive or Gerund?

Fill in the correct choice:

1) Mr. Carruthers accused me _____ *[to have laughed/of laughing]* at him behind his back.
2) They seemed _____ *[as if they were/to be]* about to attack us.
3) Mary is certainly capable _____ *[to get/of getting]* an 'A' in this course.
4) The Press suspected the senator *[to have been involved/of having been involved]* in a conflict of interest.

TO BE, NOT TO BE, OR BEING?

"UP WITH WHICH I WILL NOT PUT"

PREPOSITION PROBLEMS

The prepositions used in English often make little or no sense. What good reason is there for saying *inferior to* but *worse than*? None whatsoever, but over the centuries certain prepositions have come to be accepted as going together with certain verbs, nouns etc. There are no rules to help one learn the combinations; the only way is to read as much as possible, and to study the proper combinations. Here are some of the combinations that most commonly cause difficulty.

---

1.   **agree** with someone / with what someone says; agree to do something, to something; agree on a plan, proposal, etc.

worth checking	The union representatives did not agree with the proposed wage increase.
revised	The union representatives did not agree to the proposed wage increase.
or	The union representatives did not agree with management about the proposed wage increase.

---

2.   **angry** with someone; angry at or about something

worth checking	He was angry at me for failing to keep our appointment.
revised	He was angry with me for failing to keep our appointment.

---

3.   **annoyed** with someone; annoyed by something

worth checking	The professor is often annoyed with the attitude of the class.
revised	The professor is often annoyed by the attitude of the class.

4   **appeal** <u>to</u> someone <u>for</u> something
worth checking   The Premier appealed for the residents to help.

revised   The Premier appealed to the residents for help.

---

5.   **apply** <u>to</u> someone <u>for</u> something
worth checking   I applied for the Manager to hire me.

revised   I applied to the Manager for a job.

---

6.   **argue** <u>with</u> someone <u>about</u> something
worth checking   They argued against each other for half an hour.

revised   They argued with each other for half an hour.

---

7.   **arrive** <u>in</u> a place / <u>at</u> a place (<u>not</u> arrive a place, <u>except</u> arrive home). Airlines are perhaps to blame for the error of using both *arrive* and *depart* without prepositions.
worth checking   He won't join the Yankees until tomorrow night when they arrive Milwaukee.

    (*The Globe and Mail*, April 13, 1988)
revised   He won't join the Yankees until tomorrow night when they arrive in Milwaukee.

---

8.   **attach** two or more things (<u>not</u> attach together)
worth checking   The Siamese twins were attached together at the hip.

revised   The Siamese twins were attached at the hip.

---

9.   **borrow** something <u>from</u> someone
worth checking   I borrowed him a pair of trousers.

revised   I borrowed a pair of trousers from him.

---

10.   **cancel** something (<u>not</u> cancel out, except when the verb is used to mean *counterbalance* or *neutralize*)
worth checking   She cancelled out all her appointments.

revised   She cancelled all her appointments.

---

11.   **care** <u>about</u> something (meaning to think it worthwhile, or important to you)
worth checking   George does not care for what happens to his sister.

revised   George does not care what happens to his sister.

or   George does not care about what happens to his
         sister.

---

12. **centre:** centred <u>on</u> something (<u>not</u> around something); for one
thing to be centred <u>around</u> another is physically impossible.

 worth checking The novel is centred around the conflict between
         British imperialism and native aspirations.

 revised   The novel centres on the conflict between British
         imperialism and native aspirations.

---

13. **chase** someone/something <u>away</u> for doing something; despite
the way the word is misused in baseball slang the verb *chase* with
no preposition means *run after*, not *send away*.

 worth checking Blue Jay starting pitcher Jimmy Key was chased in
         the fifth inning.

 revised   Blue Jay starting pitcher Jimmy Key left the game in
         the fifth inning.

---

14. **collide** <u>with</u> something (<u>not</u> against something)

 worth checking The bus left the road and collided against a tree.

 revised   The bus left the road and collided with a tree.

---

15. **compare** <u>to</u>/ compare <u>with</u>: To compare something <u>to</u>
something else is to liken it, especially when speaking
metaphorically (e.g. "Can I compare thee to a summer's day?").
To compare something <u>with</u> something else is to judge how the two
are similar <u>or different</u> ("If you compare one brand with another
you will notice little difference."). Use *compare with* when noting
differences.

 worth checking The First World War was a small conflict compared
         to the Second World War, but it changed humanity
         even more profoundly.

 revised   The First World War was a small conflict compared
         with the Second World War, but it changed
         humanity even more profoundly.

---

16. **concerned** <u>with</u> something (meaning having some connection
with it, having something to do with it) and concerned <u>about</u>
something (meaning being interested in it, or worried about it)

worth checking	The Ministry is very concerned with the level of pollution in this river.
revised	The Ministry is very concerned about the level of pollution in this river.

17. **conform** to

worth checking	The building does not conform with current standards.
revised	The building does not conform to current standards.
or	The contractors did not comply with current standards.

18. **congratulate** someone on something

worth checking	The Opposition leaders congratulated the Prime Minister for his success at Meech Lake.
revised	The Opposition leaders congratulated the Prime Minister on his success at Meech Lake.

19. **connect** two things/ connect one thing with another (not connect up with)

worth checking	As soon as he connects up these wires, the system should work.
revised	As soon as he connects these wires, the system should work.

20. **conscious** of something

worth checking	He was not conscious that he had done anything wrong.
revised	He was not conscious of having done anything wrong.

(Note: unlike *conscious, aware* can be used with *of* or with a *that* clause)

21. **consist** in/ consist of: *Consist in* means to exist in, to have as the essential feature; *consist of* means to be made up of.

worth checking	Success consists of hard work.
	(i.e. The essence of success is hard work.)
revised	Success consists in hard work.
worth checking	The U.S. Congress consists in two houses – the House of Representatives and the Senate.

"UP WITH WHICH I WILL NOT PUT"

revised	The U.S. Congress consists of two houses — the House of Representatives and the Senate.

---

22. consult <u>someone</u> (<u>not</u> consult with someone)

worth checking	She will have to consult with the Board of Directors before giving us an answer.
revised	She will have to consult the Board of Directors before giving us an answer.
or	She will have to talk to the Board of Directors before giving us an answer.

---

23. **continue** something, <u>with</u> something, <u>to</u> a place (<u>not</u> continue on)

worth checking	We were told to continue on with our work.
revised	We were told to continue with our work.

---

24. **convenient** <u>for</u> someone, <u>for</u> a purpose/ convenient <u>to</u> a place

worth checking	This house is very convenient to me; it is only a short walk to work.
revised	This house is very convenient for me; it is only a short walk to work.

---

25. **cooperate** <u>with</u> someone (<u>not</u> cooperate together)

worth checking	The Provinces should cooperate together to break down inter-provincial trade barriers.
revised	The Provinces should cooperate with one another to break down inter-provincial trade barriers.

26. **correspond** <u>to</u> (be in agreement with); correspond <u>with</u> (exchange letters with)

worth checking	The fingerprints at the scene of the crime corresponded with those of the suspect.
revised	The fingerprints at the scene of the crime corresponded to those of the suspect.

27. **criticism** <u>of</u> something/somebody

worth checking	His criticisms against her were completely unfounded.
revised	His criticisms of her were completely unfounded.

28. **couple** <u>of</u> things/times/people, etc.)

worth checking	Both task forces will report sometime in the future after spending a couple million dollars.
	(The Globe & Mail, March 7, 1988)
revised	Both task forces will report sometime in the future after spending a couple of million dollars.
or	Both task forces will report sometime in the future after spending approximately two million dollars.

(In formal writing it is best to use *two* rather than *a couple of.*)

29. **depart** <u>from</u> a place.

worth checking	One woman was heard saying to a friend as they departed SkyDome...
	(*Toronto Star*, Nov. 29, 1989)
revised	One woman was heard saying to a friend as they departed from the SkyDome...
or	One woman was heard saying to a friend as they left the SkyDome...

30. **die** <u>of</u> a disease/of old age; die <u>from</u> injuries,wounds

worth checking	My grandfather died from cancer when he was only forty-two years old.
revised	My grandfather died of cancer when he was only forty-two years old.

31. **different** <u>from</u> or <u>to</u> (<u>not</u> than)

"UP WITH WHICH I WILL NOT PUT"

worth checking	These results are different than those we obtained when we did the same experiment yesterday.
revised	These results are different from those we obtained when we did the same experiment yesterday.

---

32. **discuss** something (not discuss about something; no preposition is needed)

worth checking	They discussed about what to do to ease tensions in the Middle East.
revised	They discussed what to do to ease tensions in the Middle East.

---

33. **divide** something (no preposition necessary)

worth checking	Lear wants to divide up his kingdom among his three daughters.
revised	Lear wants to divide his kingdom among his three daughters.

---

34. **do** something for someone (meaning something that will help); do something to someone (meaning something that will hurt)

worth checking	Norman Bethune did a lot to the people of China.
revised	Norman Bethune did a lot for the people of China.

---

35. **end**; at the end of something; in the end (no additional preposition): *In the end* is used when the writer does not say which end he means, but leaves this to be understood by the reader. *At the end of* is used when the writer mentions the end he is referring to.

worth checking	In the end of *Things Fall Apart*, we both admire and pity Okonkwo.
revised	At the end of *Things Fall Apart*, we both admire and pity Okonkwo.
or	In the end, we both admire and pity Okonkwo.

---

36. **end** at a place (not end up at)

worth checking	We do not want to end up at the same place we started from.

"UP WITH WHICH I WILL NOT PUT"

revised   We do not want to end at the same place we started from.

---

37. **fight** someone or with someone (not against; fight means *struggle against*, so to add *against* is redundant)

worth checking   They fought against each other for almost an hour.

revised   They fought with each other for almost an hour.

or   They fought each other for almost an hour.

---

38. **frightened** by something (when it has just frightened you); frightened of something (when talking about a constant condition)

worth checking   He was suddenly frightened of the sound of a door slamming.

revised   He was suddenly frightened by the sound of a door slamming.

---

39. **graduate** from a school

worth checking   He graduated McGill in 1986.

revised   He graduated from McGill in 1986.

---

40. **help**: not help doing (be unable to refrain from doing)

worth checking   She could not help from agreeing to his suggestion.

revised   She could not help agreeing to his suggestion.

---

41. **hurry** (not hurry up)

worth checking   She told me to hurry up if I didn't want to miss the train.

revised   She told me to hurry if I didn't want to miss the train.

---

42. **identical** with (not to)

worth checking   This hotel is identical to the Holiday Inn we stayed in last week.

revised   This hotel is identical with the Holiday Inn we stayed in last week.

---

43. **in**: Do not use *in* where *throughout* is meant; particularly when using such words as *whole* or *entire*, be careful to use *throughout*.

worth checking   Political repression is common in the whole world.

"UP WITH WHICH I WILL NOT PUT"

revised   Political repression is common throughout the world.

---

44. **independent** <u>of</u> something/someone

   worth checking   I would like to live entirely independent from my parents.

   revised   I would like to live entirely independent of my parents.

---

45. **inferior** <u>to</u> someone/something

   worth checking   Most people think that margarine is inferior than butter.

   revised   Most people think that margarine is inferior to butter.

         (*inferior* and *superior* are the only two comparative adjectives which are not followed by *than*)

---

46. **inside** or **outside** something (<u>not</u> of something)

   worth checking   Within thirty minutes a green scum had formed inside of the beaker.

   revised   Within thirty minutes a green scum had formed inside the beaker.

---

47. **interested** <u>in</u> something/ <u>in</u> doing something

   worth checking   She is very interested to find out more about plant genetics.

   revised   She is very interested in finding out more about plant genetics.

---

48. **investigate** something (<u>not</u> investigate about or into something)

   worth checking   The police are investigating into the murder in Brandon last week.

   revised   The police are investigating the murder in Brandon last week.

---

49. **join** someone (<u>not</u> join up with)

   worth checking   Conrad Black joined up with his brother Montagu in making the proposal to buy the company.

   revised   Conrad Black joined his brother Montagu in making the proposal to buy the company.

"UP WITH WHICH I WILL NOT PUT"

---

50. **jump** (<u>not</u> jump *up*)

worth checking	Unemployment has jumped up to record levels recently.
revised	Unemployment has jumped to record levels recently.

---

51. **lift** something (<u>not</u> lift *up*)

worth checking	I twisted my back as I was lifting up the box.
revised	I twisted my back as I was lifting the box.

---

52. **lower** something (<u>not</u> lower *down* something)

worth checking	They lowered the coffin down into the grave.
revised	They lowered the coffin into the grave.

---

53. **mercy**: have mercy <u>on</u> someone; show mercy to/towards someone

worth checking	We should all have mercy for anyone who is suffering.
revised	We should all have mercy on anyone who is suffering.

---

54. **meet / meet with**: *Meet with* in the sense of *attend a meeting with* is a recent addition to the language. If one is referring to a less formal or less prolonged encounter, however, there is no need for the preposition.

worth checking	Stanley finally met with Livingstone near the shores of Lake Victoria.

(The meaning here is "came face to face with for the first time"

revised	Stanley finally met Livingstone near the shores of Lake Victoria.

---

55. **near** something (<u>not</u> near to something)

worth checking	The village of Battle is very near to the place where The Battle of Hastings was fought in 1066.
revised	The village of Battle is very near the place where the Battle of Hastings was fought in 1066.

---

56. **object** <u>to</u> something.

worth checking	Some people have objected against being required to wear a seat belt.
revised	Some people have objected to being required to wear a seat belt.

---

57. **off** something (<u>not</u> off of)

worth checking	The man stepped off of the platform into the path of the moving train.
revised	The man stepped off the platform into the path of the moving train.

---

58. **opposite:** When used as a noun, *opposite* is followed by *of*; when used as an adjective, it is followed by *to* or *from*, or by no preposition.

worth checking	His conclusion was the opposite to mine.

(*Opposite* is here a noun.)

revised	His conclusion was the opposite of mine.

---

59. **partake** of something/ **participate** in something

worth checking	They have refused to partake in a new round of talks on the subject of free trade.
revised	They have refuse to participate in a new round of talks on the subject of free trade.

---

60. **prefer** one thing/person <u>to</u> another (<u>not</u> more than another)

worth checking	They both prefer tennis more than squash.
revised	They both prefer tennis to squash.

61. **protest** something (<u>not</u> protest against). *To protest* means to argue against; the preposition is redundant.

worth checking The demonstrators were protesting against the Government's decision to allow missile testing.

revised The demonstrators were protesting the Government's decision to allow Cruise missile testing.

---

62. **refer** <u>to</u> something (<u>not</u> refer back to something)

worth checking If you are confused, refer back to the diagram on page 24.

revised If you are confused, refer to the diagram on page 24.

---

63. **regard:** <u>with</u> regard <u>to</u> something/ <u>as</u> regard<u>s</u> something

worth checking I am writing in regards to the balance owing on your account.

Fair I am writing with regard to the balance owing on your account.

Better I am writing about the balance owing on your account.

---

64. **rejoice** <u>at</u> something (<u>not</u> for something)

worth checking He rejoiced for his good fortune when he won the lottery.

revised He rejoiced at his good fortune when he won the lottery.

---

65. **repeat** something (<u>not</u> repeat again)

worth checking If you miss an answer you must repeat the whole exercise again.

revised If you miss an answer you must repeat the whole exercise.

---

66. **request** something *or* request that something be done (but <u>not</u> request for something unless one is using the noun - <u>a</u> request <u>for</u> something)

worth checking He has requested for two more men to help him.

revised He has requested two more men to help him.

"UP WITH WHICH I WILL NOT PUT"

or	He has put in a request for two more men to help him.

---

67. **retroactive** <u>to</u> a date

worth checking	The tax changes are retroactive from July 1.
revised	The tax changes are retroactive to July 1.

---

68. **return** <u>to</u> a place (<u>not</u> return back)

worth checking	He wanted to return back to Edmonton as soon as possible.
revised	He wanted to return to Edmonton as soon as possible.

---

69. **seek** something/someone (<u>not</u> seek for something)

worth checking	She suggested that we seek for help from the police.
revised	She suggested that we seek help from the police.

---

70. **sight**; <u>in</u> sight (near enough to be seen); <u>out of</u> sight (too far away to be seen); <u>on</u> sight (immediately after being seen)

worth checking	The general ordered that deserters be shot in sight.
revised	The general ordered that deserters be shot on sight.

---

71. **speak** <u>to</u> someone (when one speaker is giving information to a listener); speak <u>with</u> someone (when the two are having a discussion)

worth checking	She spoke harshly with the secretary about his spelling mistakes.
revised	She spoke harshly to the secretary about his spelling mistakes.

---

72. **suffer** <u>from</u> something

worth checking	He told me that he was suffering with the flu.
revised	He told me that he was suffering from the flu.

---

73. **superior** <u>to</u> someone/something (<u>not</u> than someone/something)

worth checking	The advertisements claim that this detergent is superior than the others.

revised   The advertisements claim that this detergent is
                   superior to the others.

---

74. **surprised** at/by something: *At* is used to suggest that the
person is disappointed or scandalized; unless one wishes to suggest
this, *by* is the appropriate preposition.

worth checking   I was surprised at the unexpected arrival of my sister.

revised   I was surprised by the unexpected arrival of my
                   sister.

---

75. **underneath** something (<u>not</u> underneath of)

worth checking   When we looked underneath of the table, we found
                   what we had been looking for.

revised   When we looked underneath the table, we found
                   what we had been looking for.

---

76. **until** a time or an event (<u>not</u> up until)

worth checking   Up until 1967 the NHL was a six-team league.

revised   Until 1967 the NHL was a six-team league.

---

77. **type** <u>of</u> person/thing

worth checking   This type carburetor is no longer produced.

revised   This type of carburetor is no longer produced.

---

78. **warn** someone <u>of</u> a danger/<u>against</u> doing something/<u>not</u> to do
something

worth checking   She warned me about the danger involved in the
                   expedition.

revised   She warned me of the danger involved in the
                   expedition.

---

79. **worry** <u>about</u> something (<u>not</u> at something or for something)

worth checking   He is always worried at what will happen if he loses
                   his job.

revised   He is always worried about what will happen if he
                   loses his job.

---

80. **Prepositions in pairs or lists:** If a sentence includes two or
more nouns or verbs that take different prepositions, make sure to
include <u>all</u> the necessary words.

worth checking	The fire was widely reported in the newspapers and television.
revised	The fire was widely reported in the newspapers and on television.

---

81. **Ending a sentence with a preposition:** Some authorities have argued that it is poor English to end a sentence with a preposition. The best answer to them is Winston Churchill's famous remark upon being accused of ending with a preposition: "This is the sort of pedantic nonsense up with which I will not put." Obviously such awkwardness as this can only be avoided by ending with a preposition.

EXERCISE 19: Prepositions

Fill in the correct preposition, or leave blank if no preposition is needed.

1) My father was very angry _____ me when I did not do what he had asked me to.

2) We should arrive _____ Denver in time for dinner.

3) The three of them were chased _____ from school.

4) The group departed _____ Paris in the early morning.

5) We discussed _____ the problem with him for a whole afternoon.

6) We were told to continue _____ our work.

7) We must refer _____ to the first chapter to find the most important clue to the protagonist's identity.

8) The geopolitical situation in late 1938 was different _____ what it had been only a few months earlier.

9) He asked me what type _____ VCR we wanted.

10) She is convinced that this brand of detergent is superior _____ that one.

FOCI AND DATA

SINGULAR OR PLURAL DIFFICULTIES

1. A number of nouns are unusual in the way that a plural is **singular** formed. Here is a list of some that frequently cause mistakes. The **or plural** most troublesome — as well as a few pronouns that cause similar difficulties — are also given individual entries below:

appendix	appendices
attorney-general	attorneys-general
bacterium	bacteria
basis	bases
court martial	courts martial
crisis	crises
curriculum	curricula
datum	data
ellipsis	ellipses
emphasis	emphases
erratum	errata
father-in-law	fathers-in-law
focus	foci
governor-general	governors- general
index	indexes or indices
matrix	matrixes or matrices
medium	media
millennium	millennia
nucleus	nuclei
parenthesis	parentheses
referendum	referenda or referendums
runner-up	runners-up
stratum	strata
symposium	symposia
synthesis	syntheses
thesis	theses

2. **accommodation:** The plural form is not normally used.

worth checking   My family and my friend's family were both unable to find accommodations downtown.

Singularly Difficult Questions

by John Allemang

WORD PLAY / Singulars and plurals can be extremely tricky. For instance, are you one of those people who lives to eat, or one of those people who live to eat? Food for thought.

"YOU should be shot," said the cultured voice on my telephone message machine. I'll assume he was trying to be constructive. What I'd got wrong in the eyes of a reader who knows good from bad but lumps in bad grammar with tyrannous repression was my singulars and plurals. This is a common affliction in modern life. Singulars and plurals, I mean, not oral hate mail. Although, come to think of it, making unchallenged threats at the sound of the tone is hardly my idea of progress.

I hope that reader-assassins everywhere noticed the deft use of the singular in the last sentence. The subject of the verb is the singular verbal noun *making*, not the plural *threats*. But that's an easy one, in which I can take little pride. Where it gets more difficult, where logic seems to be at odds with easy speech, where cold-blooded readers get out their .38-calibre Smith and Wessons — but where do we start?

Let's begin with the sentence that launched an angry phone call. "But almost everyone believes that what really killed Charles Dickens were his public readings." The legislators of grammar decree that this is wrong. The subject of the verb *were* is not the plural *readings* but the singular pronoun *what* (or, if you like, the singular phrase *what really killed Charles Dickens*). A more careful writer would have written "...what really killed Charles Dickens was his public readings."

To my ears, at least, that example of good grammar sounds arch and awkward. Although postponed to the end of the sentence, *public readings* are the real killers, not the vague, stand-in pronoun *what*. Because the verb is so far away from *what* it is easily attracted into the plural *readings* that sits nearby. Me, I'd never say *was*. But I might think about rewriting: "...what really killed Dickens was the way he performed his public readings." Takes more words, means the same thing.

Now consider this sentence where the verb is also separated from its subject.

"History is a junk pile — dead ideas, clichéd language and worn-out systems — which are turned over and cast off at an enormous rate." What falls between the dashes — the contents of the junk pile — should obviously not affect the verb. But it did, because the colorful plurals are so much closer to the verb.

A more straightforward type of construction can be found on demonstration placards or in the mouths of protesters. "Native daycare centres is the issue." No, they are the issue, strange as that may seem (although the real issue is the number of centres, or their quality). But if you turn the sentence around on the axis of the copula verb, good grammar allows you to say, "The issue is native daycare centres."

I am one of those people who — what? — lives to eat, live to eat? I am one of those people who always uses the singular verb in that kind of sentence, and then wonders if I've made a mistake. And I have. Lured into the singular by egomania, I go against common sense. The plural verb is right because it is part of a generalization, the category of beings I belong to. The only argument I can muster when I get it wrong is the patent singularity of the word *one*. Which is a lonely number, but not much more.

The Simpsons is my favorite TV show. No problem there, since even a plural-looking title is singular. The Simpsons are my favorite TV family. Debatable, but I prefer the plural, since the family is here thought of as a collection of individuals first, a social unit second. The Simpsons are all out to lunch, except Maggie. No choice: clearly a plural.

There's lots more I'd like to say on this subject: how we use the singular with *lots* and how we often say *there's* with a plural, and whether the Cabinet is always singular. And who could forget *data* and *agenda*? So postpone the firing squad a week, mes amis. Seven days is not too long to wait.

From *The Globe and Mail,* Oct. 20, 1990; reprinted by permission.

FOCI AND DATA

revised	My family and my friend's family **were** both unable to find accommodation downtown.

---

3. **anyone/anybody/no one/nobody:** All are singular (119). Often it is necessary to spend a few moments puzzling over how to phrase one's ideas before one finds a way to get all the verbs and subjects to agree, and at the same time avoid awkwardness.

worth checking	Anyone may visit when they like.
Fair	Anyone may visit when he or she likes.
Better	Anyone may visit at any time.
worth checking	No one likes to leave a place that they have grown fond of.
Fair	No one likes to leave a place that he or she has grown fond of.
Better	No one likes to leave a place that has fond memories attached to it.

---

4. **bacteria:** a plural word; the singular is *bacterium*.

worth checking	There were many bacterias in the mouldy bread.
revised	There were a lot of bacteria in the mouldy bread.

---

5. **behavior:** Although some social scientists speak of a *behavior* or of *behaviors* in technical writing, in other disciplines and in conversational English the word is uncountable. Say *types of behavior*, not *behaviors*.

worth checking	He has a good behavior.
revised	His behavior is good.
or	He behaves well.

---

6. **between/among:** It is often supposed that *between* should always be used for two, *among* for more than two. As the *Oxford English Dictionary* points out, however, "in all senses *between* has been, from its earliest appearance, extended to more than two." Perhaps the most important difference is that *between* suggests a relationship of things or people to each other as individuals, whereas *among* suggests a relationship that is collective and vague.

FOCI AND DATA

Thus we say "the ball fell among the hollyhocks" where we are expressing the relationship of the ball to many flowers collectively, and where the precise location of the ball is unspecified. But we should <u>not</u> say, as we watch a baseball game, "the ball fell among the three fielders"; here we know the precise location of the ball and are expressing the relationship between it and the three individuals.

worth checking	The ball fell among the three fielders.
revised	The ball fell between the three fielders.

---

7.   **both/all:** Use *both* to refer to two, and *all* to refer to more than two.

worth checking	Harris and Waluchow were the chief speakers in the debate yesterday. They all spoke very well.
revised	Harris and Waluchow were the chief speakers in the debate yesterday. They both spoke very well.

---

8.   **brain:** One person can only have <u>one</u> *brain.* The use of the plural to refer to the *brain* of one person (e.g., "He blew his brains out") is slang, and should not be used in formal written work.

worth checking	He used his brains to solve the problem.
revised	He used his brain to solve the problem.

---

9.   **children:** Be careful when forming the possessive; the apostrophe should come before the *s.*

worth checking	All the childrens' toys had been put away.
revised	All the children's toys had been put away.

---

10.   **confusion:** uncountable — we do not normally speak of *a confusion* or of *confusions*.

worth checking	The misunderstanding about his time of arrival caused a confusion.
revised	The misunderstanding about his time of arrival caused confusion.

---

11.   **criteria:** plural; the singular is *criterion.*

worth checking	The chief criteria on which an essay should be judged is whether or not it communicates clearly.

revised	The chief criterion on which an essay should be judged is whether or not it communicates clearly.

12. **damage:** In its usual meaning, this noun has no plural, since it is uncountable. We speak of *damage,* not *a damage,* and of *a lot of damage,* not *many damages.* The word *damages* means money paid to cover the cost of any damage one has caused.

worth checking	The crash caused many damages to his car, but he was unhurt.
revised	The crash caused a lot of damage to his car, but he was unhurt.

13. **data:** Like *bacteria, media,* and *phenomena,* the noun *data* is plural. The singular form, which is rarely used, is *datum.*

worth checking	This data proves conclusively that the lake is badly polluted.
revised	These data prove conclusively that the lake is badly polluted.

14. **each/every:** Both are singular (119). The same problems experienced with *anyone* and *no one* (see above) are common here as well. Even experienced writers often must spend some time thinking how best to phrase sentences involving these words.

worth checking	Each person applying for the job must fill out this form before they will be granted an interview.
Fair	Each person applying for the job must fill out this form before he or she will be granted an interview.
Better	Each person applying for the job must fill out this form before being granted an interview.

15. **each other/one another:** Use *each other* for two, *one another* for more than two.

worth checking	The three brothers always tell stories to each other before going to sleep.
revised	The three brothers always tell stories to one another before going to sleep.
worth checking	The two men had long since begun to get on one another's nerves.

(Alan Moorehead, *The White Nile*)

FOCI AND DATA

revised	The two men had long since begun to get on each other's nerves.

16. **either/neither:** *Either* and *neither* are both singular. This can create considerable awkwardness in structuring sentences.

worth checking	Somehow, neither Sally nor Great Uncle Magnus were as tidy as they had been when they set out.

(Margaret Mahy, *Ultra-Violet Catastrophe*)

Trying to correct the error here by simply changing *were* to *was,* creates a new problem with the *they* in the second half of the sentence; a further change is also necessary.

revised	Somehow, neither Sally nor Great Uncle Magnus was as tidy as both had been when they set out.
worth checking	So far neither the Liberal rank and file nor the electorate seem satisfied with Jean Chretien's performance.

(The Globe and Mail, Sept. 20, 1990)

revised	So far neither the Liberal rank and file nor the electorate seems satisfied with Jean Chretien's performance.

17. **either/any; neither/none:** Use *either* and *neither* for two, *any* and *none* for more than two.

worth checking	Shirley has six sisters, but she hasn't seen either of them since Christmas.
revised	Shirley has six sisters, but she hasn't seen any of them since Christmas.

18. **government:** a <u>singular</u> noun.

worth checking	The government are intending to build a new terminal at this airport before 1995.
revised	The government is intending to build a new terminal at this airport before 1995.

19. **graffiti:** a plural noun; the singular form is *graffito*.

worth checking	Graffiti covers most of the subway cars in New York City.
revised	Graffiti cover most of the subway cars in New York City.

20. **media:** plural; the singular is *medium*.

worth checking   The media usually assumes that the audience has a very short attention span.

revised   The media usually assume that the audience has a very short attention span.

---

21. **money:** Some people seem to think that *monies* has a more official sound to it than *money* when they are talking of business affairs, but there is no sound reason for using this plural form in good English.

worth checking   The Council has promised to provide some monies for this project.

revised   The Council has promised to provide some money for this project.

---

22. **news:** Despite the *s*, this is a <u>singular</u> collective noun. Make sure to use a singular verb with it.

worth checking   Today's news of troubles in the Middle East are very disturbing.

revised   Today's news of troubles in the Middle East is very disturbing.

---

23. **phenomena:** plural; the singular is phenomenon.

worth checking   The great popularity of 'disco' music was a short-lived phenomena.

revised	The great populaity of 'disco' music was a short-lived phenomenon.

---

24. **police:** a <u>plural</u> noun. Be sure to use a plural verb with it.

worth checking	The police is investigating the case, and hope to make an arrest soon.
revised	The police are investigating the case, and hope to make an arrest soon.

---

25. **someone/somebody:** Both are singular. Be careful with sentences involving one of these pronouns and the pronoun *they*; getting the phrasing right is not always easy.

worth checking	Someone has forgotten to turn off the stove; they should be more careful.
Fair	Someone has forgotten to turn off the stove; he or she should be more careful.
or	Some careless person has forgotten to turn off the stove.

EXERCISE: Singular and Plural

Make the changes necessary to ensure that the parts of the sentence are in agreement:

1) Either John or his brother are responsible for causing the disturbance.

2) None of the excuses we were given are satisfactory.

3) If anyone speaks to George in the coming week, they should remind him that he has not yet paid his bill.

4) Each of the members feel that the application should be rejected.

Choose the correct alternative:

5) The aurora borealis is still a largely unexplained _____*[phenomenon/phenomena]*.

6) There appear to be at least two_____*[focuses/foci]* in Breugel's *Fall of Icarus*.

7) There were several _____*[Atorney-Generals/Atorneys-General]* during the Nixon administration.

8) Television is generally considered to be the most influential _____*[media/medium]*.

FOCI AND DATA

WHO CARES ABOUT WHOM?: Pronoun Problems

Those unfamiliar with the territory may also wish to refer to the section on pronouns in the reference guide to basic grammar (119).

pronoun problems

---

1. **extra pronoun:** It is easy to add an extra pronoun, particularly if the subject of the sentence is separated from the verb by a long adjectival clause.

worth checking	The countries which Hitler wanted to conquer in the late 1930s they were too weak to resist him.
revised	The countries which Hitler wanted to conquer in the late 1930s were too weak to resist him.
worth checking	The line that is longest in a triangle it is called the hypotenuse.
revised	The line that is longest in a triangle is called the hypotenuse.

---

2. **I and me:** Perhaps as a result of slang use of *me* as a subject pronoun ("Me and him got together for a few beer last night"), the impression seems to have lodged in many minds that the distinction between *I* and *me* is one of degree of politeness or formality rather than one of subject and object.

worth checking	There is no disagreement between you and I.
revised	There is no disagreement between you and me.

(Both *you* and *I* are here objects of a preposition — *between*. "Between you and I" is no more correct than is "I threw the ball at he.")

---

3. **than:** Does *than* take a subject or an object pronoun? Purists argue that we should say "She's brighter than *I* [am]", and "He's louder than she [is]" — that the verb is always understood in such sentences, even when we do not say it or write it, and that the unspoken verb requires a subject. It's hard to argue, however, that

the increasingly widespread use of object pronouns after *than* is either ugly or confusing.

less formal	She always sleeps later than him.
more formal	She always sleeps later than he [does].

---

4. **unreferenced or wrongly referenced pronoun:** Normally a pronoun must refer to a noun in the previous sentence or clause. In the following sentence, for example, the pronoun *she* clearly refers to the noun *Charity*, which is the subject of the first clause in the sentence:

e.g.   Charity told George that she would start work at nine.

Notice how confusing the sentence becomes, however, if there are two possible *she*s in the first part of the sentence:

e.g.   Charity told Mavis that she would start work at nine.

Does this mean that Charity will start work at nine, or that Mavis will? From the sentence it is impossible to tell. In cases like this, where it is not absolutely clear who or what a pronoun refers to, use the noun again instead:

Clear   Charity told Mavis that she (Charity) would start
                 work at nine.

In the following case the writer has gone astray by mentioning two things — one singular, one plural — and then matching only one of the two with a pronoun. In this instance the best remedy is to substitute a noun for the pronoun.

worth checking	Shields's characters are so exquisitely crafted and her plot so artfully conceived that it keeps the reader rivetted until the final page.

(The Globe and Mail)

revised	Shields's characters are so exquisitely crafted and her plot so artfully conceived that the book keeps the reader rivetted until the final page.
worth checking	My father and my brother visited me early this morning. He told me that something important had happened in Regina.
revised	My father and my brother visited me early this morning. Father told me that something important had happened in Regina.

WHO CARES ABOUT WHOM?: Pronoun Problems

Similar mistakes are often made in writing about a general class of people, such as police officers, or doctors, or football players. When writing in this way one can use either the third person singular (e.g. "A doctor helps patients. He...") or the third person plural ("Doctors help patients. They..."). Mixing the two in such situations often leads students to write unreferenced pronouns.

worth checking   A herbalist knows a lot about herbs and other plants. They can often cure you by giving you medicine.

(Here the pronoun *they* is presumably meant to refer to the plural noun, *herbalists*, but the writer has only referred to a herbalist.)

revised   A herbalist knows a lot about herbs and other plants. He can often cure you by giving you medicine.

or   Herbalists know a lot about herbs and other plants. They can often cure you by giving you medicine.

It may also not be clear what or who a pronoun refers to if it is placed too far away from the noun:

worth checking   The Finance Minister increased corporation taxes by an average of 43 per cent. Other measures in the budget included $20 million in student assistance and a 12 per cent increase in sales taxes. He also introduced a variety of measures to help small businesses.

revised   The Finance Minister increased corporation taxes by an average of 43 per cent. Other measures in the budget included $20 million in student assistance

WHO CARES ABOUT WHOM?: Pronoun Problems

> and a 12 per cent increase in sales taxes. The
> Minister also introduced a variety of measures to
> help small businesses.

Be particularly careful when using *this* as a pronoun; if the preceding sentence is a long one, it may not be at all clear what *this* refers to:

worth checking   The surplus was forecast to be $200 million, but turned out to be over $2 billion. This reflected the government's failure to predict the increase in interest rates and the onset of a recession.

(This <u>what</u>?)

revised   The surplus was forecast to be $200 million, but turned out to be over $2 billion. This vast discrepancy reflected the government's failure to predict the increase in interest rates and the onset of a recession.

Sometimes the meaning may be clear, but the omission of a pronoun may create unintended and humorous ambiguity:

worth checking   She visited a doctor with a bad case of the flu.

(Did the doctor have the flu?)

revised   She visited a doctor when she had a bad case of the flu.

worth checking   The Cougar was a sporty car aimed at the youthful-feeling who wanted luxury in their automobiles. Its buyers were similar to Mustangs, but more affluent.

revised   The Cougar was a sporty car aimed at the youthful-feeling who wanted luxury in their automobiles. Its buyers were similar to those who bought Mustangs, but more affluent.

---

5.   **who, whom.** The subject and the object pronoun (123), but of course it's not so simple as that. Nor is it — as those who don't feel it worth keeping "whom" around might have us believe — *merely* a matter of stuffiness or pedantry on the part of linguistic purists. Sound has a great deal to do with it. Even the purist must surely sometimes find herself saying, "I didn't know who I was talking to," even though the rules say it should be *whom* (subject — I; object — to whom). In similar fashion the enemies of *whom* must surely be

tempted to sacrifice principle rather than attempt such an owlish mouthful as "To who was he talking?" They would do so not on the grammatical grounds of *whom*, the object pronoun, being correct since it is acting as the object of the preposition *to*, but on the grounds of *whom*, the word with an *m* on the end, being in that sentence a lot easier to say. In such circumstances it's hard to make a good case against allowing formality to accommodate itself occasionally to convenience of pronunciation.

less formal　　Pierre Trudeau never cared who he irritated.

more formal　　Pierre Trudeau never cared whom he irritated.

EXERCISE:　　Pronouns

Correct the pronoun problem in each of the following.

1) A shopkeeper's life is usually a very busy one. They often have to work at least twelve hours a day.

2) Frank is not as good as Henry at the high jump. He usually jumps about five feet.

3) Larson argues that the sexual stereotypes of modern Western society will not be eradicated until the economic system alters, whereas Myers feels that a degree of stereotyping is an inevitable, if regrettable, result of genetic differences. This is important to recognize.

WHO CARES ABOUT WHOM?: Pronoun Problems

A QUESTION OF PRINCIPLE

Part Of Speech Conversions

part of
speech
conversions

There is no good reason why a word that has become established as one part of speech should not be used as another; the language has always been changing and growing in this way. As Tom Shippey asks.

> What can be the matter with using nouns as adjectives? Everyone does it; how about "stone wall"? It has been built into the language since before English settlers found Ireland, let alone America....As for converting nouns to verbs, what about "water"? "Watering the horses" is recorded from before the Conquest. (*TLS*, October 19-25, 1990)

The point in being aware of the conversion of one part of speech to another, then, is not that the practice is always a bad one. Rather it is to keep oneself aware of whether or not one is saying something in the best possible way. If the new creation fills a need, saying something more clearly and concisely than it is possible to do otherwise, then it deserves to survive. But if it fulfils no useful purpose — if clearer and more concise ways of saying the same thing already exist — then it's better to avoid it.

---

1. **access:** Except in the specialized vocabulary of computer science, *access* is probably best kept as a noun, not a verb; alternatives such as *enter* and *reach* don't deserve the dust bin just yet.

worth checking	The cafeteria may be accessed from either the warehouse or the accounts department.
Revised	Employees may gain access to the cafeteria from either the warehouse or the accounts department.
Better	The cafeteria may be reached through the warehouse or the accounts department.

2. **adjective for adverb:** If a word is modifying a verb, it should as a general rule be an adverb rather than an adjective. This is normally the case when the descriptive word comes directly after the verb. We say, "The boy laughed quietly", for example (rather than "The boy laughed quiet"), because the descriptive word *quietly* refers to the verb *laughed*, not the noun *boy*. Similarly, in the sentence "The quiet boy laughed" we use the adjective *quiet* to refer to the noun *boy*. The verb *to be*, however, which of course does not name an action in the way that other verbs do, is normally followed by adjectives rather than adverbs. (Verbs such as *taste, smell and feel* resemble *be* in this respect.) Thus we say "The boy is quiet", not "The boy is quietly"; we use the adjective rather than the adverb because we are again describing the boy, not the action of being. Very few would make the mistake of saying "He laughed quiet", but almost everyone occasionally chooses an adjective where the adverb should be used.

worth checking	I did good on the test yesterday.
Revised	I did well on the test yesterday.
worth checking	She asked us not to talk so loud.
Revised	She asked us not to talk so loudly.
worth checking	The premiers thought it should be worded different.
Revised	The premiers thought it should be worded differently.
worth checking	According to Mr Adams, "most books will go heavier into evolution, which is a good thing." (Washington Post, June 1987)
Revised	According to Mr Adams, "most books will go more heavily into evolution, which is a good thing."
worth checking	He performs bad whenever he is under pressure.
Revised	He performs badly whenever he is under pressure.

The pragmatists may have a point when it comes to the propriety of using comparative adjectives such as *easier* in place of more long winded adverbs such as *more easily*. Should the *Financial Post* editor have corrected the headline in the October 1987 issue that

A QUESTION OF PRINCIPLE

read "Northern Miners Breathe Easier"? Certainly it's easier to use the adjective here in place of the two-part adverb, *more easily.* Whether or not it's better is less clear; certainly many professors will not be pleased by the practice.

worth checking   The purpose of desktop publishing is to do the same old thing cheaper, easier, and quicker.

                       (*The Globe and Mail*, July 1987)

Revised   The purpose of desktop publishing is to do the same old thing more cheaply, more easily, and more quickly.

---

3.   **advice/advise:** *Advice* is the noun, *advise* is the verb.

worth checking   They refused to take our advise.

Revised   They refused to take our advice.

---

4.   **author:** a noun, not a verb; there is no need to find a substitute for "write".

worth checking   Smith is a member of the Appeals Court, and has authored two books on the judicial system.

Revised   Smith is a member of the Appeals Court, and has written two books on the judicial system.

---

5.   **critique:** a noun, not a verb

worth checking   We were asked to critique an essay by Tom Wolfe.

Revised   We were asked to write a critique of an essay by Tom Wolfe.

or   We were asked to discuss an essay by Tom Wolfe.

---

6.   **dependent/dependant:** *Dependent* is the adjective, *dependant* the noun. You are dependent on someone or something, and your young children are your dependants; they are dependent on you.

worth checking   Emily is still dependant on her parents for financial support.

Revised   Emily is still dependent on her parents for financial support.

---

7.   **dialogue:** a noun, not a verb. "Talk" serves perfectly well, even after all these years.

A QUESTION OF PRINCIPLE

worth checking	The two department heads should dialogue with each other more frequently.
Revised	The two department heads should talk to each other more frequently.

---

8. **enthuse/enthusiastic:** *Enthuse* is the verb; *enthused* is its past participle. The adjective is *enthusiastic*.

worth checking	In 1968 almost everyone was enthused about Pierre Trudeau.
Revised	In 1968 almost everyone was enthusiastic about Pierre Trudeau.
or	In 1968 almost everyone enthused over Pierre Trudeau.

---

9. **first/firstly:** *Firstly* is now generally thought of as archaic, though it is not incorrect. Be sure to be consistent, though, in the use of *first, second,* etc. in lists.

worth checking	There were several reasons for France's reluctance to commit more resources to the New World. First, she was consumed with the battle for supremacy in Europe. Secondly, the returns on previous investments had been minimal.
Revised	There were several reasons for France's reluctance to commit more resources to the New World. First, she was consumed with the battle for supremacy in Europe. Second, the returns on previous investments had been minimal.

---

10. **good/well:** the most common of the adjective-for-adverb mistakes.

worth checking	Manager Jimy Williams said of Stieb, "He pitched good, but not real good."
	(*The Toronto Star*, August 11, 1987)
Fair	He pitched well, but not really well.
Better	He did not pitch very well.

---

11. **impact:** a noun, not a verb.

worth checking	The government's decision will impact upon wholesalers in all areas of the country.
Revised	The government's decision will have an impact on wholesalers in all areas of the country.

or	The government's decision will affect wholesalers in all areas of the country.
worth checking	[The missile] apparently malfunctioned, went about 1,500 miles off course, and impacted near the Amur River.
	(Pentagon official, Sept. 17 1986)
Revised	Apparently [the missile] malfunctioned, went about 1,500 miles off course, and crashed near the Amur River.

---

12.   **like/as:** *Like* is a preposition, not a conjunction. If introducing a clause, use *as*.

e.g.	He looks like his father.
	(*Like* introduces the noun *father.*)
	He looks as his father did at his age.

(*As* introduces the clause *as his father did at his age.*)
He is acting like a drunkard.

(*Like* introduces the noun *drunkard.*)
He is acting as if he were drunk.

(*As* introduces the clause *as if he were drunk.*)

worth checking	Like I said before, smoking is forbidden.
Revised	As I said before, smoking is forbidden.
worth checking	He runs like I do — with short, choppy strides.
Revised	He runs as I do — with short, choppy strides.
or	He runs like me. We both take short, choppy strides.
worth checking	Baby Doc ran Haiti like his father had done.
Revised	Baby Doc ran Haiti the way his father had.

The attempt is also sometimes made to use *like what* in place of *as*.

worth checking	Bush wants to appear tough, like what Reagan did when he ordered the invasion of Grenada.
Revised	Bush wants to appear tough, as Reagan did when he ordered the invasion of Grenada.

A QUESTION OF PRINCIPLE

13. **its/it's:** *Its* is an adjective meaning *belonging to it.* *It's* is a contraction of *it is* — a pronoun plus a verb. (Similarly, *whose* is an adjective meaning *belonging to whom*, whereas *who's* is a contraction of *who is*.) The fact that contractions should not be used in formal writing should make distinguishing between the two easier

worth checking	Its important to remember that the population of North America in this period was less than 10 million.
Revised	It is important to remember that the population of North America in this period was less than 10 million.
worth checking	A coniferous tree continually sheds it's leaves.
Revised	A coniferous tree continually sheds its leaves.

14. **liase:** There is no good reason to transform the noun *liason* into a verb.

worth checking	He wishes to liase with other Committee members.
Revised	He wishes to consult other Committee members.

15. **loath/loathe:** *Loath* is the adjective; *loathe* is the verb.

worth checking	He told me he is beginning to loath his job.
Revised	He told me he is beginning to loathe his job.

16. **loose/lose:** *Loose* is normally used as an adjective meaning *not tight*; as a verb it means *to make loose* (e.g., "He loosed the reins"). *Lose* is of course always a verb.

worth checking	As soon as it became dark she began to loose control of herself.
Revised	As soon as it became dark she began to lose control of herself.
worth checking	If this movie doesn't bring the song back to the hit parade, then you know it's flopped — and that Spielberg is loosing his touch.
	(*Toronto Star*, Dec. 22, 1989)
Revised	If this movie doesn't bring the song back to the hit parade, then you know it's flopped — and that Spielberg is losing his touch.

A QUESTION OF PRINCIPLE

---

17. **mandate:** a noun, not a verb

worth checking   The report stated that the CBC should be properly mandated to provide a full range of Canadian programming.

(*Toronto Star*, Sept. 2 1987)

Revised   The report stated that the CBC should be given a mandate to provide a full range of Canadian programming.

---

18. **maybe/may be:** *Maybe* is an adverb that should be replaced by *perhaps* in formal writing. *May be* is a compound verb.

worth checking   May be he will come, but I doubt it.

Revised   Maybe he will come, but I doubt it.

or   Perhaps he will come, but I doubt it.

worth checking   The prototype maybe ready by Thursday.

Revised   The prototype may be ready by Thursday.

---

19. **meantime/meanwhile:** *Meantime* is a noun, used most frequently in the phrase *in the meantime. Meanwhile* is an adverb.

worth checking   The Germans were preparing for an attack near Calais. Meantime, the Allies were readying themselves for the invasion of Normandy.

Revised   The Germans were preparing for an attack near Calais. Meanwhile, the Allies were readying themselves for the invasion of Normandy.

---

20. **predominate/predominant:** *Predominate* is the verb, *predominant* the adjective, and *predominately* the adverb.

worth checking   The Social Credit movement was predominate only in Alberta and British Columbia.

Revised   The Social Credit movement was predominant only in Alberta and British Columbia.

---

21. **principal/principle:** *Principal* can be either a noun or an adjective. As a noun it means the person in the highest position of authority in an organization (e.g., a school principal) or an amount of money as distinguished from the interest on it. As an adjective it

means first in rank or importance ("The *principal* city of northern Nigeria is Kano"). *Principle* is always a noun, and is never used of a person; a *principle* is a basic truth or doctrine, a code of conduct, or a law describing how something works.

worth checking	We feel this is a matter of principal.
revised	We feel this is a matter of principle.
worth checking	Up went the shares of the two principle players in our emerging mobile telephone field.
	(*Financial Post*, June 12, 1989)
revised	Up went the shares of the two principal players in our emerging mobile telephone field.

---

22. **prophecy/prophesy:** *Prophecy* is the noun, *prophesy* the verb.

worth checking	His comment should be regarded as a prediction, not a prophesy.
Revised	His comment should be regarded as a prediction, not a prophecy.

---

23. **quality:** a noun, not an adjective. There is no good case for using it to replace *good*, or *worthwhile*.

worth checking	The salesman claims that this is a quality product.
Revised	The salesman claims that this is a product of high quality.
or	The salesman claims that this is a good product.
worth checking	"It was Mother's Day. I was trying to spend some quality time with my wife."

(An NHL vice-president explaining why he had not attended an important playoff game, as quoted in the *Toronto Star*, May 10, 1988.)

revised	"It was Mother's Day. I was trying to spend some time with my wife."

---

24. **quote/quotation:** *Quote* is the verb, *quotation* the noun.

worth checking	The following quote shows just how determined Trudeau was to patriate the Constitution.
Revised	The following quotation shows just how determined Trudeau was to patriate the Constitution.

25. **read:** In informal English the expression "a good read" has its uses. In formal English it's best to keep *read* a verb rather than a noun.

26. **real/really:** One of the most commonly made adjective-for-adverb mistakes.

worth checking   Some of the fish we caught were real big.

Revised   Some of the fish we caught were really big.

27. **Verb-noun confusion:** Where verbs and nouns have similar forms, be careful not to confuse them. Some of the most common examples are: *advice* (noun) and *advise* (verb); *extent* (noun) and *extend* (verb); *device* (noun) and *devise* (verb); *revenge* (noun) and *avenge* (verb). In Canada and Britain *practise* (verb) and *practice* (noun) should also be distinguished; in the U.S. *practice* serves as both noun and verb.

worth checking   Jimmy Carter has now to a large extend been forgotten.

Revised   Jimmy Carter has now to a large extent been forgotten.

worth checking   She wanted to revenge the harm he had caused her.

Revised   She wanted to avenge the harm he had caused her.

EXERCISE: Part of Speech Difficulties

Correct the mistake in each sentence:

1) He did not give me very good advise.

2) To some extend what you say is true, but I cannot agree with you completely.

3) There maybe a chance that you can still convince him to do what you want.

4) The above quote illustrates just how short-sighted 19th century educators could be.

5) The team's four starters voted unanimous to start on four days rest.

6) I loaned him the money to buy a car.

7) He was careful not to loose track of the argument.

PUTTING IDEAS TOGETHER

The art of combining correct clauses and sentences logically and coherently is as much dependent on taking the time to think through what we are writing — and how the reader will respond to what we write — as it is on knowledge of correct usage. It is all too easy for most of us to assume that the flow of our thoughts will be as clear to the reader as it is to us. In practical terms this leads to the omission of links in the argument or of joining words that help the reader to see those links (56). Almost as common is the tendency to give too many or contradictory cues to the reader — a tendency that is often an indication that ideas have not yet been thoroughly thought out. That in itself is nothing to be ashamed of; the key is to be willing to take the time to re-read and revise the work. Every good writer makes at least two and sometimes as many as five or six drafts of any piece of writing before considering it finished. Here are two examples, both taken from early drafts of books eventually published by Broadview Press:

> At the end of World War II there was substantial optimism that the application of Keynesian analysis would lead to economic stability and security. Over the post-war period optimistic rationalism weakened in the face of reality.

> A short report in which you request an increase in your department's budget should be written in the persuasive mode. Most reports, however, do not have persuasion as their main objective. Persuasion, though, will often be one of their secondary objectives. In reports like these, some parts will be written in the persuasive mode.

1.   **too few cues:** The first of these passages gives the reader too few cues. What is the connection between the idea of the first sentence and that of the second? One can figure it out without too much difficulty, but the flow of the argument is briefly interrupted while one does so. The problem is easily solved by the addition of

one word to the second sentence:

revised	At the end of World War II there was substantial optimism that the application of Keynesian analysis would lead to economic stability and security. Over the post-war period, however, optimistic rationalism weakened in the face of reality.

2.   **too many or contradictory cues:** The second passage suffers from the opposite problem; the use of however and though in consecutive sentences gives the reader the sense of twisting back on himself without any clear sense of direction. This sort of difficulty can be removed by rewording or rearranging the ideas:

revised	A short report in which you request an increase in your department's budget should be written in the persuasive mode. Most reports, however, do not have persuasion as their main objective. Persuasion will thus be at most a secondary objective. In reports like these, some parts will be written in the persuasive mode.

The following pages list the chief words and expressions used in English to join ideas together, and discuss problems that are often experienced with them.

WORDS TO CONNECT IDEAS THAT ARE OPPOSED TO EACH OTHER

All these words are used to indicate that the writer is saying two things which seem to go against each other, or are different from each other. For example, in the sentence, "He is very rich, but he is not very happy", the fact that he is not happy is the <u>reverse</u> of what we might expect of a rich man. The word *but* indicates this opposition of ideas to the reader.

although	nevertheless
but	though
despite	whereas
even if	while
however	yet
in spite of	

PUTTING IDEAS TOGETHER

Although

This word indicates that <u>in the same sentence</u> two things that seem to go against each other are being said. *Although* is usually used to introduce subordinate clauses, <u>not</u> phrases.

although

> Although he has short legs, he can run very quickly.

> Hume and Dr. Johnson, indeed, have a good deal in common, although Hume's attitude towards religion earned him Johnson's scorn.

---

3. Be careful not to use <u>both</u> although <u>and</u> but in the same sentence; one is enough:

worth checking   Although in most African countries the government is not elected by the people, but in Zimbabwe the government is democratically elected.

revised   Although in most African countries the government is not elected by the people, in Zimbabwe the government is democratically elected.

or   In most African countries the government is not elected by the people, but in Zimbabwe the government is democratically elected.

But

This word is usually used in the middle of a sentence to show that the two ideas in the sentence oppose or seem to oppose each other. It is also quite correct, however, to use *but* at the beginning of a sentence, if what one is saying in the sentence forms a complete clause and if the idea of the sentence seems to oppose the idea of the previous sentence.

but

e.g.   The civilization of ancient Greece produced some of the word's greatest works of art and gave birth to the idea of democracy, but the Greeks also believed in slavery.

or   The civilization of Greece produced some of the world's greatest works of art and gave birth to the idea of democracy. But the Greeks also believed in slavery.

---

4   When one is dealing with complex combinations of ideas it is sometimes easy to forget which ideas are in fact in opposition and

PUTTING IDEAS TOGETHER

which in support.

worth checking   Brandy and bourbon, with the most "congenors," have the highest hangover ratings. Red wine is a close second, followed by dark rum, sherry, scotch, rye, beer, white wine, gin and vodka. Vintage red wines have 15 times as much histamine (it triggers allergic reactions) as white wine, but vintage whites have fewer congenors.

(*The Globe and Mail*, Dec. 31, 1990)

The use of *but* is inappropriate here; that whites have both less histamine and fewer congenors is as one would expect; the two facts are both instances of white wines having fewer side effects than reds.

revised   Brandy and bourbon, with the most "congenors," have the highest hangover ratings. Red wine is a close second, followed by dark rum, sherry, scotch, rye, beer, white wine, gin and vodka. Vintage red wines also have 15 times as much histamine (it triggers allergic reactions) as white wine does.

5.   Experienced writers are careful not to use *but* more than once in a single sentence, or in consecutive sentences; they realize that doing so tends to confuse the reader.

worth checking   Chief Constable Smith said that Ryan had been legally in possession of three handguns and two rifles, but he thought it "incredible" that someone should be allowed to keep ammunition at his home. But he said any change in the firearms law was something which would not be discussed by him.

(*The Guardian*, Aug. 30 1987)

revised   Chief Constable Smith said that Ryan had been legally in possession of three handguns and two rifles. Ryan said he thought it "incredible" that someone should be allowed to keep ammunition at his home, but he would not comment directly on whether there should be a change in the firearms law.

Despite

despite

This word means the same as *although*, but it is used to introduce phrases, not clauses.

Despite his old age, his mind is active and alert.
("Despite his old age" is a phrase; it has no verb.)

PUTTING IDEAS TOGETHER

Although he is very old, his mind is active and alert.
("Although he is very old" is a clause, with *he* as a subject and *is*
as a verb.)

Despite the rain, she wanted to go out to the park.
Although it was raining hard, she wanted to go to the park.

---

6.   **despite:** Remember not to introduce clauses with *despite.*

worth checking   Despite that the drink tasted very strong, there was
very little alcohol in it.

revised   Despite its strong taste, there was very little alcohol
in the drink.

or   Although the drink tasted very strong, there was very
little alcohol in it.

Even if

This expression is used when one is introducing a clause giving a   even if
condition. The word *even* emphasizes that the condition is
surprising or unusual. Examples:

Even if I have to stay up all night, I am determined to finish the
job.
(Staying up all night would be very unusual.)

Even if Bangladesh doubled its food production, some of its
people would still be hungry.
(Doubling its food production would be very surprising.)

However

however

This word shows that what one is saying seems to go against what
one has said in the previous sentence. It should normally be placed
between commas in the middle of the sentence:

The country suffered greatly during the three-year drought.
This year, however, the rains have been heavy.

---

7.   *However* should not be used to combine ideas within one
sentence, unless a semi-colon is used.

worth checking   Hitler attempted to conquer the Soviet Union
however he was defeated.

PUTTING IDEAS TOGETHER

revised	Hitler attempted to conquer the Soviet Union; however, he was defeated.
or	Hitler attempted to conquer the Soviet Union. However, he was defeated.
or	Hitler attempted to conquer the Soviet Union but he was defeated.
worth checking	There will not be regular mail pick-up from boxes this Friday, however regular mail pick-up will resume Saturday.
	(Peterborough Examiner, Sept. 1986)
revised	There will not be regular mail pick-up from boxes this Friday, but regular mail pick-up will resume Saturday.
or	There will not be regular mail pick-up from boxes this Friday. However, regular mail pick-up will resume Saturday.

Note that *however* in the sense of *to whatever extent* may be used to introduce a clause: *However tired we are, we must finish the job tonight.*

Nevertheless

nevertheless Like *however, nevertheless* is normally used to show that the idea of one sentence seems to go against the idea of the previous sentence. It should not be used to join two clauses into one sentence. Example:

According to the known laws of physics it is not possible to walk on water. Nevertheless, this is what the Bible claims Jesus did.

Whereas

whereas This word is commonly used when one is comparing two things and showing how they differ. Like *although*, it must begin a subordinate clause, and may be used either at the beginning or in the middle of a sentence.

e.g.	Whereas Americans are usually thought of as being loud and confident, Canadians tend to be more quiet and less sure of themselves.
or	Americans are usually thought of as being loud and confident, whereas Canadians tend to be more quiet and less sure of themselves.

PUTTING IDEAS TOGETHER

8. Any sentence that uses *whereas* must have at least two clauses — a subordinate clause beginning with *whereas* <u>and</u> a main clause.

worth checking	In 'The Rain Horse' a young person feels unhappy when he returns to his old home. Whereas in 'The Ice Palace' a young person feels unhappy when she leaves home for the first time.
revised	In 'The Rain Horse' a young person feels unhappy when he returns to his old home, whereas in 'The Ice Palace' a young person feels unhappy when she leaves home for the first time.

While

9. **while:** *While* can be used in the same way as *although*. If there is any chance of confusion with the other meanings of *while*, however, it is better to use *although* in such circumstances.

while

worth checking	While I support free trade in principle, I think it would hurt this industry.
revised	Although I support free trade in principle, I think it would hurt this industry.

Yet

yet

This word can be used either to refer to time (e.g. "He is not yet here"), or to connect ideas in opposition to each other. When used in this second way, it may introduce another word or a phrase, or a completely new sentence.

His spear was firm, yet flexible.

Barthes decries the language of "realism" — the pretence that one can represent on the page life as it really is. Yet it is difficult to see how following his prescriptions for an art of signs that "draw attention to their own arbitrariness" can entirely escape a tendency towards art that calls too much attention to its own surface, even art that is self-indulgent.

10. *Yet*, like the other words in this group, should not be paired with another conjunction in such a way as to create too many twists and turns in the argument.

worth checking	Varying the pace, altering the tone, [director Joseph] Rubens keeps us off balance. Ultimately, though, that pedestrian script catches up with him, yet not

before *Sleeping with the Enemy* has made its point.
(*The Globe and Mail*, Feb. 8, 1991)

(The combination of *yet* and *though* is confusing for the reader.)

revised   Varying the pace, altering the tone, [director Joseph] Rubens keeps us off balance. Ultimately, that pedestrian script catches up with him, yet not before *Sleeping with the Enemy* has made its point.

WORDS TO JOIN LINKED OR SUPPORTING IDEAS

also	indeed
and	in fact
as well	moreover
further	similarly
furthermore	: [colon]
in addition	; [semi-colon]
not only...but also	

Also, as well

also, as well   These two are very similar both in meaning and in the way that they are used. It is best not to use *also* to start sentences or paragraphs. Examples:

He put forward his simplistic credo with enormous conviction. "To do well at school," he assured us, "you must be willing to study. It is also important to eat the right foods, exercise regularly, and get plenty of sleep." While the one thing we all wanted, and none of us had managed to get, was plenty of sex.

He put forward his simplistic credo with enormous conviction. "To do well at school," he assured us, "you must be willing to study. It is also important to eat the right foods, exercise regularly, and get plenty of sleep." While the one thing we all wanted, and none of us had managed to get, was plenty of sex.

---

11.   *Also* should not be used in the way that we often use *and* — to join two clauses together into one sentence.

worth checking   We performed the experiment with the beaker half full also we repeated it with the beaker empty.

revised   We performed the experiment with the beaker half full and we repeated it with the beaker empty.

or   We performed the experiment with the beaker half
         full. We also repeated it with the beaker empty.

---

12. **and:** If this word appears more than once in the same sentence, it's worth stopping to ask if it would not be better to start a new sentence. Usually the answer will be yes.

worth checking   All my family attended the celebration and most of
                     my friends were there and we enjoyed ourselves
                     thoroughly.

revised   All my family attended the celebration and most of
                     my friends were there too. We enjoyed ourselves
                     thoroughly.

---

13. **as well:** To avoid repetition, do not use *as well* in combination with *both*.

worth checking   This method should be rejected, both because it is
                     very expensive as well as because it is inefficient.

revised   This method should be rejected, both because it is
                     very expensive and because it is inefficient.

In addition, further, furthermore, moreover

All of these are commonly used to show that what the writer is saying gives additional support to an earlier statement she has made. An example:]

moreover

> It is easy to see why many countries still trade with South Africa, despite their intense dislike of apartheid. For one thing, it is the richest country in Africa. Many of its resources, moreover, are of strategic importance.

Notice that all four expressions are often used after sentences that begin with words such as *for one thing* or *first*.

Indeed, in fact

Both of these are used to indicate that what the writer is saying is a restatement or elaboration of the idea he has expressed in the previous sentence. Notice that a colon or semi-colon may also be used to show this. Examples:

indeed, in fact

PUTTING IDEAS TOGETHER

Asia is the world's most populous continent. In fact, more people live there than in all the other continents combined.

Asia is the world's most populous continent: more people live there than in all the other continents combined.

not only...but also

not only...but also This combination is used to join two pieces of supporting evidence in an argument. The combination can help to create balanced, rhythmic writing, but if it is to do so it must be used carefully (73). Notice that it is not necessary to use *but also* in all cases, but that if the phrase is omitted a semi-colon is normally required in order to avoid a run-on sentence.

worth checking   Not only were the Police a commercial success, they were also among the first New Wave acts to achieve musical respectability.

(*Network*, Winter 1987)

revised   Not only were the Police a commercial success; they were also among the first New Wave acts to achieve musical respectability.

or   The Police were not only a commercial success, but also a critical one; they were among the first New Wave acts to achieve musical respectability.

Plus

plus 14. **plus:** Do not use this word in the same way as *and* or *as well*.

worth checking   For one thing, the Council did not much like the design for the proposed new City Hall. Plus, there was not enough money available to build it that year.

revised   For one thing, the Council did not much like the design for the proposed new City Hall. As well, there was not enough money available to build it that year.

WORDS USED TO INTRODUCE CAUSES OR REASONS

The core of most arguments involves reasons why the writer's statements can be claimed to be true, and relationships of cause and effect (44). It is common to experience some difficulty at first in understanding such relationships clearly. The discussion below of the word *because* may be helpful in this respect. To begin with, though, here is a list of words that are used to introduce causes or reasons:

as   for
as a result of   on account of
because   since
due to

As

This word can either be used to show the relationship between two events in time, or to indicate that one event is the cause of another. This sometimes leaves room for confusion about meaning (ambiguity). The following sentence is a good example:

> As he was riding on the wrong side of the road, he was hit by a car.

This can mean either "When he was riding on the wrong side of the road,..." or "Because he was riding on the wrong side of the road,...". Unless the writer is absolutely certain that the meaning is clear, it may be better to use *while* or *when* instead of *as* to indicate relationships in time, and *because* instead of *as* to indicate relationships of cause and effect.

as

Because

because

This word creates many problems for students. The first thing to remember is that any group of words introduced with *because* must state a cause or reason. It must *not* state a result or an example.

---

15.   In the following sentences, *because* has been wrongly used:

worth checking   The wind was blowing because the leaves were moving to and fro.

worth checking   He had been struck by a car because he lay bleeding in the road.

A moment's reflection leads to the realization that both of these sentences are the wrong way round. The movement of the leaves is the <u>result</u> of the blowing of the wind, and the man's bleeding is the <u>result</u> of his having been hit. When the sentences are turned around, they become correct:

revised   The leaves were moving to and fro because the wind was blowing.

revised   He lay bleeding on the road because he had been struck by a car.

What leads many people to make mistakes like these is the sort of question that begins, "How do you know that..." or "Prove that..." or "Show that...". The person who is asked, "How do you know that the wind is blowing?" is likely to answer wrongly, "The wind is blowing because the leaves are moving to and fro."

What he really means is, "I know the wind is blowing because I see the leaves moving to and fro." That answer is quite correct, since here the <u>seeing</u> is the cause of the <u>knowing</u>. Similarly, someone who is asked to show that the man in a story he has read has been hit by a car might answer wrongly, "He had been struck by a car because he lay bleeding in the road." What he really means is, "I <u>know</u> that he had been struck by a car because I <u>read</u> that he lay bleeding in the road."

It is of course awkward to use a lot of phrases such as "I know that" and "I see that". Here are some easier and better ways of answering such questions:

The movement of the trees shows that the wind is blowing.

The fact that the leaves are moving proves that the wind is blowing.

Since the man lay bleeding in the road, it seems likely that he had been hit by a car.

---

16. *Because* is also often used incorrectly to introduce examples. Look carefully at the following sentences:

worth checking   The Marcos regime detained people in jail for long periods without ever bringing them to trial **because** it had little respect for the law.

worth checking   In the story, 'The Hero', Dora feels sorry for Julius because she sheds tears when he is expelled from school.

In these sentences the source of confusion may not be immediately clear. If we ask ourselves whether the fact that the regime did this <u>caused</u> it to have little respect for the law, however, we realize that the answer is no. Is the fact that Dora sheds tears a <u>cause</u> of her feeling sorry for Julius? Again, no. It may be a result of her feeling sorry, or an example chosen to show that she felt sorry, but it is certainly not a cause. Again, it is possible to correct these sentences as we did the ones above — by reversing the order of the ideas. But this may not always be an appropriate solution to the problem, particularly if what the writer is trying to show is an example or an illustration rather than a relationship of cause and effect. If, for example, one had been asked, "How do you know that Dora feels sorry for Julius?", or told to "Show that the Marcos regime had little respect for the law," one would not normally want to answer using *because*. Here are various ways of dealing with such difficulties:

> Dora feels sorry for Julius when he is expelled, as we can see when she sheds tears for him.

> It is clear that Dora feels sorry for Julius, since she sheds tears for him.

> We can see from the fact that Dora sheds tears for Julius that she feels sorry for him.

> The fact that the Marcos regime detained people for long periods without ever bringing them to trial

PUTTING IDEAS TOGETHER

> shows that it had little respect for the law.
>
> The Marcos regime showed little respect for the law. It detained people for long periods, for example, without ever bringing them to trial.
>
> The Marcos regime had little respect for the law; it detained people for long periods without ever bringing them to trial.

Of all these the last is perhaps the best, since it is the most succinct.

---

17.   It is best not to use *because* when listing several reasons for something. Otherwise the writer gives the reader the impression that the first reason given is to be the <u>only</u> reason. The reader will then be surprised when others are mentioned.

worth checking	He was happy because it was Friday. He was also happy because his team had won the game that morning and he had scored the winning goal. Finally, he was happy because he had done well on his exams.
revised	He was happy for several reasons: it was Friday, he had scored the winning goal for his team that morning, and he had done well on his exams.
worth checking	Frederick was able to enjoy such success because he was enormously adroit at waiting for the right opportunity, and seizing it when it was handed him. He was also successful because he created a military machine that had no equal.
revised	One reason Frederick was able to enjoy such success was that he was enormously adroit at waiting for the right opportunity, and seizing it when it was handed him. But none of this would have been possible had he not also created a military machine that had no equal.

---

18.   Some students like to answer "How...?" questions by using *because*. Instead, the word *by* should be used.

worth checking	How did she help him? She helped him because she lent him some money.
revised	How did she help him? She helped him by lending him some money.

Due to

19.   **due to:** *Due* is an adjective and therefore should always modify a noun (as in the common phrase *with all due respect*). When followed by *to* it can suggest a causal relationship, but remember that the word *due* must in that case refer to the previous noun:

e.g.   The team's success is due to hard work.

(*Due* refers to the noun *success*.)

It is not a good idea to begin a sentence with a phrase such as "Due to unexpected circumstances..." or "Due to the fact that...". To avoid such difficulties it is best to use *because*.

worth checking	Due to the departure of our Sales Manager, the Marketing Director will take on additional responsibility for a short time.
revised	Because our Sales Manager has resigned suddenly, the Marketing Director will take on additional responsibility for a short time.

Since

When used to introduce causes or reasons (rather than as a time word) *since* is used in essentially the same way as *because*.

WORDS USED TO INTRODUCE RESULTS OR CONCLUSIONS

as a result	therefore
consequently	thus
hence	to sum up
in conclusion	in consequence
it follows that...	so, and so

As a result, hence

Both of these are used to show that the idea being talked about in one sentence follows from, or is the result of what was spoken of in the previous sentence.

e.g.   His car ran out of gas. As a result, he was late for his appointment.

hence

or   His car ran out of gas. Hence, he was late for his
                        appointment.

Notice the difference between these two and words such as
because and *since*; we would say "Because [or since] his car ran out
of gas, he was late for the appointment."

---

21. *Hence* should not be used to join two clauses into one
sentence.

worth checking   Her phone is out of order hence it will be impossible
                        to contact her.

revised   Her phone is out of order. Hence, it will be
                        impossible to contact her.

worth checking   It is not the film but the advertising that is
                        exploitative, hence pornographic.

revised   It is not the film but the advertising that is
                        exploitative, and hence pornographic.

So

so

This word may be used to introduce results when one wants to
mention both cause and result in the same sentence (e.g., "Her
phone is out of order, so it will be impossible to contact her"). It is
usually best not to use *so* to begin a sentence, in order to avoid
writing sentence fragments.

---

22. If *so* is used, *because* is not needed, and vice versa. One of the
two is enough.

worth checking   Because he was tired, so he went to bed early.

revised   Because he was tired, he went to bed early.

or   He was tired, so he went to bed early.

WORDS USED TO EXPRESS PURPOSE

in order to	so that
in such a way as to	so as to

PUTTING IDEAS TOGETHER

So that

23. **so that:** When used beside each other (see also *so...that* below) these two words show purpose; they indicate that we will be told <u>why</u> an action was taken. Examples:

> He sent the parcel early so that it would arrive before Christmas.
>
> She wants to see you so that she can ask you a question.

The words *such that* should never be used in this way to indicate purpose.

worth checking	The doctor will give you some medicine such that you will be cured.
revised	The doctor will give you some medicine so that you will be cured.

worth checking	Fold the paper such that it forms a triangle.
revised	Fold the paper so that it forms a triangle.
or	Fold the paper in such a way that it forms a triangle.

WORDS USED TO INTRODUCE EXAMPLES

for example   such as
for instance   : [colon]
in that

For example, for instance, such as

The three expressions are used differently, even though they all introduce examples. *Such as* is used to introduce a single word or short phrase. It always relates to a plural noun that has appeared just before it. Examples:

> Crops such as tea and rice require a great deal of water.
> > (Here *such as* relates to the noun crops.)
> Several African tribes, such as the Yoruba of Nigeria and the Makonde of Tanzania, attach a special ceremonial importance to masks.
> > (*Such as* relates to tribes.)

For example and *for instance*, on the other hand, are complete phrases in themselves, and are normally set off by commas. Each is used to show that the entire sentence in which it appears gives an example of a statement made in the previous sentence. Examples:

> Some crops require a great deal of water. Tea, for example, requires an annual rainfall of at least 1500 mm.

> Several African tribes attach a special ceremonial importance to masks. The Yoruba and the Makonde, for example, both believe that spirits enter the bodies of those who wear certain masks.

> Tornadoes are not only a Deep South phenomenon. In 1987, for instance, over 20 people were killed by a tornado in Edmonton, Alberta.

24. *For example* and *for instance* should not be used to introduce phrases that give examples. In such situations use *such as* instead.

worth checking	In certain months of the year, for example July and August, Penticton receives very little rainfall.
revised	In certain months of the year, such as July and August, Penticton receives very little rainfall.
or	In certain months of the year Penticton receives very little rainfall. July and August, for example, are almost always extremely dry.

In that

in that

25. **in that:** Do not confuse with *in the way that*.

worth checking	He is cruel in the way that he treats his wife harshly.
revised	He is cruel in that he treats his wife cruelly.
or	He is cruel in the way that he treats his wife.

Such as

such as

26. **such as:** The addition of *and others* at the end of a phrase beginning with *such as* is redundant.

worth checking	Teams such as Philadelphia, Boston and others have been successful with a very physical style of hockey.
revised	Teams such as Philadelphia and Boston have been successful with a very physical style of hockey.

PUTTING IDEAS TOGETHER

or Philadelphia, Boston and other teams have been
successful with a very physical style of hockey.

WORDS USED TO INDICATE ALTERNATIVES

either...or	otherwise
if only	rather than
instead, instead of	unless
in that case	whether...or
neither...nor	or

If only

This expression is normally used when we wish that something   *if only*
would happen, or were true, but it clearly will not happen, or is not
true. Examples:

> If only he were here, he would know what to do.
>> (This indicates that he is not here.)

> "If only there were thirty hours in a day..." she kept saying.

In that case

This expression is used when we wish to explain what will happen if   *in that case*
the thing spoken of in the previous sentence happens, or turns out
to be true. Examples:

> He may arrive before six o'clock. In that case we can all go
> out to dinner.

> It is quite possible that many people will dislike the new law.
> In that case the government may decide to change it.

Do not confuse *in that case* with *otherwise*, which is used in the
reverse situation (i.e., when one wishes to explain what will happen
if the thing spoken of in the previous sentence does <u>not</u> happen, or
turns out to be false.

Otherwise

This word has two meanings. The first is *in other ways* (e.g. "I have   *otherwise*
a slight toothache. Otherwise I am healthy"). The second meaning
can sometimes cause confusion: *otherwise* used to mean *if not*.

PUTTING IDEAS TOGETHER

Here the word is used when we want to talk about what will or may happen if the thing spoken of in the previous sentence does not happen. Examples:

> I will have to start immediately. Otherwise I will not finish in time.
>> (This is the same as saying, "If I do not start now, I will not finish in time.")
>
> The general decided to retreat. Otherwise, he believed, all his troops would be killed.
>> (This is the same as saying, "The general believed that if he decided not to retreat, all his troops would be killed.")
>
> You must pay me for the car before Friday. Otherwise I will offer it to someone else.
>> (i.e. "If you do not pay me for the car before Friday, I will offer it to someone else.")

---

27. When used to mean *if not*, *otherwise* should normally be used to start a new sentence. It should not be used in the middle of a sentence to join two clauses.

worth checking	I may meet you at the party tonight, otherwise I will see you tomorrow.
revised	I may see you at the party tonight. Otherwise I will see you tomorrow.

WORDS USED TO SHOW DEGREE OR EXTENT

for the most part
so...that
such...that
to a certain extent

to some extent
too...for...to
to some degree

So...that

so...that

---

28. **so...that:** When separated from each other by an adjective or adverb, these two words express degree or extent, answering questions such as "How far...?", "How big...?", "How much...?". Examples:

> How fat is he? He is so fat that he cannot see his feet.
>
> How large is Canada? It is so large that you need about six

days to drive across it.

So...that is the only combination of words that can be used in this way; it is wrong to say "very fat that..." or "too large that", just as it is wrong to leave out the word *so* and simply use *that* in such sentences.

worth checking	She was very late for dinner that there was no food left for her.
revised	She was so late for dinner that there was no food left for her.
worth checking	Dominic speaks quickly that it is often difficult to understand him.
revised	Dominic speaks so quickly that it is often difficult to understand him.

Such...that

29. **such...that:** Like *so...that*, the expression *such...that* is used to   such that express degree or extent, answering questions such as, "How big...?", "How long...?", "How fast...?". Notice the difference in the way the two are used.

	How far is it? It is <u>such</u> a long way <u>that</u> you would never be able to get there walking.
or	It is <u>so</u> far <u>that</u> you would never be able to reach there walking.
	How fat is he? He is <u>such</u> a fat man <u>that</u> his trousers need to be made specially for him.
or	He is <u>so</u> fat <u>that</u> his trousers need to be made specially for him.

The difference between the two is of course that only <u>one</u> word is normally used between *so* and *that*, whereas two or three words (usually an article, an adjective and a noun) are used between *such* and *that*. Be careful not to confuse the two, or to leave out *such*.

worth checking	It was a hot day that nobody could stay outside for long.
revised	It was such a hot day that nobody could stay outside for long.

PUTTING IDEAS TOGETHER

That and which

To understand when to use *that* and when to use *which* one must understand the difference between a restrictive and a non-restrictive clause. A restrictive clause restricts the application of the noun it modifies. Here is an example:

> The horse that was injured yesterday should recover.

Here the clause *that was injured yesterday* restricts the meaning of the subject of the sentence—*horse*—to a particular horse. The clause helps to define the subject. A non-restrictive clause does not restrict the application of the noun it modifies.

> The injured horse, which was the favourite to win the race, should recover in time for the Derby.

Here the clause *which was the favorite to win the race* tells us more about the horse but is not necessary to its definition. Notice that the non-restrictive clause is set off by commas. Restrictive clauses, on the other hand, follow directly on after the noun they describe. As you can see, *that* is used with restrictive clauses, and *which* with non-restrictive ones.

PUTTING IDEAS TOGETHER

30. **which:** The use of the word which provokes a violent reaction among many English instructors. They are frequently irritated by the number of times *which* is used incorrectly in restrictive clauses:

worth checking	The only store which sells this brand is now closed.
revised	The only store that sells this brand is now closed.
worth checking	The position which Marx adopted owed much to the philosophy of Hegel.
revised	The position that Marx adopted owed much to the philosophy of Hegel.

There are some instances, however, in which one is quite justified in using *which* in a restrictive clause. Such is the case when the writer is already using at least one *that* in the sentence:

worth checking	He told me that the radio that he bought was defective.
revised	He told me that the radio which he had bought was defective.

Better yet is to avoid the use of a second relative pronoun by rephrasing:

revised	He told me that the radio he had bought was defective.

Indeed, instructors who object to *which* point out that often rephrasing can make the sentence shorter and crisper:

Fair	The ending, which comes as a surprise to most readers, is profoundly unsettling.
revised	The ending is both surprising and unsettling.
Fair	The campaign, which had been carefully planned, was an enormous success.
revised	The carefully-planned campaign was an enormous success.

But *which* is not a special case in this regard. *That, who* and *whose* can often be fruitfully removed in the same way:

Fair	The deficit that we ran last year will probably be exceeded this year.

PUTTING IDEAS TOGETHER

revised	Last year's deficit will probably be exceeded this year.
Fair	Eisenhower hired as his personal driver a woman who turned into a long-term friend.
revised	Eisenhower and his driver became close friends.

The vice, then, is not *which* per se, but wordiness in general. Those who focus their attention on the one word and rail that "witches ride on broomsticks" might do better to treat the excessive use of *which* as a symptom of a much broader disease.

WORDS USED TO MAKE COMPARISONS

by comparison
in contrast

on the one hand...
...the other hand

OTHER JOINING WORDS AND EXPRESSIONS

as illustrated above/below
as mentioned above/below
as we can see/we can see that
assuming that
as shown in the diagram
above/below
firstly/in the first place
secondly/in the second place
for one thing

in other words
in the event of
the light of
in this respect/in some
respects
in that
these findings indicate that
to begin with
whereby

EXERCISE 30: Putting Ideas Together

Fill in *but, although, however, despite, because* or *as a result*. Pay close attention to the punctuation.

1) _____ he was sick, he could not come to work yesterday.

2) _____ he was sick, he came to work yesterday.

3) He was sick yesterday. _____, he still came to work.

4) _____ his sickness, he still came to work yesterday.

5) He was sick yesterday. _____, he did not come to work.

6) He was sick yesterday, _____ he still came to work.

7) She has practised for many long hours. _____, she is now a good player.

8) She has practised for many long hours, _____ she is still not a good player.

9) She is now a good player _____ she has practised for many long hours.

10) _____ she has practised for many long hours, she is not yet a good player.

11) She has practised for many long hours. _____, she is not yet a good player.

12) _____ her long hours of practice, she is not yet a good player.

EXERCISE: Putting Ideas Together

In each of the following there is one mistake. Correct it.

1) He went away in the morning and he came home the same night and he told me that he had had a good trip.

2) Although he has short legs, but he is a fast runner.

3) Despite that the teacher marked hard, we all passed.

4) Mark was sick because he stayed in bed all day.

5) Because the players would not give up, so they achieved victory.

6) Michipicoten Island on Lake Superior is very beautiful, but it is also very inaccessible. However, it is possible to reach it by private boat.

EXERCISE: Putting Ideas Together

Fill in appropriate joining words or expressions, choosing from those in the lists provided.

For (1), choose from:

as well	however
and	though
as a result	despite
; [semi-colon]	

1) The idea of building a canal from the Mediterranean Sea to the Red Sea is centuries old_____ it was considered even in the time of the Roman Empire. _____, it was not until the late nineteenth century that the project was actually begun. _____many difficulties, the canal was finally completed early in this century, _____for many years most ships bypassed the Cape of Good Hope. In the late 1960's and the 1970's, _____, ships that were too large for the canal began to be built. _____, the conflict between Israel and Egypt caused the canal to be closed at various times. _____, a great deal of sea traffic now once again travels right around Africa, just as it did before the Suez Canal was built.

For (2), choose from:

despite	such as
and	however
although	as a result
moreover	

2) Zimbabwe is one of Africa's most developed countries. _____ it has certain natural disadvantages, _____being land-locked, it has an excellent transportation system, _____ its agricultural sector is very productive. _____, it produces many manufactured goods. _____a three-year drought and the efforts of South Africa to subvert its neighbour, the economy of the country remains strong. _____, many of the S.A.D.C.C. nations look to Zimbabwe for economic leadership. _____, Zimbabwe is still less developed than most European countries.

WORD ORDER PROBLEMS

Word order problems are of many sorts. See also, for example, the discussions elsewhere in this book of syntax; of ambiguity; of split infinitives; of indefinite pronouns such as *each*, *every*, and *anyone*; and of *not only...but also*.

---

1.   **Amounts:** For no good reason, adjectives having to do with amounts or quantities (e.g. *much, few, many*) normally precede the noun or pronoun to which they refer, even when the verb *to be* is used. In this way such adjectives differ from other adjectives. For example, we can talk about "a happy man", putting the adjective *happy* before the noun *man*, or we can use the present tense of the verb *to be* and say "The man is happy", in which case the adjective *happy* comes after the noun *man*. In contrast, it is not correct to say, "We were many at the meeting," or "The people here are few". Instead the sentence must be changed around, and the adjectives put before the nouns. The easiest way to do this is by using *There* and the verb *to be*. The revised versions of the above sentences are,

revised   There were many of us at the meeting.

revised   There are few people here.

A further example:

worth checking   The students at the football game were many.

revised   There were many students at the football game.

---

2.   **Direct object position:** The normal position for direct objects (129) is after the verb. When the direct object is put at the beginning of a sentence it sounds awkward, and the word order may lead students to include an extra, unwanted pronoun later in the sentence. It is therefore best to always keep the direct object after the verb.

worth checking   Some of the money I put it in the bank.

(Notice the extra pronoun *it*.)

revised   I put some of the money in the bank.

(*I* is the subject, *some of the money* is the direct object.)

---

3.   **either...or:** These words should directly precede the pair of things to which they refer. The same applies to *neither...nor*.

worth checking   I will either pick an apple or a banana.

(*Either* and *or* refer to *apple* and *banana*. Therefore they must come immediately before those words.)

revised   I will pick either an apple or a banana.

worth checking   He will go either to New York for the holiday or remain here.

(The choice is between going and remaining.)

revised   He will either go to New York for the holiday or remain here.

---

4.   **except:** A phrase beginning with *except* should appear directly after the noun or pronoun to which *except* refers.

worth checking   We all had to wait except for those who had bought tickets in advance.

revised   All except those who had bought tickets in advance had to wait.

---

5.   **first person last rule:** When speaking about both yourself and another person (or other people), always mention the other person first. The first person pronoun (*I, me*) should come last.

worth checking   I and my brother decided to go shopping yesterday.

revised   My brother and I decided to go shopping yesterday.

---

6.   **only:** *Only* should come before the word or words it refers to.

worth checking   She asked six people to the party only.

revised   She asked only six people to the party.

---

7.   **questions in indirect speech:** In a question we normally reverse the order of the subject and the verb. For example, to change the statement "She was sad" to a question we reverse the

order of *she* and *was* and ask, "Was she sad?". The same rule does not apply, however, to questions in indirect speech. These are considered to be part of a statement and, as in any other statement, the entire verb should come after the subject. For example, to turn the above sentence into indirect speech we would say, "I asked her whether she was sad" (<u>not</u> "I asked her was she sad.")

worth checking   I asked him how was he.

revised   I asked him how he was.

worth checking   She asked her brother where was he going.

revised   She asked her brother where he was going.

Notice as well that these sentences are statements, not questions. They therefore do not end with a question mark.

8.   **relative pronouns** (123) : Relative pronouns (*who, which, whom, whose,* etc.) normally refer to the word that has come immediately before them. This may sometimes turn out to be difficult, in which case the word order may have to be changed.

worth checking   He purchased his friend's shop, whom he had

WORD ORDER PROBLEMS

known for many years.

(The relative pronoun *whom* refers to *friend*, not *shop*. Change
the word order to put *whom* directly after *friend*.)

revised   He purchased the shop from his friend, whom he
                 had known for many years.

worth checking On Saturday I went to my brother's wedding, whose
                 new wife is a senior government official.

revised   On Saturday I went to the wedding of my brother,
                 whose new wife is a senior government official.

WORD ORDER PROBLEMS

EXCESS WORDS, MISSING WORDS

Wordiness is perhaps the most persistent disease afflicting modern writing; references to it permeate this book. The mistake of including too few words in a sentence is much less common; most of the following entries, therefore, are instances of too many words rather than too few.

excess words/
missing words

---

1. **actual/actually:** usually redundant

worth checking Many people assume that the Switzerland is made up entirely of bankers and watchmakers. In actual fact, the Swiss economy is very diversified.

revised Many people assume that the Switzerland is made up entirely of bankers and watchmakers. In fact, the Swiss economy is very diversified.

---

2. **as regards:** Use *about*, or rephrase.

worth checking As regards your request for additional funding, we have taken the matter under advisement.

revised We are considering your request for more money.

---

3. **as stated earlier:** If so, why state it again?

worth checking The Venus flytrap, which as stated earlier is an insectivorous plant, grows only in a restricted area of New Jersey.

revised The Venus flytrap grows only in a restricted area of New Jersey.

---

4. **aspect:** often a pointer to an entire phrase or clause that can be cut

worth checking The logging industry is a troubled one at the present time. One of the aspects of this industry that is a cause for concern is the increased production of cheaper timber in South America.

revised The logging industry is now a troubled one.

Increased production of cheaper timber in South America has reduced the market for North American wood.

---

5. **at a later date:** later

worth checking   We can decide this at a later date.

revised   We can decide this later.

---

6. **at the present time:** *now*, or nothing

worth checking   At the present time the company has ten employees.

revised   The company has ten employees.

---

7. **attention:** *It has come to my attention that* is almost always unecessarily wordy.

worth checking   It has come to my attention that shipments last month were 15% below targeted levels.

revised   Shipments last month were 15% below targeted levels.

---

8. **basis/basically:** Both are often pointers to wordiness.

worth checking   On the basis of the information we now possess it is possible to see that William Bligh was not the ogre he was once thought to be. Basically, he was no harsher than most captains of the time.

revised   Recent research suggests that William Bligh was not the ogre he was once thought to be. He was no harsher than most captains of the time.

---

9. **cause:** Sentences using *cause* as a verb can often be rephrased more concisely; try to think of other verbs.

worth checking   The increased sales tax caused the people to react with fury.

revised   The increase in sales tax infuriated the people.

worth checking   The change in temperature caused the liquid to freeze within seventeen minutes.

revised   The liquid froze within seventeen minutes of the temperature change.

10. **close proximity to:** *near*

worth checking   The office is situated in close proximity to shops and transportation facilities.

revised   The office is near a shopping centre and a bus stop.

---

11. **exists:** often a pointer to wordiness

worth checking   A situation now exists in which voters suspect the government's motives, regardless of whether or not they approve of its actions.

revised   Voters now suspect the government's motives even if they approve of its actions.

---

12. **fact:** Be wary of *the fact that*.

worth checking   Due to the fact that we have discontinued this product, we are unable to provide spare parts.

revised   Because we have discontinued this product we are unable to provide spare parts.

worth checking   The fact that every member nation has one vote in the General Assembly does not give each one equal influence.

revised   Each member nation has one vote in the General Assembly, but some have more influence than others.

worth checking   Despite the fact that virtually no one in those days could foresee the end of American surpluses, Jones could.

revised   Jones was one of the few to foresee the end of American surpluses.

---

13. **factor:** heavily overused, and a frequent cause of wordiness

worth checking   An important factor contributing to the French Revolution was the poverty of the peasantry.

revised   The poverty of the peasantry was a major cause of the French Revolution.

---

14. **from my point of view, according to my point of view, in my opinion:** All three expressions are usually redundant.

worth checking   From my point of view, basic health care is more

	important than esoteric and expensive machines or procedures that benefit few.
Fair	I think that basic health care is more important than esoteric and expensive machines or procedures that benefit few.
revised	Basic health care is more important than esoteric and expensive machines or procedures that benefit few.

---

15. **I myself:** In almost all cases the addition of *myself* is needlessly repetitive.

worth checking	I myself believe in freedom of speech.
revised	I believe in freedom of speech.

---

16. **include:** Often a needed word or two is omitted after this verb. The best solution may be to rephrase or find another verb.

worth checking	The report includes both secondary and post-secondary education.
revised	The report includes material on both secondary and post-secondary education.
or	The report deals with both secondary and post-secondary education.
worth checking	The Thirty Years War included most countries in Europe.
revised	The list of countries that fought in the Thirty Years War includes almost every European nation.
revised	Almost every European country fought in the Thirty Years War.

---

17. **in all probability:** *probably*

worth checking	In all probability we will be finished tomorrow.
revised	We will probably be finished tomorrow.

---

18. **interesting:** In most cases the writer should not have to tell the reader that what he is saying is interesting.

worth checking	It is interesting to observe that illiteracy affects almost as high a proportion of native-born Americans as it does immigrants.
revised	Illiteracy affects almost as high a proportion of

native-born Americans as it does immigrants.

---

19. **as you know, as we all know:** usually better omitted

worth checking   As we all know, Ronald Reagan was first elected in 1980.

revised   Ronald Reagan was first elected in 1980.

---

20. **mean for:** The preposition is unnecessary.

worth checking   I did not mean for him to do it all himself.

revised   I did not mean that he should do it all himself.

---

21. **nature:** often contributes to wordiness

worth checking   The nature of the brain is to process information incredibly swiftly.

revised   The brain processes information extremely swiftly.

---

22. **personally:** It is safe to let your reader take it for granted that you are a person.

worth checking   Personally, I feel that the Supreme Court has too much power.

revised   I feel that the Supreme Court has too much power.

---

23. **point in time:** *now* or *then*

worth checking   At that point in time central Africa was very sparsely populated.

revised   Central Africa was then very sparsely populated.

---

24. **really:** If an intensifier must be used, *very* is preferable.

worth checking   It is really important that this be done today.

revised   It is very important that this be done today.

or   This must be done today.

---

25. **regard, with regard to, as regards:** Try *about*, *over*, or rephrase.

worth checking   I am writing with regard to your proposal to centralize production.

revised   I am writing about your proposal to centralize production.

EXCESS WORDS, MISSING WORDS

worth checking	As regards the trend in interest rates, it is likely to continue to be upward.
revised	Interest rates are likely to continue to increase.
worth checking	This Act gave the government powers with regard to the readjustment of industry.
revised	This Act gave the government powers over the readjustment of industry.

26. **repetition and redundancy:** Part One drew a distinction between repetition and repetitiveness (56). Writers who pay attention to the meaning of the individual words they use often also catch themselves using redundancies — words or expressions that unecessarily repeat an already expressed meaning in different words.

worth checking	This property will appreciate greatly in value.
revised	This property will appreciate greatly.
worth checking	The house is very large in size.
revised	The house is very large.
worth checking	"It was decided it would be mutually beneficial to both of us if he left."

(*The Globe and Mail*, Sept. 20, 1990)

EXCESS WORDS, MISSING WORDS

revised   "It was decided it would be mutually beneficial if he left."

or   "We agreed it would be better for both of us if he left."

---

27. **situation:** By avoiding this word you will usually make your sentence shorter and better.

worth checking   This treaty created a situation in which European countries gave up a degree of autonomy in return for greater security.

revised   Through this treaty European countries gave up a degree of autonomy in return for greater security.

---

28. **too few words:** This mistake can happen anywhere in a sentence. One of the best tests of whether or not a writer has checked over her work is whether or not there are missing words. In almost all cases, such omissions will be noticed through careful proofreading (103).

worth checking   She rushed home to tell my family and about the accident.

revised   She rushed home to tell my family and me about the accident.

worth checking   Mrs. Gandhi reminded the Conference that just one intercontinental ballistic missile could plant 200 million trees, irrigate 1 million hectares of land, or build 6,500 health care centers.

(United Nations official)

revised   Mrs. Gandhi reminded the Conference that the money spent on just one intercontinental ballistic missile could be used to plant 200 million trees, irrigate 1 million hectares of land, or build 6,500 health care centers.

---

29. **There is/are/was/were:** These constructions often produce sentences that are needlessly long.

worth checking   There were many factors which undermined the government's popularity in this period.

revised   Many things undermined the government's popularity in this period.

worth checking   There are many historians who accept this thesis.

EXCESS WORDS, MISSING WORDS

revised	Many historians accept this thesis.

---

30. too many words: Many of the causes of this problem have been given separate entries.

worth checking	So far as the purpose of this essay is concerned, it will concentrate on the expansion of Soviet power.
revised	This essay will concentrate on the expansion of Soviet power.
worth checking	Although the author does not claim to be writing a social study, the question arises whether the social implications of his analysis can be ignored.
revised	Although the author does not claim to be writing a social study, his analysis does have social implications.

---

31. would like to take this opportunity to: *would like*

worth checking	I would like to take this opportunity to thank my cousin in Peoria.
revised	I am very grateful to my cousin in Peoria.

EXERCISE: Too Many Words or Too Few Words

In each of the following there are either too many or too few words. Improve each sentence.

2) I myself I think that it is not wise to have more than three or four children.

3) In my opinion I think men are just as intelligent as women.

4) It was the general consensus of opinion that no new projects of an expensive nature should be embarked upon at that point in time.

5) The protagonist has fallen in love a girl he met at the fair the previous weekend.

6) She said that she did not to work at the factory, no matter how much she was paid.

IN TO EVERY THING

TWO WORDS OR ONE WORD?

A number of very commonly used English words have over many years become accepted as one word because they are combined so often. Other similar combinations, however, should still be written as two words. In a few cases one can see English usage changing on this point right now. A generation ago, for example, *alright* as one word could not have been found in any dictionary. Now a few authorities are beginning to regard *alright* as acceptable, and perhaps in another generation or two it will have completely replaced *all right*. For the moment, though, it is best to stick with *all right* rather than the more colloquial *alright*.

---

1.   What has been written as two words should be one. Here are some common examples:

already: one word when used as an adverb ("He has finished already.")
altogether: one word when used as an adverb to mean *completely* or *entirely* ("He is not altogether happy with the result.")
awhile: one word when used as an adverb
another   **anybody**
anyone: one word unless it is followed by *of.*
bathroom   **bloodshed**
businessman
cannot: *can not* is less common, but still acceptable.
everybody
everyday: one word when used as an adjective ("Brushing your teeth should be part of your everyday routine"- here *everyday* is an adjective modifying the noun *routine*.)
everyone: one word unless it is followed by *of.*
everything   **forever**
furthermore   **indeed**
into: one word except in the relatively few cases where the senses of *in* and *to* are clearly separate. (Fowler uses the example, "the Prime Minister took her in to dinner.")
maybe: when used as an adverb meaning *perhaps* ("Maybe I will join you later" - here the verb is *will join* and *maybe* is an adverb.)

nearby	nobody
onto: see *into*	**ourselves**
somebody	**someone**
straightforward	**themselves**
wartime	**whatever**
whenever	

---

2. What has been written as one word should be two words. Here are some common examples:

a lot
all ready: two words when not used as an adverb ("We are all ready to go.")
all right
all together: two words when not used as an adverb ("They were all together when I left them.")
every day: two words when not used as an adjective ("We see each other every day.")

every time	**in fact**
in front	**in order**
in spite of	

may be: two words when used as a verb ("He may be here later tonight" - *may be* is the verb in the sentence.)
no one

IN TO EVERY THING

SUPPOSED TO BE: Mistakes of Usage

1. **according to:** This expression normally is used only when one is referring to a <u>person</u> or to a group of people (e.g. "According to his lawyer, the accused was nowhere near the scene when the crime was committed", "According to Shakespeare, Richard III was an evil king").

worth checking	According to geography, Zaire is larger than all of Western Europe.
revised	As we learn in geography, Zaire is larger than all of Western Europe.
worth checking	According to the story of <u>Cry the Beloved Country</u>, Stephen Kumalo has a quick temper.
revised	The events of the story show that Stephen Kumalo has a quick temper.

2. **age/aged:** Do not use the noun *age* as a participle.

worth checking	A woman age 35 was struck and killed by the car.
revised	A woman aged 35 was struck and killed by the car.

3. **all of:** Many authorities advise that the expression *all of* should be avoided in the interests of economy. Perhaps so, but there is certainly no error involved, and in many cases the addition of the word *of* improves the rhythm of the sentence; Lincoln's famous maxim "You can not fool all the people all of the time" would not be improved by dropping the *of*.

4. **amount:** This word should only be used with things that are uncountable (sugar, rice, etc.).

worth checking	A large amount of books were stolen from the library last night.

| *revised* | A large number of books were stolen from the library last night. |

---

5. **and:** In most cases *or* rather than *and* should be used as a connective if the statement is negative.

| *worth checking* | Moose are not found in South America, Africa and Australia. |
| *revised* | Moose are not found in South America, Africa, or Australia. |

---

6. **anyways/anywheres:** There is never a need for the *s*.

| *worth checking* | We were unable to find him anywheres. |
| *revised* | We were unable to find him anywhere. |

---

7. **as:** When this word is used to relate the times at which two actions happened, the actions must have happened <u>at the same time</u> (e.g., "As I got out of bed, I heard the sound of gunfire," where the hearing happens <u>during</u> the action of getting out; "As he was walking to work, he remembered that he had left the stove on," where the remembering happens <u>during</u> the walking). *As* <u>cannot</u> be used in this way if the two actions happened at <u>different</u> times; if one action is completed before the other begins, always use *when*.

| *worth checking* | As I had finished my geography homework, I started my history essay. |

(The finishing happens before the starting.)

| *revised* | When I had finished my geography homework, I started my history essay. |

| *worth checking* | As she discovered that the engine was overheating, she stopped the car immediately. |

(The discovering happens before the stopping.)

| *revised* | When she discovered that the engine was overheating, she stopped the car immediately. |

Note: Since *when* can be used both when actions happen simultaneously and when they happen at different times, any student who is at all uncertain about this point is wise to avoid using *as* to refer to time, and always stick to *when*. This has the added advantage of avoiding the possible ambiguity as to whether *as* is being used to mean *because* or to mean *when*.

SUPPOSED TO BE: Mistakes of Usage

8.   **as/that/whether:** Do not use *as* to mean *that* or *whether*.

worth checking   I don't know as how I can do the job in time.

revised   I don't know whether I can do the job in time.

9.   **because of the following reasons/some reasons/many reasons:** The word *because* makes it clear that a cause or reason is being introduced. The addition of a phrase such as *of the following reasons* is redundant. Either use *because* on its own, or use <u>for</u> *the following reasons/many reasons*, etc.

worth checking   During her first few years in Canada, Susanna Moodie was unhappy because of several reasons.

revised   During her first few years in Canada, Susanna Moodie was unhappy for several reasons.

10.   **both:** The expressions *both alike, both equal,* and *both together* involve repetition.

Poor   Macdonald and Cartier both arrived together at about eight o'clock.

Better   Macdonald and Cartier arrived together at about eight o'clock.

11.   **can be able:** *I can do it* and *I am able to do it* mean the same thing. Using both verbs together is redundant.

worth checking   He thinks Hartford can be able to win the Cup.

revised   He thinks Hartford can win the Cup.

or   He thinks Hartford will be able to win the Cup.

12.   **cannot help but:** one too many negatives; use *can but* or *cannot help*.

worth checking   He couldn't help but think he had made a mistake.

revised   He couldn't help thinking he had made a mistake.

or   He could but think he had made a mistake.

13.   **change:** You <u>make</u> a *change* (<u>not</u> do a *change*).

worth checking   The manager did several changes to the roster before the match with the Soviet Union.

revised   The manager made several changes to the roster before the match with the Soviet Union.

SUPPOSED TO BE: Mistakes of Usage

---

14. **comment:** We <u>make</u> comments (<u>not</u> say or do them).

| *worth checking* | Anyone who wishes to say any comments will have a chance to speak after the lecture. |
| *revised* | Anyone who wishes to make any comments will have a chance to speak after the lecture. |

---

15. **compared to/than:** The use of *compared to* as a participial phrase often leads to ambiguity and error. Unless one is speaking of one person *comparing* something to something else, it is usually better to use *than*.

| *worth checking* | There were many more trilliums in 1987 compared to previous years. |
| *revised* | There were many more trilliums in 1987 than there had been in previous years. |

---

16. **convince:** You *convince* someone *that* they should do something, or *persuade* them *to* do it.

| *worth checking* | Reagan's advisers convinced him to approve the arms for hostages deal with Iran. |
| *revised* | Reagan's advisers persuaded him to approve the arms for hostages deal with Iran. |

---

17. **decimate:** Most etymologists agree that originally this word meant *kill one of every ten*. It has come to be used more loosely to mean *destroy a considerable number of*, and sometimes *kill nine of every ten*, but it is best not to use it in a way that some authorities feel, as H.W. Fowler puts it, "expressly contradicts the proper sense."

| *worth checking* | The regiment was decimated; less than 40 per cent survived. |
| *revised* | The regiment suffered extreme losses; less than 20 per cent survived. |

---

18. **elder/older:** *Elder* can act as an adjective ("my *elder* son") or a noun ("the *elder* of the two"). *Older* can act only as an adjective. If using *than*, use *older*.

| *worth checking* | She is four years elder than her sister. |
| *revised* | She is four years older than her sister. |

SUPPOSED TO BE: Mistakes of Usage

19. **etc.:** The Latin *et cetera*, or *etc.* for short, means *and the rest* or *and others*. To say *and etc.* is really to say *and and others*. Beware as well of combining *etc.* with expressions such as *such as.*

worth checking	During recent years several countries (Mexico, Argentina and etc.) have amassed huge debts, which they are now unable to pay.
revised	During recent years several countries (Mexico, Argentina, etc.) have amassed huge debts, which they are now unable to pay.
worth checking	Plants such as venus flytraps, pitcher plants, etc. feed on insects.
revised	Plants such as venus flytraps and pitcher plants feed on insects.
or	Some plants (venus flytraps, pitcher plants, etc.) feed on insects.

20. **for:** One use of this preposition is to show purpose. Normally, however, *for* can only be used in this way when the purpose can be expressed in one word (e.g., *for safety, for security*). It is <u>not</u> usually correct to try to express purpose by combining *for* with a pronoun and an infinitive: expressions such as *for him to be happy, for us to arrive safely* are awkward and should be avoided. Instead, one can express purpose either by beginning with an infinitive (e.g. *in order to make life easier, in order to increase yield per hectare*), or by using *so that* (e.g., *so that life will be made easier, so that yield per hectare will be increased*).

worth checking	Please speak slowly for me to understand what you say.
revised	Please speak slowly so that I can understand what you say.
worth checking	The team must work hard for it to have a chance at the Grey Cup.
revised	The team must work hard if it is to have a chance at the Grey Cup.

21. **forget:** To *forget* something is to fail to remember it, <u>not</u> to leave it somewhere.

worth checking	I forgot my textbook at home.

revised	I left my textbook at home.
or	I forgot to bring my textbook from home.

---

22.   had ought/hadn't ought: Use *ought* or *ought not* instead.

worth checking	He hadn't ought to have risked everything at once.
revised	He ought not to have risked everything at once.
or	He should not have risked everything at once.

---

23.   hardly: *Hardly* acts as a negative; there is thus no need to add a second negative.

worth checking	The advertisers claim that you can't hardly tell the difference.
revised	The advertisers claim that you can hardly tell the difference.

---

24.   how/what: One may talk about *how* something (or someone) *is*, or *what* something (or someone) is *like*, but <u>not</u> *how* they are *like*.

worth checking	Tell me how it looks like from where you are.
revised	Tell me how it looks from where you are.
or	Tell me what it looks like from where you are.
worth checking	I do not know how the roads are like between St. John's and Cornerbrook.
revised	I do not know what the roads are like between St. John's and Cornerbrook.
or	I do not know how the roads are between St. John's and Cornerbrook.

---

25.   increase: Numbers can be *increased* or *decreased*, as can such things as *production* and *population* (nouns which refer to certain types of numbers or quantities). Things such as *houses*, however, or *books* (nouns which do not refer to numbers or quantities) cannot be *increased*; only the <u>number</u> of houses, books etc. can be *increased* or *decreased*, *raised* or *lowered*.

worth checking	The government has greatly increased low-rent houses in the suburbs of Toronto.
revised	The government has greatly increased the number of low-rent houses in the suburbs of Toronto.

SUPPOSED TO BE: Mistakes of Usage

26. **information:** One <u>gives</u> *information* (<u>not</u> *tells* it).

worth checking	He told me all the information I wanted about how to apply.
revised	He gave me all the information I wanted about how to apply.

27. **investigation:** We <u>make</u>, <u>carry out</u>, or <u>hold</u> an *investigation* (<u>not</u> do one).

worth checking	The manager did a thorough investigation into the disappearance of funds from his department.
revised	The manager made a thorough investigation into the disappearance of funds from his department.

28. **irregardless:** The result of confusion between *regardless* and *irrespective*. Use *regardless*.

worth checking	She told us to come for a picnic, irregardless of whether it is rainy or sunny.
revised	She told us to come for a picnic, regardless of whether it is rainy or sunny.

29. **is when/is where:** Many people use these phrases when attempting to define something. There is always a better way.

worth checking	Osmosis is when a fluid moves through a porous partition into another fluid.
revised	Osmosis occurs when a fluid moves through a porous partition into another fluid.
or	Osmosis is the movement of a fluid through a porous partition into another fluid.

30. **journey:** You <u>make</u> a journey (<u>not</u> *do* one)

worth checking	If we do not stop along the way, we can do the journey in an hour.
revised	If we do not stop along the way, we can make the journey in an hour.

31. **law:** A law is *passed*, *made*, or *put into effect* by the government, and *enforced* by the police. Laws are <u>not</u> *put* or *done*.

worth checking	I think the government should put a law increasing the penalty for drunken driving.

revised	I think the government should pass a law increasing the penalty for drunken driving.

---

32. less/fewer: When something can be counted (e.g., people, books, trees), use *fewer*. Use *less* only with <u>uncountable</u> nouns (e.g., *sugar, meat, equipment*).

worth checking	There are less people here than there were last week.
revised	There are fewer people here than there were last week.
worth checking	There are less steps and that means there is more room for error. (*Financial Post*, Nov. 20, 1989)
revised	There are fewer steps and that means there is more room for error.

---

33. lie (meaning *speak falsely*): You *lie* <u>about</u> something, <u>not</u> that something.

worth checking	He lied that he was eighteen years old.
revised	He lied about his age, stating that he was eighteen.
or	He lied when he said he was eighteen years old.

---

34. mistake: *Mistakes* are <u>made</u> (<u>not</u> done).

worth checking	He did seven mistakes in that short spelling exercise.
revised	He made seven mistakes in that short spelling exercise.

---

35. more/most: To use *more* with a comparative adjective, or *most* with a superlative adjective is to repeat oneself.

worth checking	The bride looked like the most happiest person in the world.
revised	The bride looked like the happiest person in the world.
or	The bride looked like the most happy person in the world.
worth checking	Gandalf is much more wiser than Frodo.
revised	Gandalf is much wiser than Frodo.

36. **nor:** This word is usually used together with *neither*. Do <u>not</u> use it together with *not*; when using *not*, use *or* instead of *nor*.

worth checking	She does not drink nor smoke.
revised	She does not drink or smoke.
or	She neither drinks nor smokes.

worth checking	[Liberal organizer Senator Al] Graham does not have the money nor the organization to work with that Atkins enjoys.
	(*The Toronto Star*, May 1987)
revised	Graham does not have the money or the organization to work with that Atkins enjoys.
or	Graham has neither the money nor the organization to work with that Atkins enjoys.

37. **nothing/nobody/nowhere:** These words should not be used with another negative word such as *not*. If one uses *not*, then one should use *anything* instead of *nothing*, *anybody* instead of *nobody*, *anywhere* instead of *nowhere*.

worth checking	He could not do nothing while he was in prison.
revised	He could not do anything while he was in prison.

38. **opposed:** You are opposed <u>to</u> something or someone (<u>not</u> with or against)

worth checking	Charles Darwin was opposed against the literal interpretation of the story of Creation, as found in *Genesis*.
revised	Charles Darwin was opposed to the literal interpretation of the story of Creation, as found in *Genesis*.

39. **preclude:** To *preclude* something is to exclude any possibility of it happening; people cannot be *precluded*.

worth checking	Our cash flow problem precludes us from entering into any new commitments.
revised	Our cash flow problem precludes any new commitments.
or	We do not have enough money to make a commitment to you now.

40. **position/theory.** Positions and theories are held or argued; they do not hold or argue themselves. Philosophy students beware!

worth checking	Devlin's position holds that a shared public morality is essential to the existence of society.
revised	Devlin's position is that a shared public morality is essential to the existence of society.
or	Devlin holds that a shared public morality is essential to the existence of society.

41. **reason:** The phrase "the reason is because" involves repetition; use *that* instead of *because*, or eliminate the phrase completely.

worth checking	The reason ice floats is because it is lighter than water.
revised	The reason ice floats is that it is lighter than water.
or	Ice floats because it is lighter than water.

worth checking	The reason I have come is because I want to apply for a job.
revised	I have come to apply for a job.

Housing is short.

42. **short/scarce:** If a person is *short* of something, that thing is *scarce*.

SUPPOSED TO BE: Mistakes of Usage

worth checking	Food is now desperately short throughout the country.
revised	Food is now extremely scarce throughout the country.
or	The country is now desperately short of food.

---

43. **since/for:** Both these words can be used to indicate length (or duration) of time, but they are used in slightly different ways. *Since* is used to mention the point at which a period of time began (*since 6 o'clock, since 1980, since last Christmas*, etc.). *For* is used to mention the amount of time that has passed (*for two years, for six months, for centuries*, etc.).

worth checking	She has been staying with us since three weeks.
revised	She has been staying with us for three weeks.
or	She has been staying with us since three weeks ago.

---

44. **so:** When used to show degree or extent, *so* is normally used with *that*: "so big that...", "so hungry that..." , etc. *So* should not be used as an intensifier in the way that *very* is used.

worth checking	When she stepped out of the church she looked so beautiful.
revised	When she stepped out of the church she looked very beautiful.
or	When she stepped out of the church she looked so beautiful that it was hard to believe she had once been thought of as plain.

---

45. **some/any/someone/anyone:** With negatives (*not, never*, etc.) *any* is used in place of *some*.

worth checking	He never gives me some help with my work.
revised	He never gives me any help with my work.

---

46. **speech:** You make a *speech* or give a speech (not *do a speech*).

worth checking	The Dean was asked to do a speech at the Convocation.
revised	The Dean was asked to give a speech at the Convocation.

SUPPOSED TO BE: Mistakes of Usage

47. **start:** If <u>both</u> the time at which an event begins <u>and</u> the time that it finishes are mentioned, it is not enough to use only the verb *start*.

worth checking	The dance started from 9 p.m. till midnight.
revised	The dance started at 9 p.m. and finished at midnight.
or	The dance continued from 9 p.m. until midnight.
or	The dance lasted from 9 p.m. until midnight.

48. **supposed to/should:** These two are very similar in meaning, and may often be used interchangeably; if a person is *supposed to* do something, then that is what she *should* do. In the <u>past</u> tense, however, the question of when and when not to use *supposed to* is quite tricky. You <u>may</u> use it when you are clearly talking about a <u>fixed plan</u> that has not been carried out (e.g. "He was supposed to arrive before two o'clock, but he is still not here"). You <u>should not</u> use it to apply to any action that you think was wrong, or you feel should not have been carried out. The safe solution to this problem is to always use *should* instead of *supposed to*.

worth checking	What she said was impolite, but he was not supposed to hit her for saying it.
revised	What she said was impolite, but he should not have hit her for saying it.

worth checking	The South African government was not supposed to keep Nelson Mandela in jail for so many years.
revised	The South African government should not have kept Nelson Mandela in jail for so many years.

49. **suppose/supposed:** Be sure to add the *d* in the expression *supposed to*.

worth checking	We are suppose to be there by eight.
revised	We are supposed to be there by eight.

50. **thankful/grateful:** We are *thankful* that something has happened, and *grateful* for something we have received.

worth checking	I am very thankful for the kind thoughts expressed in your letter.

revised	I am very grateful for the kind thoughts expressed in your letter.

---

51. too: The word *too* suggests that something is <u>more</u> than necessary, or <u>more</u> than desired. Do not use it indiscriminately to lend emphasis.

worth checking	She looked too beautiful in her new dress.
revised	She looked very beautiful in her new dress.

---

52. try/sure: Perhaps the most common error of all, in published books and articles as well as in student writing, is the use of *and* rather than *to* after *try* and *sure*.

worth checking	No Montrealers stepped in to try and save the franchise.
	(*The Toronto Star*, June 27, 1987)
revised	No Montrealers stepped in to try to save the franchise.
worth checking	Burton had agreed with the Sultan not to try and convert the Africans to Christianity.
	(Alan Moorehead, *The White Nile*)
revised	Burton had agreed with the Sultan not to try to convert the Africans to Christianity.
worth checking	Be sure and take out the garbage before you go to bed.
revised	Be sure to take out the garbage before you go to bed.

---

53. use/used: Be sure to add the *d* in the expression *used to*.

worth checking	He use to be much more reckless than he is now.
revised	He used to be much more reckless than he is now.

---

54. where: Do not use *where* for *that*.

worth checking	I read in the paper where the parties are now tied in popularity.
revised	I read in the paper that the parties are now tied in popularity.

EXERCISE: Usage

In each of the following sentences there is one mistake. Correct it.

1)   According to science, it is impossible to travel faster than the speed of light.

2)   As he has got into the car, he turned the key in the ignition.

3)   The European powers wanted to colonize Africa because of the following reasons.

4)   There are several birds (penguins, ostriches and etc.) which cannot fly.

5)   He often forgets his office key at home.

6)   It is a difficult problem in the way that you have to go through several steps in order to solve it.

7)   Students at this school will be substantially increased next year.

8)   The police did a thorough investigation, and could find no evidence or wrongdoing.

9)   She lied that she had not stolen any money.

10)   He is opposed against legalizing abortion.

11)   The reason she likes him is because he is a well-known personality.

12)   The college would like to increase the places available in residence.

13)   A revolution is when the government changes hands as a result of a violent uprising.

14)   The reason the ozone layer is being destroyed is because of the effects of aerosol sprays.

15)   The plaintiff now intends to try and regain custody of the child.

SUPPOSED TO BE: Mistakes of Usage

PUNCTUATION

The Period

The most important mark of punctuation is the full stop (or period), which is used to separate one sentence from another, and the most common punctuation mistakes involve the use of the full stop. The first of these is the run-on sentence: a sentence that continues running on and on instead of being broken up into two or more sentences. (Where a comma has been used instead of a period, the term *comma splice* is often used to denote a run-on sentence.) The second is the incomplete sentence (or *sentence fragment*): a group of words that has been written as if it were a full sentence, but that needs something else to make it complete.

period ∎

---

1. **run-on sentence:** The basic idea of a sentence is that it expresses one complete idea. Often simply remembering this simple fact will be enough to keep run-on sentences at bay, particularly if one reads work over to oneself (aloud, if it's not too embarrassing) and notice where one pauses naturally.

worth checking	Early last Thursday we were walking in the woods it was a bright and clear morning.
revised	Early last Thursday we were walking in the woods. It was a bright and clear morning.

In the above example it should be quite clear that there are two separate ideas, and that these should be put into two separate sentences. Sometimes, though, it is not so simple. In particular, certain words may be used to join two clauses into one sentence, while other words should not be used in this way. We have already seen (in our survey of joining words) some examples of words that cause problems of this sort. Here is a review:

and: The appearance of more than one *and* in a sentence is often a sign that the ideas would be better rephrased.

worth checking	Beaverbrook effectively mobilized the resources of the country to serve the war effort overseas and he later was knighted and he is also well-known for creating a media empire.
revised	Beaverbrook effectively mobilized the resources of the country to serve the war effort — an accomplishment for which he later was knighted. He is also well-known for creating a media empire.
or	Beaverbrook, who had created a vast media empire before the war, then distinguished himself by effectively mobilizing the resources of the country to serve the war effort. It was in recognition of this service that he was knighted.

hence:

worth checking	With the exception of identical twins no two people have exactly the same genetic makeup hence it is impossible for two people to look exactly the same.
revised	With the exception of identical twins no two people have exactly the same genetic makeup. Hence, it is impossible for two people to look exactly the same.

however:

worth checking	During the rainy season more water flows over Victoria Falls than over any other falls in the world however several other falls are higher than Victoria.
revised	During the rainy season more water flows over Victoria Falls than over any other falls in the world. However, several other falls are higher than Victoria.

otherwise:

worth checking	You had better leave now otherwise we will call the police.
revised	You had better leave now. Otherwise, we will call the police.

An even more common cause of run-on sentences than any of the above is the word *then*.

2.   **then:** Unlike *when, then* should not be used to join two clauses together into one sentence. *And then* may be used, or a semi-colon, or a new sentence may be begun.

worth checking	We applied the solution to the surface of the leaves then we made observations at half-hour intervals ovcer the next twelve hours.
revised	We applied the solution to the surface of the leaves. Then we made observations at half-hour intervals over the next twelve hours.
or	We applied the solution to the surface of the leaves; then we made observations at half-hour intervals over the next twelve hours.
or	We applied the solution to the surface of the leaves and then we made observations at half-hour intervals ovcer the next twelve hours.

worth checking	The Lancaster House agreement was finally signed in 1980, then the war ended.
revised	The Lancaster House agreement was finally signed in 1980. Then the war ended.
worth checking	The Montreal Canadiens produced vital late-period goals then they wrapped their iron defense around the Calgary Flames to take an upper hand in the Stanley Cup final Tuesday night.
	(Canadian Press story, May 21, 1986)
revised	The Montreal Canadiens produced vital late-period goals and then wrapped their iron defense around the Calgary Flames to take an upper hand in the Stanley Cup final Tuesday night.

PUNCTUATION

3.   **incomplete sentences:** A good writer always asks herself as she checks her work if each sentence is complete in itself; in this way the more obvious errors will almost always be caught. For example, if "When the meeting ends tomorrow" is in the rough draft as a complete sentence, re-reading will probably lead to the realization that the idea is not complete; the group of words needs another group of words to finish it. (e.g., "When the meeting ends tomorrow we should have a comprehensive agreement.") Be particularly careful with longer sentences to make sure they are complete. For example, the group of words "Marina walked to the sea" is a complete sentence, but the following sentence is incomplete, even though it is much longer; it doesn't tell us what happened when she was walking.

worth checking	While Marina was walking to the sea and thinking of her father and the sound of a woodthrush.
revised	While Marina was walking to the sea she heard the sound of a woodthrush and thought of her father.
worth checking	Unemployment is a serious problem in Canada. In fact, throughout the world.
revised	Unemployment is a serious problem both in Canada and abroad.
worth checking	So long as you have a place to live and enough to eat.
revised	So long as you have a place to live and enough to eat, you have some reason to be thankful.

The three words which most frequently lead students to write incomplete sentences are *and*, *because* and *so*.

4.   **and:** Although there are certain cases in which it is possible to begin a sentence with *and*, these are extremely difficult to sense. It is usually better for all except professional writers not to begin sentences with *and* if they wish to avoid incomplete sentences.

worth checking	To make this crop grow well you should add Compound 'D' fertilizer to the soil. And you should add top dressing a few months later.

PUNCTUATION

| *revised* | To make this crop grow well you should add Compound 'D' fertilizer to the soil, and top dressing a few months later. |

---

5.   **because:** In order to prevent young children who have difficulty in writing long sentences from writing incomplete sentences, many primary school teachers wisely tell their pupils not to begin sentences with *because*. In fact it is not incorrect to begin with *because*, so long as the sentence is complete. The rule to remember is that any sentence with *because* in it must mention both the cause and the result. Whether the word *because* comes at the beginning or in the middle of the sentence does not matter; what is important is that the sentence have two parts.

| *worth checking* | Sandinista leaders told their people to be ready for war. Because the United States had been trying to destabilize Nicaragua. |
| *revised* | Sandinista leaders told their people to be ready for war, because the United States had been trying to destabilize Nicaragua. |

| *worth checking* | Because of the cold and wet weather which affected the whole area. Many people were desperately trying to find more firewood. |
| *revised* | Because of the cold and wet weather which affected the whole area many people were desperately trying to find more firewood. |

---

6.   **so:** This word is probably the biggest single cause of incomplete sentences. As is the case with *and*, there are certain situations in which professional writers manage to get away with beginning sentences with *so*, but the student should not normally attempt this. *So* should be used to join ideas together into one sentence, not to separate them by starting a new sentence.

| *worth checking* | I did not know what was happening. So my friends explained the procedure to me. |
| *revised* | I did not know what was happening, so my friends explained the procedure to me. |

| *worth checking* | The meat was too heavily spiced. So most of it had to be thrown away. |

revised   The meat was too heavily spiced, so most of it had
to be thrown away.

The Comma

comma **,** Although the omission or wrong use of a comma sounds like a
small mistake, it can be very important. The following group of
words, for example, forms a sentence only if a comma is included.

worth checking Because of the work that we had done before we
were ready to hand in the assignment.

revised   Because of the work that we had done before, we
were ready to hand in the assignment.

The omission or addition of a comma can also completely alter
the meaning of a sentence − as it did in the Queen's University
Alumni letter that spoke of the warm emotions still felt by alumni
for "our friends, who are dead," (rather than "our friends who are
dead"). The second would have been merely a polite
rememberance of those Alumni who have died; the first suggests
that *all* the friends of the reader are dead.

7. **omission of commas:** Commas very commonly come in pairs,
and it is common as well to omit the second comma in a pair. Be
particularly careful when putting commas around a name, or
around an adjectival subordinate clause.

worth checking My sister Caroline, has done very well this year in
her studies.

revised   My sister, Caroline, has done very well this year in
her studies.

worth checking The snake which had been killed the day before,
was already half-eaten by ants.

revised   The snake, which had been killed the day before,
was already half-eaten by ants.

The Question Mark

question mark **?** 8. All students know that a question should be followed by a
question mark, but it is easy to forget, particularly if one is writing
quickly and forgets to check over the work afterwards.

worth checking	Would Britain benefit from closer ties with Europe. More than 20 years after the UK joined the Common Market, the question continues to bedevil British political life.
revised	Would Britain benefit from closer ties with Europe? More than 20 years after the UK joined the Common Market, the question continues to bedevil British political life.

The Exclamation Mark

This mark is used to give extremely strong emphasis to a statement. It should be used very sparingly, if at all, in formal written work: most good writers avoid it completely, since they realize that it does not help to make what they say sound more important.

exclamation mark!

The Semi-colon

This mark is used to separate ideas that are closely related to each other. In most cases a period could be used instead; the semi-colon simply signals to the reader the close relationship between the two ideas. In the following example the second sentence reinforces the statement of the first; a semi-colon is thus appropriate, although a full stop is also correct.

semi-colon ;

	This book is both exciting and profound. It is one of the best books I have read.
or	This book is both exciting and profound; it is one of the best books I have read.

Similarly in the following example the second sentence gives evidence supporting the statement made in the first sentence. Again, a semi-colon is appropriate.

	The team is not as good as it used to be. It has lost four of its past five games.
or	The team is not as good as it used to be; it has lost four of its last five games.

The semi-colon is also used occasionally to divide items in a series that includes other punctuation:

> The following were told to report to the coach after practice: Jackson, Form 2B; Marshall, Form 3A; Gladys, Form 1B.

The Colon

colon **:**

This mark is often believed to be virtually the same as the semi-colon in the way it is used. In fact, there are some important differences. The most common uses of the colon are as follows:

- in headings, to announce that more is to follow, or that the writer is about to list a series of things
- introducing a quotation
- in between two clauses, indicating that the second one provides an explanation of what was stated in the first

This last use is very similar to the main use of the semi-colon. The subtle differences are that the semi-colon can be used in such situations when the ideas are not quite so closely related, and the colon asks the reader to pause for a slightly longer period. Note that a colon must be preceded by an independent clause; what comes before it, in other words, could be a full sentence on its own. Here are some examples:

> In the last four weeks he has visited five different countries: Mexico, Venezuela, Panama, Haiti and Belize.

> The theory of the Communists may be summed up in the single phrase: abolition of private property.

---

9. Be sure to use a colon to introduce a list.

worth checking The operation in Toronto has supplied Mr. Bomersbach with four luxury cars, two Cadillacs, a Mercedes, and a Jaguar.

(*The Globe and Mail*, April 4, 1987)

PUNCTUATION

revised   The operation in Toronto has supplied Mr.
Bomersbach with four luxury cars: two Cadillacs, a
Mercedes, and a Jaguar.

The Hyphen

This mark may be used to separate two parts of a compound word   hyphen ▪
(e.g. tax-free, hand-operated). Notice that many such word
combinations are only hypohenated if the combination acts as an
adjective:

No change is planned for the short term.

(*Term* acts here as a noun, with the adjective *short* modifying
it.)

This is only a short-term plan.

(Here the compound acts as a single adjective, modifying the
noun *plan*.)

Hyphens are also used to break a word at the end of a line if
there is not enough space.

---

10.   A hyphen should never be used to break up proper nouns,
and should only be used to break up other words when it is placed
between syllables. Any noun beginning with a capital letter (e.g.
Halifax, Mulroney, January, Harriet) is a proper noun.

worth checking   Thomas Huxley coined the word "agnostic" to refer
to someone who does not believe in the existen-·
ce of God, but is not prepared to rule out the
possibility either.

revised   Thomas Huxley coined the word "agnostic" to refer
to someone who does not believe in the existence of
God, but is not prepared to rule out the possibility
either.

Whenever one is uncertain about whether or not to use a hyphen,
the easy solution is to put the entire word on the next line.

The Dash

Dashes are often used in much the same way as parentheses, to set   dash ──
off an idea within a sentence. Dashes, however, call attention to
the set-off idea in a way that parentheses do not:

> Peterborough, Ontario (home of Broadview Press) is a
> pleasant city of 60,000.
>
> Peterborough, Ontario — home of Broadview Press—is a
> pleasant city of 60,000.

A dash may also be used in place of a colon to set off a word or phrase at the end of a sentence:

> He fainted when he heard how much he had won: one million
> dollars.
>
> He fainted when he heard how much he had won — one
> million dollars.

Most typewriters and word processors do not have a dash on the keyboard; in such circumstances use -- (instead of -) to distinguish a dash from a hyphen.

Parentheses

parentheses ( ) Parentheses are used to set off an interruption in the middle of a sentence, or to make a point whch is not part of the main flow of the sentence. They are frequently used to give examples, or to express something in other words using the abbreviation *i.e.*. Example:

> Several world leaders of the 1980s (Deng in China, Reagan in
> the US, etc.) were very old men.

Square brackets are used for parentheses within parentheses, or to show that the words within the parentheses are added by another person.

Apostrophe

apostrophe ' The two main uses of the apostrophe are to show possession (e.g. "Peter's book") and to shorten certain common word combinations (e.g., *can't, shouldn't, he's*)

11. We use contractions frequently in this book, which is addressed to the student, and is relatively informal in its style. Abbreviations or contractions, however, should not be used in formal written work. Use *cannot*, not *can't; did not*, not *don't*; and so on.

worth checking   The experiment wasn't a success, because we'd heated the solution to too high a temperature.

revised   The experiment was not a success, because we had heated the solution to too high a temperature.

The correct placing of the apostrophe to show possession can be a tricky matter. When the noun is singular, the apostrophe must come before the *s* (e.g., *Peter's, George's, Canada's*), whereas when the noun is plural and ends in an *s* already, add the apostrophe after the *s*.

worth checking   We have been asked to dinner by Harriets mother.

revised   We have been asked to dinner by Harriet's mother.

worth checking   His parent's house is filled with antiques.

revised   His parents' house is filled with antiques.

worth checking   All three groups of parents attended their infant's one month pediatric checkup, and observations were made of father's interactions with their infants.

revised   All three groups of parents attended their infants' one month pediatric checkup, and observations were made of fathers' interactions with their infants.

When a singular noun already ends in *s*, authorities differ as to whether or not a second *s* should be added after the apostrophe:

correct   Ray Charles' music has been very influential.

correct   Ray Charles's music has been very influential.

Whichever convention a writer chooses, he should be consistent. And be sure in such cases not to put the apostrophe before the first *s*.

worth checking   Shield's novel is finely, yet delicately constructed. (concerning novelist Carol Shields)

revised   Shields' novel is finely, yet delicately constructed.

[or "Shields's novel")

EXERCISE: Run-on and Incomplete Sentences

Correct each of the following run-on or incomplete sentences.

1) "She's miniature, her hands are about the size of my thumb," he said.   (*Peterborough Examiner*, July 28, 1986)

2) How much influence the book might have, how it compares to other philosophical books, how it fits in with the current trends in philosophy, these are all very hard to determine.

3) It had taken the best part of an hour to put the plan forward, it took another five minutes before I got my answer.

                                        (F.H. Winterbotham, *Ultra Secret*)

4) The informant did not lie to us, he gave us his idea of what the people believed they were doing. (Anthropological essay)

5) Another positive element is that outside firms will bring new or substantially revitalized agricultural resources into use, they will create new employment to operate the production facilities.

6) Suppose an industry which is threatened by foreign competition is one which lies at the very heart of your National defence, where are you then?   (Economist W. Hewins, quoted in the *Atlantic*)

7) Hydrochloric acid is a very dangerous substance. So always handle it very carefully.

8) We occasionally expel Soviet diplomats who get caught with their fingers in briefcases, otherwise the government is more concerned with not rocking diplomatic boats, and in preventing embarrasssing facts about itself from reaching the media—hence our penchant for secrecy.   (columnist Peter Worthington, July 12, 1987)

9) Rookie sidearmer Mark Eichhorn didn't merely have a fine year in the Blue Jay's bullpen in 1986, his campaign ranks at the very top, the very best season in baseball history. (*The Toronto Star*, October 1986)

10) In Heriot, Scotland, a run on the bank isn't a sign of financial instability, it's just the way things always have been and still are, every Thursday from 3:30 to 4:30. The only time the bank is open. The good things in life stay that way. (Advertisement, March 1987)

11) The freedom fighter spun around just in time, then he fired quickly.

12) The issue of political reform—which in essence means democratising the Communist Party—was sidestepped at the central committee meeting last autumn, to do so again will mean burying it.

                                        (*The Guardian*, April 1987)

13) Getting the right price for your residence is not just good luck, it's getting the right agent to help you.   (Advertisement, 1987)

14) At first Bauer had no trouble with the climbing. At 7.8 km. he was second best, only Delgado was faster. (*The Toronto Star*)

15) A major breakthrough came in 1912, two BASF scientists made the world's first synthetic ammonia, which remains the key ingredient in most fertilizer. (*Financial Post*, Nov. 1986)

16) Credit Unions. Where you're more than a customer, you're a shareholder. (Advertisement, *Macleans* Magazine, Sept. 15, 1986)

17) Jones argues that the world is overpopulated. This doesn't make sense because Jones says that the world has too many people but in some areas they don't have enough. (Sociology essay)

18) Do not park illegally, you will be tagged.... Use the GO service, it's still going.... Leave early, it may be a long trip. (*The Toronto Star*, 1989)

19) Television executives don't really care if a show is good or not, so long as it is popular, the larger the audience the better, TV is a mass medium. (Communications essay)

20) When Coca Cola altered its formula it forgot that the biggest ingredient in the brand's success was its traditional place in North American culture. They weren't just tampering with a recipe, they were changing a social institution. (*The Toronto Star*, June 1987)

EXERCISE: Punctuation

Correct the punctuation mistake in each of the following.

1) Mbabane which is the capital of Swaziland, is a small town encircled by hills.

2) "Why did you come here," he asked me.

3) We all rode in my brothers car to Ottawa.

4) There are several reasons why apartheid can't last much longer.

EXERCISE: Punctuation

Punctuate the following passages:

1) what did you think of the election he asked me i was surprised and disappointed that the republicans took so many seats i think they should bring in proportional representation soon he agreed

2) i just dont know what to do said don i cant seem to punctuate properly in english so i keep on writing incomplete sentences and run on sentences mary suggested several things that might help first of all she said you should read each word out loud and notice when you pause also she added remember that the words so and and and should not begin sentences

DIRECT AND INDIRECT SPEECH

Direct Speech

direct speech Direct speech is a written record of the exact words used by the person speaking. The main rules for writing direct speech in English are as follows:

- **The exact words spoken — and no other words — must be surrounded by quotation marks (inverted commas).**
- **A comma should precede a quotation, but other punctuation should be placed inside the quotation marks.**

He said, "I think I can help you."
> (The period after *you* comes before the quotation marks.)
> "Drive slowly," she said, "and be very careful."
> (The comma after *slowly* and period after *careful* both come inside the quotation marks.)

- **With each change in speaker a new paragraph should be begun.** Example:

"Let's go fishing this weekend," Mary suggested. "It should be nice and cool by the water."
"Good idea," agreed Charity. "I'll meet you by the store early Saturday morning."

The most common difficultiues experienced when recording direct speech are as follows:

1. **omission of inverted commas:** This happens particularly frequently at the end of a quotation.

worth checking   She said, "I will try to come to see you tomorrow. Then she left.

revised   She said, "I will try to come to see you tomorrow." Then she left.

2. **placing punctuation outside the inverted commas:**

worth checking	He shouted, "The house is on fire"!
revised	He shouted, "The house is on fire!"

---

3. **including the word "that" before direct speech:** *That* is used before passages of indirect speech, <u>not</u> before passages of direct speech.

worth checking	My brother said that, "I think I have acted stupidly."
revised	My brother said, "I think I have acted stupidly."
or	My brother said that he thought he had acted stupidly.
worth checking	The official indicated that, "we are not prepared to allow galloping inflation."
revised	The official said, "We are not prepared to allow galloping inflation."
or	The official indicated that his government was not prepared to allow galloping inflation.

---

4. In a formal essay, any quotation longer than three lines should normally be indented to set it off from the body of the text. Any quotation of more than two lines of poetry should also be and indented. (Two lines of poetry may be quoted in the body of the text, with a slash (/) to indicate the separation between lines.) Quotations set off from the body of the text should not be preceded or followed by quotation marks.

worth checking

Larkin's last great poem, 'Aubade', is haunted by the

fear of death: "Not to be here, Not to be anywhere, And soon;

nothing more terrible, nothing more true." Some have called

the vision of the poem unremittingly grim, but throughout the

revised

> Larkin's last great poem, 'Aubade', is haunted by the
>
> fear of death:
>
>> Not to be here,
>> Not to be anywhere,
>> And soon; nothing more terrible, nothing more true.
>
> Some have called the vision of the poem unremittingly grim,
>
> but throughout there are moments in which Larkin

See under Sequence of Tenses (161) for other difficulties in using quotation; under Plagiarism (95) for the importance of attributing quotations used in written work; and under Citation (96) for methods used to cite quotations used.

Indirect Speech

indirect speech Indirect speech reports what was said without using the same words that were used by the speaker. The rules for writing indirect speech are as follows:

- **Do not use quotation marks.**

- **Introduce statements with the word** *that*, **and do not put a comma after** *that*. Questions should be introduced with the appropriate question word (*what, why, whether, if, how, when*, etc.)

- **Change first person pronouns and adjectives** (e.g., *I, me, we, us, my, our*) **to third person ones** (*he, she, they, him, her, them, his, hers*, etc.).

> "I am not happy with our team's performance," said Paul.
>
> (direct speech)
>
> Paul said that he was not happy with his team's performance.
>
> (indirect speech)

Second person pronouns must also sometimes be changed.

- **Change the tenses of the verbs to agree with the main verb of the sentence.** Usually this involves moving the verbs one step back into the past from the tenses that were used by the speaker in direct speech. Notice in the above example, for instance, that the present tense *am* has been changed to the past tense *was* in indirect speech. Here are other examples:

"We will do everything we can," he assured me.

He assured me that they would do everything they could.
(*Will* and *can* change to *would* and *could*.)

"You went to school near Brandon, didn't you?" he asked me.

He asked me if I had gone to school near Brandon.
(*Went* changes to *had gone*.)

- **Change expressions having to do with time.** This is made necessary by the changes in verbs discussed above. For example, *today* in direct speech normally becomes *on that day* in indirect speech, *yesterday* becomes *on the day before*, *tomorrow* becomes *the next day* and so on.

The most common problems made when indirect speech is being used are as follows:

---

5.   **confusion of pronouns:** Many students do not remember to change all the necessary pronouns when shifting from direct to indirect speech.

When I met him he said, "You have cheated me."
(direct speech)

worth checking   When I met him he said that you had cheated me.

revised   When I met him he said that I had cheated him.

He will probably say to you, "I am poor. I need money."

worth checking   He will probably tell you that he is poor and that I need money.

revised   He will probably tell you that he is poor and that he needs money.

DIRECT AND INDIRECT SPEECH

6. **verb tenses:** Remember to shift the tenses of the verbs one step back into the past when changing something into indirect speech.

> She said, "I will check my tires tomorrow."

worth checking   She said that she will check her tires the next day.

revised   She said that she would check her tires the next day.

> "Can I go with you later this afternoon?" he asked.

worth checking   He asked if he can go with us later that afternoon.

revised   He asked if he could go with us later that afternoon.

See the section on Plagiarism (95) for a discussion of what sorts of phrases one can safely use without attributing a source. And, for those students who have difficulty in paraphrasing or summarizing without relying too heavily on direct speech (or unconsciously plagiarizing), Janet Giltrow's *Academic Writing* should be of use.

DIRECT AND INDIRECT SPEECH

WRITERS ARE NEVER STATIONERY

DIFFICULTIES WITH MEANING

1. **accept/except:** two words often confused because of their similar sounds. *Accept* is a verb meaning to receive something favourably (or at least without complaining). Examples:

We accepted the invitation to his party.

We will have to accept the decision of the judge.

Except, on the other hand, is a conjunction (or sometimes a preposition) which means *not including* or *but.*

worth checking All the permanent members of the Security Council accept China voted to authorize the use of force against Iraq.

revised All the permanent members of the Security Council except China voted to authorize the use of force against Iraq.

---

2. **adapt/adopt/adept:** To *adapt* something is to alter or modify it; to *adopt* something is to approve it or accept responsibility for it; *adept* is an adjective meaning *skillful.*

worth checking The Board adapted the resolution unanimously.

revised The Board adopted the resolution unanimously.

---

3. **adverse/averse:** *Adverse* means *unfavourable*; *averse* means *reluctant or unwilling.*

worth checking The plane was forced to land because of averse weather conditions.

revised The plane was forced to land because of adverse weather conditions.

---

4. **affect/effect:** *Effect* is normally used as a noun meaning *result.* (It can also be used as a verb meaning *put into effect,* as in "The

changes were effected by the Committee.") *Affect* is a verb meaning *cause a result*.

worth checking	When the acid is added to the solution, there is no visible affect.
revised	When the acid is added to the solution, there is no visible effect.
worth checking	"The issues that effect us here on the reserve are the same issues that effect the whole riding," Mr. Littlechild said. (*The Globe and Mail*)
worth checking	"The issues that affect us here on the reserve are the same issues that affect the whole riding," Mr. Littlechild said.

---

5. **aggravate/annoy/irritate:** *Aggravate* means *make worse*.

e.g.	The injury was aggravated by the bumpy ride in the ambulance.

Aggravate should <u>not</u> be used to mean *annoy* or *irritate*.

worth checking	She found his constant complaints very aggravating.
revised	She found his constant complaints very irritating.

---

6. **alliterate/illiterate:** *Alliterate* is a verb meaning to use consecutively two or more words that begin with the same sound.

e.g.	The big, burly brute was frighteningly fat.

Illiterate is an adjective meaning either *unable to read* or *unable to read and write well*. Those who confuse the two are sometimes, if unfairly, accused of being illiterate.

worth checking	Over forty per cent of the population of Zambia is functionally alliterate.
revised	Over forty per cent of the population of Zambia is functionally illiterate.

---

7. **alternately/alternatively:** *Alternately* means *happening in turn, first one and then the other*; *alternatively* means *instead of*. Be careful as well with the adjectives *alternate* and *alternative*.

worth checking	An alternate method of arriving at this theoretical value would be to divide the difference between the two prices by the number of warrants.
revised	An alternative method of arriving at this theoretical value would be to divide the difference between the two prices by the number of warrants.

(*or* "Another method of...")

worth checking	Professor Beit-Hallahmi seems to have trouble alternatively in reading his own book accurately and in reading my review of it correctly.

(Stanley Hoffman, *The New York Review of Books*)

worth checking	Professor Beit-Hallahmi seems to have trouble alternately in reading his own book accurately and in reading my review of it correctly.

---

8.   **ambiguity:** There are many types of ambiguity; for other references see, for example, under Syntax (70) and Pronoun Problems (198). But see the box on the next page too.

---

9.   **amoral/immoral:** *Amoral* means *not based on moral standards*; *immoral* means *wrong according to moral standards.*

worth checking	The modern reader is unlikely to share Alexander Pope's views as to what constitutes amoral behavior.
revised	The modern reader is unlikely to share Alexander Pope's views as to what constitutes immoral behavior.

---

10.   **anti/ante:** If you remember that *anti* means *against* and *ante* means *before* you are less likely to misspell the many words that have one or the other as a prefix.

worth checking	The UN had many anticedents — most notably the League of Nations formed after World War I.
revised	The UN had many antecedents — most notably the League of Nations formed after World War I.

---

11.   **anxious/eager:** The adjective *anxious* means *uneasy, nervous, worried*; it should not be used in formal writing to mean *eager.*

worth checking	He was anxious to help in any way he could.
revised	He was eager to help in any way he could.

---

12.   **appraise/apprise:** To *appraise* something is to estimate its value; to *apprise* someone of something is to inform him or her of it.

worth checking	The house has been apprised at $120,000.
revised	The house has been appraised at $120,000.

BRITISH LEFT WAFFLES ON FALKLAND ISLANDS

The following are all examples of ambiguity in newspaper headlines. In some cases it may take several moments to decipher the intended meaning.

ambiguity

- TWO PEDESTRIANS STRUCK BY BRIDGE
- MAN HELD OVER GIANT L.A. BRUSH FIRE
- ILLEGAL ALIENS CUT IN HALF BY NEW LAW
- PASSERBY INJURED BY POST OFFICE
- RED TAPE HOLDS UP NEW BRIDGE
- BRITISH LEFT WAFFLES ON FALKLAND ISLANDS
- VILLAGE WATER HOLDS UP WELL
- JERK INJURES NECK, WINS AWARD
- BISHOP THANKS GOD FOR CALLING

(The above examples come courtesy of columnist Bob Swift of Knight-Ridder Newspapers, and of Prof. A. Levey of the University of Calgary.)

And, from the Global News weather telecast, September 13, 1990, the following gem:

- "OUT WEST TOMORROW, THEY'RE GOING TO SEE THE SUN, AS WELL AS ATLANTIC CANADA."

Who ever suggested that Canadians lacked vision?

Pedestrian struck by bridge.

WRITERS ARE NEVER STATIONERY

13. **assure/ensure/insure:** To *assure* someone of something is to tell them with confidence or certainty; to *ensure* (or, in the US, to *insure*) that something will happen is to make sure that it does; to *insure* something is to purchase insurance on it so as to protect yourself in case of loss.

worth checking   Our inventory is ensured for $1,000,000.

revised   Our inventory is insured for $1,000,000.

14. **be/become:** The difference between the two is that *to be* simply indicates existence, while *to become* indicates a process of change. Whenever you are talking about a <u>change</u>, use *become* instead of *be*.

worth checking   I had been quite contented, but as time went by I was unhappy.

revised   I had been quite contented, but as time went by I became unhappy.

worth checking   After years of struggle, Zimbabwe finally was independent in 1980.

revised   After years of struggle, Zimbabwe finally became independent in 1980.

15. **bored, boring:** *Bored* is the opposite of *interested* and *boring* is the opposite of *interesting*. In other words, one is quite likely to be bored when someone reads out what one has already read in the textbook, or when one is watching a football game when the score is 38-0, or when one is doing an uninteresting job. To be bored, however, is <u>not</u> the same as being sad, or depressed, or irritated, or angry.

worth checking   She was so bored with her husband that she tried to kill him.

revised   She was so angry with her husband that she tried to kill him.

16. **can/may:** In formal writing *can* should be used to refer to ability, *may* to refer to permission.

worth checking   He asked if he could leave the room.

(This only makes literal sense if one is talking about an injured person conversing with his doctor.)

revised	He asked if he might leave the room.

---

17. **capital/capitol:** As a noun *capital* can refer to wealth, to the city from which the government operates, to an upper case letter, or to the top of a pillar. It can also be used as an adjective to mean most important or principal. Capitol is much more restricted in its meaning — a specific American legislative building or Roman temple.

worth checking	The prosecution alleged that he had committed a capitol offence.
revised	The prosecution alleged that he had committed a capital offence.

---

18. **careless/uncaring:** *Careless* means *negligent* or *thoughtless*; you can be careless about your work, for example, or careless about your appearance. Do not use *careless*, however, when you want to talk about not caring enough about other people.

worth checking	He acted in a very careless way towards his mother when she was sick.
revised	He acted in a heartless way towards his mother when she was sick.

---

19. **censor/censure:** To *censor* something is to prevent it, or those parts of it that are considered objectionable, from being available to the public. To *censure* someone is to express strong criticism or condemnation.

worth checking	The Senate censored the Attorney-General for his part in the Iran-Contra affair.
revised	The Senate censured the Attorney-General for his part in the Iran-Contra affair.

---

20. **classic/classical:** As an adjective *classic* means of such a high quality that it has lasted or is likely to last for a very long time. *Classical* is used to refer to ancient Greece and Rome, or, particularly when speaking of music, to refer to a traditional style.

worth checking	Sophocles was one of the greatest classic authors; his plays are classical.
revised	Sophocles was one of the greatest classical authors; his plays are acknowledged classics.

WRITERS ARE NEVER STATIONERY

21. **childish/childlike:** The first is a term of abuse, the second a term of praise.

worth checking   Her writing expresses an attractive childish innocence.

revised   Her writing expresses an attractive childlike innocence.

---

22. **collaborate/corroborate:** To *collaborate* is to work together, whereas to *corroborate* is to give supporting evidence.

worth checking   He collaborated her claim that the Americans had corroborated with the Nazi colonel Klaus Barbie.

revised   He corroborated her claim that the Americans had collaborated with the Nazi colonel Klaus Barbie.

---

23. **compliment/complement:** To *compliment* someone is to praise him, and a *compliment* is the praise; to *complement* something is to add to it to make it better or complete, and a *complement* is the number or amount needed to make it complete.

worth checking   None of the divisions had its full compliment of troops.

revised   None of the divisions had its full complement of troops.

worth checking   I paid her the complement of saying that her scarf complimented her dress.

revised   I paid her the compliment of saying that her scarf complemented her dress.

---

24. **comprise/compose:** The whole *comprises* or includes the various parts; the parts *compose* the whole.

worth checking   The British government is comprised of far fewer Ministries than is the Canadian government.

revised   The British government comprises far fewer Ministries than does the Canadian government.

or   The British government is composed of far fewer Ministries than is the Canadian government.

---

25. **conscience/conscious/consciousness:** To be *conscious* is to be awake and aware of what is happening, whereas *conscience* is the

part of your mind that tells us it is right to do some things and wrong to do other things (such as steal or murder). *Conscience* and *consciousness* are both nouns; the adjectives are *conscientious* (aware of what is right and wrong) and *conscious* (aware).

worth checking   She was tempted to steal the chocolate bar, but her conscious told her not to.

revised   She was tempted to steal the chocolate bar, but her conscience told her not to.

---

26. **contemptuous/contemptible:** We are *contemptuous* of anyone or anything we find *contemptible*.

worth checking   The judge called the delinquent's behavior utterly contemptuous.

revised   The judge called the delinquent's behavior utterly contemptible.

---

27. **continual/continuous:** If something is *continuous* it <u>never stops</u>; something *continual* is frequently repeated but not unceasing. The same distinction holds for the adverbs *continually* and *continuously*.

worth checking   He has been phoning me continuously for the past two weeks.

    (Surely he stopped for a bite to eat or a short nap.)

revised   He has been phoning me continually for the past two weeks.

---

28. **copyright:** *Copyright* is the right to make copies of something. The fact that these are often of written material has encouraged a confusion of spelling.

worth checking   The software company plans to copywrite some of the advances it will introduce this year.

    (*Financial Post*, March, 1989)

---

29. **council/counsel; councillor/counsellor:** A *council* is an assembled group of officials, and a *councillor* is a member of that group. *Counsel* is advice, or in the special case of a lawyer, the person offering advice. In other situations the person offering *counsel* is a *counsellor*.

worth checking   The city counsel met to discuss the proposed bylaw.

revised	The city council met to discuss the proposed bylaw.

---

30. credible/credulous: Someone *credulous* (believing) is likely to believe anything, even if it is not *credible* (believable).

worth checking	"Maybe I'm too credible," she said. "I believe everything my husband tells me."
revised	"Maybe I'm too credulous," she said. "I believe everything my husband tells me."

---

31. deduce/deduct: *Deduction* is the noun stemming from both these verbs, which is perhaps why they are sometimes confused. To *deduce* is to draw a conclusion, whereas to *deduct* is to subtract.

worth checking	Sherlock Holmes deducted that Moriarty had committed the crime.
revised	Sherlock Holmes deduced that Moriarty had committed the crime

---

32. degradation/decline: *Degradation* carries the connotation of shame and disgrace; certain military spokespeople have been making every attempt to corrupt it. To *degrade* something is not to reduce it, or downgrade it, or destroy it.

worth checking	Among those units in which women played a combat role there was no degradation in operational effectiveness.
	(CBC news, April 30, 1987)
revised	Among those units in which women played a combat role there was no decline in operational effectiveness.
or	...there was no reduction in operational effectiveness.
worth checking	According to US authorities, the Iraqi threat has now been significantly degraded.
	(Global news, January 24, 1991)
revised	According to US authorities, the Iraqi threat has now been significantly reduced.

---

33. definite/definitive: If something is *definite* then there is no uncertainty about it; a *definitive* version of something fixes it in its final or permanent form — just as a dictionary definition attempts to fix the meaning of a word. Often a sentence is better with neither of these words.

worth checking	Glenn Gould's recording of Bach's <u>Brandenburg Concertos</u> is often thought of as the definite modern version.
revised	Glenn Gould's recording of Bach's <u>Brandenburg Concertos</u> is often thought of as the definitive modern version.
worth checking	Once we have completed our caucus discussion I will be making a very definitive statement.
revised	Once we have completed our caucus discussion I will be making a statement.
or	Once we have completed our caucus discussion I will have something definite to say.

---

34. **deprecate/depreciate:** To *deprecate* something is to suggest that it is not valuable or worthy of praise; something that *depreciates* loses its value.

worth checking	Robert Stanfield is very self-depreciating man.
revised	Robert Stanfield is a very self-deprecating man.

---

35. **discrete/discreet:** *Discrete* means separate or distinct, whereas *discreet* means prudent and tactful; unwilling to give away secrets.

worth checking	Johnny Carson is not renowned for being discrete.
revised	Johnny Carson is not renowned for being discreet.

---

36. **disinterested/uninterested:** A *disinterested* person is unbiased; uninfluenced by self-interest, especially of a monetary sort. It is thus quite possible for a person who is entirely *disinterested* in a particular matter to be completely fascinated by it. If one is *uninterested* in something, on the other hand, one is bored by it.

worth checking	He was so disinterested in the game that he left after the fifth inning with the score at 2-2.
revised	He was so uninterested in the game that he left after the fifth inning with the score at 2-2.
worth checking	It was vintage Reagan: stumbling over his text, unsure of his facts, disinterested in the topic at hand.

(*The Toronto Star*, Nov. 15, 1987)

WRITERS ARE NEVER STATIONERY

revised   It was vintage Reagan: stumbling over his text,
                 unsure of his facts, uninterested in the topic at hand.

---

37. **dissociate/disassociate:** There is no need for the extra
syllable.

worth checking T.S. Eliot speaks of the disassociation of sensibility
                  that began in the seventeenth century.

revised   T.S. Eliot speaks of the dissociation of sensibility
                  that began in the seventeenth century.

---

38. **disorient/disorientate:** Both are considered correct by many
authorities, but the extra syllable of the second grates on the ear.

Poor   I was entirely disorientated in the darkness.

Better   I was entirely disoriented in the darkness.

---

39. **dissemble/disassemble:** To *dissemble* is to disguise your
feelings — a mild form of lying. To *disassemble* is to take apart.

worth checking For the test we are required to first assemble and
                  then dissemble a V-8 engine.

revised   For the test we are required to first assemble and
                  then disassemble a V-8 engine.

---

40. **distinct/distinctive:** *Distinct* means able to be seen or
perceived clearly; easily distinguishable from those around it.
Distinctive means *unusual*; not commonly found. There is a similar
contrast between the adverbs *distinctly* and *distinctively* and the
nouns *distinction* and *distinctiveness*.

worth checking I distinctively heard the sound of a car engine.

revised   I distinctly heard the sound of a car engine.

---

41. **economic/economical:** *Economic* means pertaining to
economics, or sufficient to allow a reasonable return for the
amount of money or effort put in. *Economical* is a word applied to
people, which means thrifty. The difference applies as well to
uneconomic and *uneconomical*.

worth checking The controversy over whether it's economical to
                  develop Hibernia continues.

                  (Robert Skully, *Venture*, July 18, 1990)

         [The Hibernia project will cost billions of dollars.]

WRITERS ARE NEVER STATIONERY

revised   The controversy over whether it's economic to develop Hibernia continues.

42.   **effective/efficacious/effectual/efficient:** *Effective, efficiacious and effectual* all mean *sufficient to produce the desired effect. Efficacious*, however, applies only to things: a person cannot be efficacious. *Effectual* was once applied only to actions, but is now sometimes applied to people as well. *Effective* can apply to actions or people, and has an added connotation: producing results with little waste of money or effort. Thus a promotional campaign to persuade people to buy a product by giving away free samples to every man, woman and child in the country might be effective, but it would certainly not be efficient; a good deal of waste would be involved. The same difference applies to the nouns *effectiveness* and *efficiency. (Efficacy* is a rather pretentious noun that is usually best avoided.)

wrth checking   The Board wants to increase the efficacy of the machinery we use.

revised   The Board wants to increase the efficiency of the machinery we use.

WRITERS ARE NEVER STATIONERY

Poor	It would not be efficacious to launch a direct mail campaign with a product of this sort.
Better	It would not be effective to launch a direct mail campaign with a product of this sort.

---

43. **eligible/illegible:** One is *eligible* to be considered for a job or membership in an organization if one meets the standard set for applicants. One of the requirements might be that one's handwriting not be *illegible*.

worth checking	He regretted that I was not illegible to join his Club.
revised	He regretted that I was not eligible to join his Club.

---

44. **elicit/illicit:** *Elicit* is a verb; one *elicits* information about something. *Illicit* is an adjective meaning *illegal* or *not approved*.

worth checking	She has been dealing in elicit drugs for some time.
revised	She has been dealing in illicit drugs for some time.

---

45. **emigrant/immigrant:** To *migrate* is to move from one place to another. The prefix *ex*, shortened to *e*, means *out of*, so an *emigrant* from a country is someone who is moving out of it. The prefix *in* or *im* means *in* or *into*, so an *immigrant* to a country is someone moving into it. Similarly, *emigration* is the movement of people out of a country, while *immigration* is the movement of people into a country. Notice the spelling in both cases; e-migrant (one *m*), im-migrant (two *m*s)

worth checking	More than 100,000 emigrants entered America last year.
revised	More than 100,000 immigrants entered America last year.

---

46. **eminent/imminent/immanent:** A person is *eminent* if she is well-known and well-respected; an event is *imminent* if it is about to happen; a quality (or a god) is *immanent* if it pervades everything.

worth checking	Even those working for the Ontario NDP in the 1990 campaign did not believe that a majority victory was immanent.

WRITERS ARE NEVER STATIONERY

revised	Even those working for the Ontario NDP in the 1990 campaign did not believe that a majority victory was imminent.

47. enormity/enormousness: Originally the adjective *enormous* simply meant deviating from the norm, but it had come by the early nineteenth century to also mean *abnormal, monstrous,* or *extraordinarily wicked.* Today the only meaning is of course *vast* in size or quantity, but the connotation of wickedness is preserved in the noun *enormity.* We may speak of the *enormity* of a person's crime, but if we want a noun to express vast size we should use *enormousness* or *vastness.*

worth checking	What most impresses visitors to the Grand Canyon is usually its sheer enormity.
revised	What most impresses visitors to the Grand Canyon is its sheer enormousness.
Better	What most impresses visitors to the Grand Canyon is its vastness.

48. epithet/epigraph/epitaph/epigram: four words often confused. Here are their meanings:

Epithet	an adjective or short phrase describing someone (*"The Golden Brett,* the epithet often used to discribe Brett Hull, involves an allusion to the nickname of his famous father.")
Epigraph	an inscription, especially one placed upon a building, tomb or statue to indicate its name or purpose
Epitaph	words describing a dead person, often the words inscribed on the tomb
Epigram	a short, witty or pointed saying
worth checking	His epigram will read, "A good man lies here."
revised	His epitaph will read, "A good man lies here."

49. explicit/implicit: If something is *explicit* it is *unfolded* — stated in precise terms, not merely suggested or implied. Something that is *implicit* is *folded in* — not stated overtly. By extension *implicit* has also come to mean complete or absolute in expressions such as *implicit trust* (i.e. trust so complete that it does not have to be put into words).

worth checking	I told you implicitly to have the report on my desk first thing this morning.
revised	I told you explicitly to have the report on my desk first thing in the morning.

50. **financial/fiscal/monetary/economic:** The terms used in personal, business and government finance are not always the same. Here are four that are often not clearly understood:

Financial	having to do with finance or the handling of money
Fiscal	having to do with public revenue
Monetary	having to do with the currency of a country (Only in very limited circumstances, such as the expression *monetary value*, can monetary have the more general meaning of having to do with money.)
Economic	having to do with the economy. Thus a government's *economic* program embraces both *fiscal* and *monetary* policies.
worth checking	My brother is a nice person, but he has no monetary ability.
revised	My brother is a nice person, but he has no financial ability.

51. **finish/be finished/have finished:** In slang usage to *be finished* means to be at the end of one's life or career ("If Andre Dawson's

knee is seriously injured again, he is finished"). This special use should not be extended to the verb *finish* in its normal meaning.

| *worth checking* | Are you finished your work? |
| *revised* | Have you finished your work? |

---

52. **flout/flaunt:** To *flout* is to disobey or show disrespect for; to *flaunt* is to display very openly.

| *worth checking* | The students flaunted the authority of the University administration by refusing to attend classes. |
| *revised* | The students flouted the authority of the University administration by refusing to attend classes. |

---

53. **formerly/formally:** The similarity of sound often leads to confusion.

worth checking	In August Mr. Laurel formerly broke with Mrs. Aquino.
	(*The Globe and Mail*, Feb. 9, 1989)
revised	In August Mr. Laurel formally broke with Mrs. Aquino.

---

54. **fortunate/fortuitous:** *Fortunate* means lucky; *fortuitous* means happening by chance.

| *worth checking* | This combination of circumstances is not a fortuitous one for our company; we shall have to expect reduced sales in the coming year. |
| *revised* | This combination of circumstances is not a fortunate one for our company; we shall have to expect reduced sales in the coming year. |

---

55. **forward/foreword:** You find a *foreword* before the other words in a book.

| *worth checking* | The author admits in a forward that his research was not comprehensive. |
| *revised* | The author admits in a foreword that his research was not comprehensive. |

---

56. **founder/flounder:** As a verb, *founder* means to get into difficulty; to stumble or fall, to sink (when speaking of a ship), or to fail (when speaking of a plan). To *flounder* is to move clumsily or with difficulty, or to become confused in an effort to do something.

worth checking	He foundered about in a hopeless attempt to solve the problem.
revised	He floundered about in a hopeless attempt to solve the problem.

---

57. further/farther: *Farther* refers only to physical distance.

worth checking	Eisenhower argued that the plan should receive farther study.
revised	Eisenhower argued that the plan should receive further study.

---

58. historic/historical: *Historic* means of sufficient importance that it is likely to become famous in history; *historical* means having to do with history (historical research, historical scholarship, etc.).

worth checking	We are gathered here for a historical occasion – the opening of the city's first sewage treatment plant.
revised	We are gathered here for a historic occasion – the opening of the city's first sewage treatment plant.

---

59. hopefully: one of the greatest causes of disagreement among grammarians. Traditionalists argue that the correct meaning of the adverb *hopefully* is *filled with hope,* and that the use of the word to mean *it is to be hoped that* is therefore incorrect. On the other side it is plausibly argued that many adverbs can function as independent comments at the beginning of a sentence. ("Finally, let me point out that..."; "Clearly, we have much to do if we are to..."; "Obviously, we will....") Why should *hopefully* be treated differently? Why indeed? Using *hopefully* for this purpose may not make for beautiful English, but it should not be regarded as a grievous error.

Poor	Hopefully, it will be possible to finish before tomorrow.

(As usually happens, "hopefully" is here used with the passive, making for a wordy sentence.)

Better	We hope we can finish before tomorrow.

Poor	Hopefully, we will arrive before dusk.

(This sentence should be rewritten in order to ensure that the sentence does not suggest the meaning, "we will arrive filled with hope before dusk.")

Better	I hope we will arrive before dusk.

WRITERS ARE NEVER STATIONERY

60. **human/humane:** Until the eighteenth century there was no distinction made between the two in either meaning or pronunciation; they were simply alternative ways of spelling the same word. In recent centuries *humane* has come to be used to refer exclusively to the more attractive human qualities – kindness, compassion and so forth.

worth checking   Their group is campaigning for the human treatment of animals.

revised   Their group is campaigning for the humane treatment of animals.

61. **illusion/allusion:** An *allusion* is an indirect reference to something; an *illusion* is something falsely supposed to exist.

worth checking   Joyce is making an illusion in this passage to a Shakespearean sonnet.

revised   Joyce is making an allusion in this passage to a Shakespearean sonnet.

62. **imply/infer:** To *imply* something is to suggest it without stating it directly; the other person will have to *infer* your meaning. It may be a comfort to the many who have confused the two to know that the mistake goes back at least as far as Milton:

worth checking   Great or Bright infers not Excellence.

(*Paradise Lost* viii, 91)

revised   Great or Bright implies not Excellence.

(The fact that a thing is great or bright does not imply that it is also excellent.)

worth checking   I implied from his tone that he disliked our plan.

revised   I inferred from his tone that he disliked our plan.

63. **in/into:** The difference is that *into* is used to indicate movement from outside to inside.

worth checking   Writers in Canada and Britain expressed sympathy for Mr. Rushdie's decision, although some said he was caving into pressure. (*The Globe and Mail*, Dec. 30, 1990)

revised

Writers in Canada and Britain expressed sympathy
for Mr. Rushdie's decision, although some said he
was caving in to pressure.

---

64. **incidents/incidence:** *Incidents* is the plural of *incident* (happening), whereas *incidence* is a singular noun meaning the rate at which something occurs.

worth checking   The incidents of lung cancer is much lower in
                    Zambia than it is in North America.

revised   The incidence of lung cancer is much lower in
                    Zambia than it is in North America.

---

65. **ingenious/ingenuous:** *Ingenious* means clever; *ingenuous* means pleasantly open and unsophisticated.

worth checking   Her manner was completely ingenious; I cannot
                    imagine she was trying to deceive us.

revised   Her manner was completely ingenuous; I cannot
                    imagine she was trying to deceive us.

---

66. **innumerable:** so numerous that it is impossible to count; do not use as synonym for *many*.

worth checking   Scholars have advanced innumerable explanations
                    for the dinosaurs' disappearance.

revised   Scholars have advanced many explanations for the
                    dinosaurs' disappearance.

---

67. **insist/persist:** To *insist* (that something be done, *or* on doing something) is to express yourself very forcefully. To *persist* in doing something is to keep on doing it, usually despite some difficulty or opposition.

worth checking   Even after he had been convicted of the crime, he
                    persisted that he was innocent.

revised   Even after he had been convicted of the crime, he
                    insisted that he was innocent.

---

68. **instinctive/instinctual:** There is no difference in meaning; it is thus better to stay with the older (and more pleasant sounding) *instinctive*.

Poor

	Biologists disagree as to what constitutes instinctual behavior.
Better	Biologists disagree as to what constitutes instinctive behavior

---

69. judicial/judicious: *Judicial* means having to do with law courts and the administration of justice. *Judicious* means having good judgement.

worth checking	He made one or two judicial comments about the quality of the production.
revised	He made one or two judicious comments about the quality of the production.

---

70. know: When one *knows* something, that piece of knowledge has been in one's mind for some time. The process of gathering or acquiring knowledge is called *discovering*.

worth checking	Although I noticed the new employee on Monday, I did not know her name until today.
revised	Although I noticed the new employee on Monday, I did not discover her name until today.

---

71. later/latter: *Later* means afterwards in time, whereas the *latter* is the last mentioned (of two things).

worth checking	I looked up the battle of Stalingrad in both the *World Book* and the *Encyclopaedia Britannica*. The later provided much more information.
revised	I looked up the battle of Stalingrad in both the *World Book* and the *Encyclopaedia Britannica*. The latter provided much more information.

---

72. laudable/laudatory: *Laudable* means worthy of praise; *laudatory* means expressing praise.

worth checking	His efforts to combat poverty are very laudatory.
revised	His efforts to combat poverty are very laudable.

---

73. liable/likely: *liable* means obliged by law ("You will be liable for any damage caused when you are driving the vehicle"), or in danger of doing or suffering from something undesirable ("That chimney is liable to fall"). Since in the latter meaning *likely* can often be used in place of *liable,* it is often assumed that there is really no distinction between the two. Careful writers, however, do not use *liable* unless they are referring to possible consequences of an <u>undesirable</u> nature.

Poor   Last Sunday Clearwater won the Colonial Open.
He's liable to win again before the Canadian Open.

(*The Globe and Mail,* June 1987)

Better   Last Sunday Clearwater won the Colonial Open.
He's likely to win again before the Canadian Open.

---

74.   **lightning/lightening:** One is not likely to see the sky *lightening* until after the thunder and *lightning* are over.

worth checking   Three of the men were severely injured by the lightening.

revised   Three of the men were severely injured by the lightning.

---

75.   **literally:** *Literal* means by the letter — in exact agreement with what is said or written. A literal meaning is thus the opposite of a figurative or metaphorical meaning. Do not use the adverb *literally* simply to emphasise something.

worth checking   As silviculturalists we are — literally — babes in the woods.

(Ken Drushka, *Stumped: The Forest Industry in Transition*)

[Silviculturalists may be literally in the woods, but they are not literally babes.]

WRITERS ARE NEVER STATIONERY

[Silviculturalists may be literally in the woods, but they are not literally babes.]

revised   As silviculturalists we are babes in the woods.

---

76. **make/allow/make possible:** To *make* someone do something is to force them to do it (often against their wishes); to *allow* someone to do something is to permit them or *make it possible* for them to do something that they want to do.

worth checking The government is building a new wing to the hospital; this will make many more people come for treatment.

revised   The government is building a new wing to the hospital; this will allow many more people to come for treatment.

or   The government is building a new wing to the hospital; this will make it possible for many more people to come for treatment.

---

77. **mitigate/militate:** To *mitigate* something is to make it less harsh or severe; thus *mitigating* circumstances are those that make a criminal offence less serious. To *militate* against something is to act as a strong influence against it.

worth checking The natural history orientation of early anthropology also mitigated against studies of change.

        (Bruce G. Trigger in *Natives and Newcomers*)

revised   The natural history orientation of early anthropology also militated against studies of change.

---

78. **momentarily:** *Momentarily* means *lasting only a moment* ("He was *momentarily* confused"). Common usage also allows the word to mean *in a moment* or *soon*; in formal writing it is best to avoid this use.

Poor   Ms. Billings has informed me that she will join us momentarily.

Better   Ms. Billings told me that she will join us soon.

---

79. **need/want:** The verb *need* conveys the idea that it would be difficult or impossible for you to do without the needed thing. If

one really *needs* a television. Be careful too not to commit to paper the slang use of *need to* for *should.*

worth checking	I need to marry a woman who is very beautiful, very intelligent, very kind and very rich.
revised	I want to marry a woman who is very beautiful, very intelligent, very kind and very rich.
worth checking	The government needs to improve the roads in this area.
revised	The government should improve the roads in this area.

---

80. **of/have:** The difference in meaning is obvious, but the similarity in sound consistently leads people to write sentences involving such meaningless expressions as *should of, would of, could of, may of, might of* and *must of.*

worth checking	The experiment would of succeeded if the solution had been prepared correctly.
revised	The experiment would have succeeded if the solution had been prepared correctly.
worth checking	Hitler believed that Rommel should of been able to defeat Montgomery at El Alamein.
revised	Hitler believed that Rommel should have been able to defeat Montgomery at El Alamein.

---

81. **other:** if one uses the words <u>the</u> *other* it suggests that the thing or person one is about to mention is the <u>only</u> *other* one is going to write about. If there are several *others* to be mentioned, *another* is the word to choose.

worth checking	One reason why Germany lost the Second World War was that she underestimated the importance of keeping the United States out of the conflict. The other reason was that her intelligence network was inferior to that of the Allies. Moreover, Hitler's decision to invade Russia was a disastrous mistake.

(Here the use of *the other* in the second sentence leads the reader to believe this is the <u>only</u> other reason. When a third reason is mentioned in the next sentence, the reader is taken by surprise.)

WRITERS ARE NEVER STATIONERY

revised One reason why Germany lost the Second World War was that she underestimated the importance of keeping the United States out of the conflict. Another reason was that her intelligence network was inferior to that of the Allies. Moreover, Hitler's decision to invade Russia was a disastrous mistake.

---

82. **our/are:** Like the substitution of *of* for *have* (307), the confusion of *our* and *are* should never survive the rough draft stage. Unfortunately, it very frequently does.

worth checking Almost all are time is spent together.

revised Almost all our time is spent together.

---

83. **partake/participate:** *Partake* refers to things (especially food and drink), *participate* to activities.

worth checking The Governor General made a brief appearance, but did not partake in the festivities.

revised The Governor General made a brief appearance, but did not participate in the festivities.

---

84. **per cent/percentage:** If you use *per cent,* you must give the number. Otherwise, use *percentage.*

worth checking The per cent of people surveyed who reported any change of opinion was very small.

revised The percentage of people surveyed who reported any change of opinion was very small.

or Only six per cent of the people surveyed reported any change of opinion.

---

85. **persecute/prosecute:** To *persecute* someone is to treat them in a harsh and unfair manner, especially because of their political or religious beliefs. To *prosecute* someone is to take legal action against them in the belief that they have committed a crime.

worth checking Catholics began to be prosecuted in England in the sixteenth century.

revised Catholics began to be persecuted in England in the sixteenth century.

---

86. **persuade:** To *persuade* someone of something is to make them believe that it is true. To persuade them to do something is to lead

them, through what one says, to do the desired thing. If one does not succeed in making them believe or do what one wants, then one has not persuaded or convinced them, but only <u>tried</u> to persuade them.

worth checking After all Portia's persuasion Shylock still refuses to change his mind.

revised After all Portia's attempts to persuade him, Shylock still refuses to change his mind.

---

87. **phase:** an overused word; remember that it refers only to time; it should not be thought of as a synonym for *part*.

worth checking The federal bureaucracy has a bewildering number of phases.

revised The federal bureaucracy has a bewildering number of levels and departments.

---

88. **pore/pour:** As *The Globe and Mail Style Book* puts it, one should "not write of someone pouring over a book unless the tome in question is getting wet."

worth checking After pouring over the evidence, the committee could find no evidence of wrongdoing.

revised After poring over the evidence, the committee could find no evidence of wrongdoing.

---

89. **practical/practicable:** *Practical* means suitable for use, or involving activity rather than theory. *Practicable* means able to be done. Changing the railway system back to steam locomotives would be *practicable* but extremely *impractical.* In most cases *practical* is the word the writer wants; excessive use of *practicable* will make writing sound pretentious rather than important.

worth checking We do not feel that the construction of a new facility would be practicable at this time.

revised It would not be practical to construct a new facility now.

---

90. **presently:** The subject of much disagreement among grammarians; should *presently* be restricted to its original meaning of *soon*, or should common usage of the word to mean *now* be

allowed to spread unopposed? Traditionalists argue that the acceptance of both meanings encourages ambiguity, but in fact the verb tense usually makes clear whether the speaker means *soon* or *now* ("I will be there presently", "I am presently working on a large project", etc.). Perhaps the best solution is to avoid the rather pompous *presently* altogether, and stick to those fine Anglo-Saxon words *soon* and *now*.

Poor	I am seeing Mr. Jones presently.
Better	I am seeing Mr. Jones now.
or	I will be seeing Mr. Jones soon.

91. **prove:** To *prove* something is to eliminate any doubt whatsoever as to its truth. Outside of Mathematics, Science or philosophical logic *proof* is rarely possible; what you are doing in a History or Political Science or English essay is presenting an argument, not a *proof*. Be cautious in the claims you make in formal writing.

worth checking	The following passage proves that T.S. Eliot was anti-Semitic.
revised	The following passage strongly suggests that T.S. Eliot was anti-Semitic.

92. **proposition/proposal:** The only formally correct meaning of *proposition* is a statement that expresses an idea, as in "This country is dedicated to the proposition that all men are created equal." It is better not to use it to mean *proposal*.

Poor	The department has put forward a proposition for increasing sales.
Better	The department has put forward a proposal for increasing sales.

93. **raise/rise:** *raise* means to lift; *rise* means to come up.

worth checking	They rose the curtain at 8 o'clock.
revised	They raised the curtain at 8 o'clock.
or	The curtain rose at 8 o'clock.

94. **rational/rationale:** *rational* is an adjective meaning logical or sensible. A *rationale* is an explanation for something.

WRITERS ARE NEVER STATIONERY

worth checking	The underlying rational for the proliferation of soaps and detergents is not to make our skin or clothes any cleaner, but to increase the profits of the manufacturers.
revised	The underlying rationale for the proliferation of soaps and detergents is not to make our skin or clothes any cleaner, but to increase the profits of the manufacturers.

---

95. ravish/ravage: *Ravish* has two quite unrelated meanings — to rape, or to fill with delight. To *ravage* is to damage or destroy.

worth checking	The tree had been ravished by insects.
revised	The tree had been ravaged by insects.

---

96. real/genuine: The basic meaning of *real* is *existing*; the opposite of *fake* or *forged* is *genuine*.

Poor	The buyer had thought the painting was a Cézanne, but he soon discovered it was not real.
Better	The buyer had thought the painting was a Cézanne, but he soon discovered it was not genuine.

---

97. respectively/respectfully: *Respectively* means in the order mentioned; *respectfully* means done with respect.

worth checking	San Diego, Chicago, and Miami were, respectfully, the three best teams in the NFL last season.
revised	San Diego, Chicago, and Miami were, respectively, the three best teams in the NFL last season.

---

98. sensory/sensuous/sensual: Advertising and pornography have dulled the distinction among these three adjectives. The meanings of *sensory* and *sensuous* are similar — *sensual* is the sexy one:

Sensory	having to do with the senses
Sensuous	having to do with the senses, or appealing to the senses
Sensual	offering physical pleasure, especially of a sexual sort

worth checking	Boswell suggested they go to a house of ill repute, but Johnson had no desire for sensuous pleasures.
revised	Boswell suggested they go to a house of ill repute, but Johnson had no desire for sensual pleasures.

WRITERS ARE NEVER STATIONERY

---

99. **set/sit:** *Set* means to place something somewhere.

worth checking	I could remember everything, but I had difficulty sitting it down on paper.
revised	I could remember everything, but I had difficulty setting it down on paper.
worth checking	He asked me to set down on the couch.
revised	He asked me to sit down on the couch.

---

100. **simple/simplistic:** *Simplistic* is a derogatory word meaning *too simple* or *excessively simplified*.

worth checking	The questions were so simplistic that I was able to answer all but one correctly.
revised	The questions were so simple that I was able to answer all but one correctly.

---

101. **somehow:** *Somehow* means *by some method* ("Somehow I must repair my car so that I can arrive in time for my appointment"). It does not mean *in some ways, to some extent,* or *somewhat.*

worth checking	His brother is somehow mentally disturbed.
revised	His brother is mentally disturbed in some way.
or	His brother is somewhat disturbed mentally.

---

102. **stationary/stationery:** *Stationary* means *not moving*; *stationery* is what you write on.

worth checking	As Mr. Blakeney remembered it, Lord Taylor "would always park his car in the no-parking zone outside the Bessborough Hotel, leaving House of Lords stationary on the windshield."
	(*The Toronto Star*, June 1987)
revised	As Mr. Blakeney remembered it, Lord Taylor "would always park his car in the no-parking zone outside the Bessborough Hotel, leaving House of Lords stationery on the windshield."

---

103. **stimulant/stimulus:** *Stimulus* (plural *stimuli*) is the more general word for anything that produces a reaction; *stimulant* normally refers to a drink or drug that has a *stimulating* effect.

WRITERS ARE NEVER STATIONERY

worth checking	The shocks were intended to act as stimulants to the rats that we used as subjects for the experiment.
revised	The shocks were intended to act as stimuli to the rats that we used as subjects for the experiment.

---

104. **tack/tact:** *Tack* is a sailing term; a different tack means a different direction relative to the wind. *Tact* is skill in saying or doing the right or polite thing.

worth checking	We will have to exercise all our tack in the coming negotiations.
revised	We will have to exercise all our tact in the coming negotiations.

---

105. **than/that:** The difference in meaning is obvious, but slips of the pen or typewriter are too often allowed to make it to the final draft.

worth checking	It turns out that the company needs more money that we had expected.
revised	It turns out that the company needs more money than we had expected.

---

106. **they/their/there/they're:** Four words that are confused perhaps more frequently than any others. *They* is a pronoun used to

replace any plural noun (e.g., books, people, numbers). *There* can be used to mean *in* (or *at*) *that place*, or can be used as an introductory word before various forms of the verb *to be* (*There is, There had been*, etc.). *Their* is a possessive adjective meaning *belonging to them.* Beware in particular of substituting *they* for *there*:

| *worth checking* | They were many people in the crowd. |
| *revised* | There were many people in the crowd. |

The easiest way to check whether one is making this mistake is to ask if it would make sense to replace *they* with a noun. In the above sentence, for example, it would obviously be absurd to say, "The people were many people in the crowd."

The confusion of *they, there,* and *their* is the sort of mistake that all writers are able to catch if they check their work carefully before writing the final draft.

worth checking	Soviet defenceman Mikhail Tatarinov is considered to be there enforcer.
	(*Peterborough Examiner*, Feb. 12 1987)
revised	Soviet defenceman Mikhail Tatarinov is considered to be their enforcer.
worth checking	There all going to the dance this Saturday.
revised	They're all going to the dance this Saturday.
or	They are all going to the dance this Saturday.

---

282. tiring/tiresome: Something that is *tiring* makes you feel *tired*, though you may have enjoyed it very much. Something that is *tiresome* is tedious and unpleasant.

| *worth checking* | Although it is tiresome for him, my father likes to play tennis at least twice a week. |
| *revised* | Although it is tiring for him, my father likes to play tennis at least twice a week. |

---

107. to/towards: *Towards* indicates motion.

| *worth checking* | The deer moved slowly to me through the tall grass. |
| *revised* | The deer moved slowly towards me through the tall grass. |

WRITERS ARE NEVER STATIONERY

108. to/too/two: *Too* can mean *also* or be used (*too many, too heavy*) to indicate excess; *two* is of course the number.

worth checking   She seemed to feel that there was to much to do.

revised   She seemed to feel that there was too much to do.

---

109. unexceptional/unexceptionable: *Unexceptional* means ordinary, not an exception; *unexceptionable* means you do not object (or take exception) to the thing or person in question.

worth checking   One way Reagan pays for this is in the confusion and controversy that surround the unexceptional White House plan to reflag 11 Kuwaiti tankers with the Stars and Stripes. It is a modest proposal that in itself should not cause the handwringing now being observed on Capitol Hill.

(*Washington Post*, July 20 1987)

(The plan to reflag the tankers clearly <u>was</u> an exception; the U.S. had not done anything similar for years. What the writer means to say is that the plan is unexceptionable — that no one should have any objection to it.)

revised   One way Reagan pays for this is in the confusion and controversy that surround the unexceptionable White House plan to reflag 11 Kuwaiti tankers with the Stars and Stripes. It is a modest proposal that...

---

110. unique/universal/perfect/complete/correct: None of these can be a matter of degree. Something is either unique or not unique, perfect or imperfect, and so on.

worth checking   Fathers may have a relatively unique contribution to make to family functioning and the development of the child.

revised   Fathers may have a unique contribution to make to family functioning and the development of the child.

---

111. valid/true/accurate: An *accurate* statement is one that is factually correct. A combination of *accurate* facts may not always give a *true* picture, however. For example, the statement that former Canadian Prime Minister Mackenzie King often visited prostitutes is entirely *accurate*, but gives a false impression; in fact King visited prostitutes to try to convince them of the error of their ways, not to use their services. *Valid* has become so overused and fuzzy in its meaning that it is best avoided. Properly used it can mean *legally acceptable,* or *sound in reasoning.* Usually it is best to use *accurate* or *true,* or *well-founded.*

Poor	Churchill's fear that the Nazis would become a threat to the rest of Europe turned out to be valid.
Better	Churchill's fear that the Nazis would become a threat to the rest of Europe turned out to be well-founded.

---

112. **vein/vain:** *Veins* run through your body; to be *vain* is to be conceited; an effort that brings no results is in *vain.*

worth checking	Shakespeare portrays Sir John Oldcastle – or Falstaff, as he is usually known – as vein and irresponsible but immensely amusing and likeable.
revised	Shakespeare portrays Sir John Oldcastle – or Falstaff, as he is usually known – as vain and irresponsible but immensely amusing and likeable.

---

113. **verbal/oral:** *Oral* means spoken rather than written, whereas *verbal* means having to do with words. A person who is unable to speak may have a high level of *verbal* skill.

worth checking	I can write well enough, but I have difficulty in expressing ideas verbally.
revised	I can write well enough, but I have difficulty in expressing ideas orally.

---

114. **were/where:** *Were* is of course a past tense form of the verb *to be,* while *where* refers to a place.

worth checking	This is the place were Dante met Beatrice.
revised	This is the place where Dante met Beatrice.

EXERCISE: Difficulties with Meaning

Choose the correct word or expression.

1) Do you think your action will have any _____ [effect/affect]?

2) The shopkeeper did not want to _____ [accept/except] a check.

3) The tape recording _____ [compliments/complements] the study guide.

4) The _____ [council/counsel] deliberated for seven hours before reaching a decision.

5) One approach is to break down the questionnaire results by age and sex. _____ [Alternately/Alternatively], we may study the variations among different income levels.

6) He is very conservative and would never wish to _____ [flout/flaunt] the university administration.

7) The stage can be _____ [dissembled/disassembled] within two hours.

8) The two elements must be seen as entirely _____ [discreet/discrete].

9) She told me _____ [definitely/definitively] that she would not support the motion.

10) Britain is considering whether or not to restore _____ [capitol/capital] punishment.

11) The majority believe that theft is _____ [amoral/immoral] in any circumstances.

12) No politician is _____ [adverse/averse] to publicity.

13) They were eager to declare the amount as a _____ capitol/capital gain.

14) The company always purchases _____ [stationary/stationery] in bulk.

15) The book is laden with a preface, a _____ [foreword/forward] and an introduction.

16) The spokesman _____ [inferred/implied] that the withdrawal would be made, but he would not state it _____ [explicitly/implicitly].

17) Many non-religious people believe that the Ten Commandments are good _____ [principals/principles] to follow.

18) The judge felt that the guilt of the accused was _____ [mitigated/militated] by the manner in which he had been provoked; the victim was his supervisor at work, and had been _____ [persecuting/prosecuting] him for years.

WRITERS ARE NEVER STATIONERY

EXERCISE: *Of* and *Have*

Fill in either *of* or *have*:

1) I would _____ come if I had been able to.
2) I should _____ done more work at the beginning _____ the term.
3) The tragedy could not _____ been prevented.
4) It was very kind _____ you to write.

EXERCISE: They, There, Their

Fill in the correct choice.

1) The boys told _____ mother that they would be late.
2) _____ were many people at the political rally.
3) _____ are very happy to live in such a nice house.
4) _____ are a great many machines in that factory.
5) _____ car is old, but _____ keep it in good condition.
6) _____ are many students who have not yet handed in _____ work.

SPELLING

Spelling and Sound

Many spelling mistakes result from similarities in the pronunciation of words with very different meanings. These are covered in the list below. Other words that cause spelling difficulties are listed separately.

spelling

absent (adjective)	absence (noun)
absorb	absorption
accept	except
access (entry)	excess (too much)
advice (noun)	advise (verb)
affect (to influence)	effect (result)
allowed (permitted)	aloud
alter (change)	altar (in a church)
appraise (value)	apprise (inform)
bitten	beaten
base (foundation)	bass (in music)
bath (noun)	bathe (verb)
believe (verb)	belief (noun)
berry (fruit)	bury (the dead)
beside (by the side of)	besides (as well as)
birth	berth (bed)
bizarre (strange)	bazaar (market)
bloc (political grouping)	block
breath (noun)	breathe (verb)
buoy (in the water)	boy
buy (purchase)	by
cash	cache (hiding place)
casual (informal)	causal (to do with causes)
cause	case
ceiling (above you)	sealing
ceased (stopped)	seized (grabbed)
chick	cheek
check (make sure)	cheque (worth money)
chose (past tense)	choose (present tense)
cite (make reference to)	sight site (place)
climatic	climactic
cloths (fabrics)	clothes
coma (unconscious)	comma (punctuation)
compliment (praise)	complement (make complete)

conscious (aware)	conscience (sense of right)
contract	construct
convinced	convicted (of a crime)
conventional (usual)	convectional
conversation	conservation concentration
council (group)	counsel (advice)
cord (rope)	chord (music)
course	coarse (rough)
credible (believable)	creditable (deserving credit)
critic (one who criticises)	critique (piece of criticism)
defer (show respect)	differ
deference (respect)	difference
deprecate (criticise)	depreciate (reduce in value)
desert (dry place)	dessert (sweet)
device (thing)	devise (to plan)
died/had died	dead/was dead
dissent (protest)	descent (downward motion)
distant (adjective)	distance (noun)
edition (of a book etc.)	addition (something added)
emigrate	immigrate
emigrant	immigrant
envelop (verb)	envelope (noun)
except	expect
fear	fair fare (payment)
feeling	filling
fell	feel fill
flaunt (display)	flout
forward	foreword (in a book)
forgo (do without)	forego (go before)
formally	formerly (previously)
forth (forward)	fourth (after third)
foul	fowl (birds)
future	feature
genus (biological type)	genius (creative intelligence)
greet	great grate (scrape)
guided (led)	guarded (protected)
had	heard head
heat	heart hate
heir (inheritor)	air
hordes (masses)	hoards (keeps)
human	humane (kind)
illicit (not permitted)	elicit (bring forth)
illusion (unreal image)	allusion (reference)
immigrate	emigrate
independent (adjective)	independence (noun)
inhabit (live in)	inhibit (retard)
instance (occurrence)	instants (moments)
intense (concentrating)	intents
isle (island)	aisle (to walk in)
know	no now

SPELLING

lack	lake
later	latter letter
lath (piece of wood)	lathe (machine)
leave	leaf
lead	led
lessen (reduce)	lesson
let	late
leave	live
leaving	living
liable (responsible)	libel (legal action)
lightning (from clouds)	lightening (becoming lighter)
lose (be unable to find)	loose (not tight)
mad (insane)	made maid (servant)
man	men
martial (to do with fighting)	marshal
mental	metal
merry	marry
met	meet mate
minor (underage)	miner (underground)
mist (light fog)	missed
moral (ethical)	morale (spirit)
mourning (after death)	morning
new	knew
of	off
on	own
ones	once
pain	pane (of glass)
patients (sick people)	patience (ability to wait)
peer (look closely)	pier (wharf)
perpetrate (be guilty of)	perpetuate (cause to continue)
perquisite (privilege)	prerequisite (requirement)
personal (private)	personnel (employees)
perspective (vision)	prospective (anticipated)
poor	pour (liquid) pore
precede (go before)	proceed (continue)
precedent	president
presents (gifts)	presence (being there)
price (cost)	prize (reward)
principle	principal (of a school)
prostate (gland)	prostrate (lie down)
quay (wharf - pronounced *key*)	key
quite	quiet (not noisy)
rein (to control animals)	rain reign (of a king)
release (let go)	realizse / realise (discover)
relieve (verb)	relief (noun)
response (noun)	responds (verb)
rid	ride
ridden	written
rise	rice
rite (ritual)	right write

SPELLING

rod	rode	reared
rote (repetition)	wrote	
saved	served	
saw	so	sew
secret	sacred (holy)	
seam (in clothes etc.)	seem (appear)	
scene (location)	seen	
sell (verb)	sale (noun)	sail (boat)
senses	census (population count)	
shed	shade	
shone	shown	
shot	short	
sit	sat	set
smell	smile	
snake	snack (small meal)	
soar	sore (hurt)	
sole (single)	soul (spirit)	
sort (type or kind)	sought (looked for)	
stationery (paper)	stationary (not moving)	
steal (present tense)	stole (past tense)	
straight (not crooked)	strait (of water)	
striped (e.g. a zebra)	stripped (uncovered)	
suit	suite (rooms or music)	sweet
super	supper (meal)	
suppose	supposed to	
sympathies (noun)	sympathize (verb)	
tale (story)	tail	
talk	took	
tap	tape	
than	then	
they	there	their
thing	think	
this	these	
throw	threw (past tense)	
through	thorough	
tied	tired	
urban (in cities)	urbane (sophisticated)	
vanish (disappear)	varnish	
vein (to carry blood)	vain	
vision (sight)	version	
waist (your middle)	waste	
wait	weight (heaviness)	
waive (give up)	wave	
weak (not strong)	week	
wants	once	
weather (sunny, wet, etc.)	whether (or not)	
wedding	weeding	
were	where	
wholly (completely)	holy (sacred)	holly
woman (singular)	women (plural)	

SPELLING

won
yoke (for animals)

worn
yolk (of an egg)

Other Commonly Misspelled Words

abbreviation
absence
accident
accidentally
accommodation
achieve
ackowledge
acquire
acquisition
acquit
across
address
adjacent
advertisement
affidavit
ambulance
amoeba
among
amount
analogous
analysis
anxious
apparatus
apparently
appreciate
approach
architect
argument
asinine
author
auxiliary
bacteria
basically
battery
beautiful
beginning
behavior or behaviour
believe
boast
boastful
breakfast

bulletin
burglar
burial
buried
business
candidate
Caribbean
carpentry
cautious
ceiling
changeable
character
chlorophyll
choir
chrome
chronological
cigarette
coincidence
colleague
colonel
colossal
column
commitment
committee
comparative
competition
competitor
complexion
conceive
condemn
conjunction
connoisseur
consensus
consistent
controller
convenience
cooperation
cooperative
courteous
courtesy
creator

creature
criticism
decisive
definite
delicious
description
desirable
despair
despise
destroy
develop
diesel
different
dilemma
dilapidated
dining
disappear
disappoint
disastrous
discrimination
disease
disintegrate
dissatisfied
dominate
dormitory
double
doubtful
drunkard
drunkenness
duchess
due
dying
eclipse
effective
efficient
eighth
embarrass
employee
encourage
enemy
enmity

enormous
entertain
enthusiasm
entitle
entrepreneur
environment
enzyme
epidermis
epididymis
especially
espresso
essential
exaggerate
excessive
excite
exercise
existence
existent
experience
extraordinary
Fahrenheit
faithful
faithfully
fault
favor
  or favour
favorite
  or favourite
financial
foreigner
foretell
forty
fourth
fulfil or fulfill
gamete
germination
government
grammar
grateful
gruesome
guarantee
guerrillas
guilty
happened
happiest
hard-hearted
hatred
hectare

helpful
humor
  or humour
hyena
hypothesis
imaginary
imagine
immigration
importance
indispensable
inoculate
intention, intentional
interrupt
irrelevant
isosceles
itinerary
jealous
jeopardy
journalist
jump
junction
kneel
knowledge
knowledgeable
laboratories
laboratory
language
lazy, laziness
ledger
leisure
liberation
library
licence (noun)
license (verb)
lieutenant
likeable or likable
liquid, liquefy
literature
lying
manoeuvre
  or maneuver
marvelous
medicine
medieval
melancholy
membrane
merciful
mermaid

millennia
millennium
millionaire
mischief
mischievous
misled
misspell
modern
naked
naughty
necessary
necessity
neighbour
  or neighbor
noticeable
nuclear
nucleus
obscene
obsolescent
obsolete
occasion
occasional
occupy
occur
occurred
occurrence
omelet
  or omelette
omit
ourselves
paid
parallel
parliament
party
permissible
permission
perpendicular
perseverance
photosynthesis
playful
possess
possession
poignant
poultry
predictable
pregnancy
pregnant
prerogative

SPELLING

prescription
privilege
program
  or programme
properly
psychiatric
psychological
punctuation
pursue
questionnaire
really
receipt
recommend
referee
reference
regret
repeat
repetition
replies
reply
residence (place)
residents (people)
restaurant
revolutionary
rhyme
rhythm
saddest
sandals
scene
schedule
science
scissors
scream
search
seize
sense
separate

Shakespearian
  or Shakespearean
shining
shotgun
sigh
significant
simultaneous
sincerely
skilful or skillful
slippery
slogan
smart
solemn
spaghetti
speech
spongy
sponsor
stale
stingy
stomach
stubborn
studious
studying
stupefy
stupid
subordinate
subpoena
substitute
subtle, subtlety
suburbs
succeed
success, successful
sue, suing
summary
surprised
surreptitious
surrounded

survive
symbol
talkative
tarred
television
temperature
tendency
theatre
  or theater
theoretical
theory
title
tough
tragedy
trophy
truly
unique
until
vacancy
vacillate
valuable
vegetable
vehicle
vicious
visitor
volume
voluntary
Wednesday
welcome
whisper
writer
writing
written
yield

INDEX

CORRECTION KEY (symbols listed in the MLA Handbook)

(Numbers refer to pages in this book.)

Ab	Faulty abbreviation
Adj	Improper use of adjective (122-3, 205-6, 260)
Adv	Improper use of adverb (125, 205-6, 301-2)
Agr	Faulty agreement (137-9, 191-8)
Amb	Ambiguous (70, 286-7)
Awk	Awkward expression or construction
Cap	Faulty capitalization
D	Faulty diction (59-65)
Dgl	Dangling construction (155-60)
Frag	Fragment (270-72)
lc	Use lowercase
Num	Error in use of numbers
‖	Lack of parallelism (73-5)
P	Faulty punctuation (267-77)
Ref	Unclear pronoun reference (200-202)
Rep	Unnecessary repetition (56-7, 248)
R-O	Run-on (267-72)
Sp	Error in spelling (319-25)
SS	Faulty sentence structure (58-9, 70-5)
T	Wrong tense of verb (135-54)
tr ⁀	Transpose elements (e.g., to quickly go, recieve)
V	Wrong verb form (135-54)
Wdy	Wordy (58-61, 157, 235-6, 243-50)
ᵛ	Add apostrophe or single quotation mark (276-7)
⌒	Close up
⌃	Add comma (272)
ℓ	Delete
⋏	Insert
¶	Begin a new paragraph (53-5)
No ¶	Do not begin a new paragraph (53-5)
⊙	Add a Period (267-9)
ᵛ ᵛ	Double quotation marks (280-4)
#	Add space